R Machine Learning
By Example

Understand the fundamentals of machine learning with R and build your own dynamic algorithms to tackle complicated real-world problems successfully

Raghav Bali

Dipanjan Sarkar

[PACKT]
PUBLISHING

open source
community experience distilled

BIRMINGHAM - MUMBAI

R Machine Learning By Example

First published: March 2016

Production reference: 1220316

Published by Packt Publishing Ltd.
Livery Place
35 Livery Street
Birmingham B3 2PB, UK.

ISBN 978-1-78439-084-6

www.packtpub.com

Credits

Authors
Raghav Bali
Dipanjan Sarkar

Reviewer
Alexey Grigorev

Commissioning Editor
Akram Hussain

Acquisition Editors
Kevin Colaco
Tushar Gupta

Content Development Editor
Kajal Thapar

Technical Editor
Utkarsha S. Kadam

Copy Editors
Vikrant Phadke
Alpha Singh

Project Coordinator
Shweta H Birwatkar

Proofreader
Safis Editing

Indexer
Monica Ajmera Mehta

Graphics
Disha Haria
Kirk D'Penha

Production Coordinator
Arvindkumar Gupta

Cover Work
Arvindkumar Gupta

About the Authors

Raghav Bali has a master's degree (gold medalist) in IT from the International Institute of Information Technology, Bangalore. He is an IT engineer at Intel, the world's largest silicon company, where he works on analytics, business intelligence, and application development. He has worked as an analyst and developer in domains such as ERP, finance, and BI with some of the top companies in the world. Raghav is a shutterbug, capturing moments when he isn't busy solving problems.

I would like to thank Packt Publishing for this opportunity, Kajal Thapar and Utkarsha S. Kadam for their fantastic support and editing, and everyone from the R community for making life simpler and data science interesting.

Finally, I would to thank my family, especially my parents and brother for their faith in me and for whom this book will be a surprise. I would also like to thank my mentors, teachers, and friends, who have always been an inspiration. Last but not least, special thanks to my partner in crime, Dipanjan Sarkar, without whom this wouldn't have been possible.

Dipanjan Sarkar is an IT engineer at Intel, the world's largest silicon company, where he works on analytics, business intelligence, and application development. He received his master's degree in information technology from the International Institute of Information Technology, Bangalore. His areas of specialization includes software engineering, data science, machine learning, and text analytics.

Dipanjan's interests include learning about new technology, disruptive start-ups, and data science. In his spare time, he loves reading, playing games, and watching popular sitcoms. He has also reviewed *Data Analysis with R*, *Learning R for Geospatial Analysis*, and *R Data Analysis Cookbook*, all by Packt Publishing.

I would like to thank my good friend and colleague, Raghav Bali, for co-authoring this book with me. Without his support, it would have been impossible to make this book a reality. I would also like to thank Kajal Thapar and Utkarsha S. Kadam for giving me timely feedback on the book's content and making the whole writing process really interactive and enjoyable. Much gratitude goes without saying to Packt Publishing for giving me this wonderful opportunity to share my knowledge with the machine learning and R enthusiasts out there who are doing truly amazing things every day.

Last but never the least, I am indebted to my family, friends, teachers, and colleagues for always standing by my side and supporting me in all my endeavors. Your support keeps me going day in, day out to take on new challenges!

About the Reviewer

Alexey Grigorev is a skilled data scientist and software engineer with more than 5 years of professional experience. He currently works as a data scientist at Searchmetrics. In his day-to-day job, he actively uses R and Python for data cleaning, data analysis, and modeling. He has been a reviewer on other Packt Publishing books on data analysis, such as *Test-Driven Machine Learning* and *Mastering Data Analysis with R*.

www.PacktPub.com

eBooks, discount offers, and more

Did you know that Packt offers eBook versions of every book published, with PDF and ePub files available? You can upgrade to the eBook version at www.PacktPub.com and as a print book customer, you are entitled to a discount on the eBook copy. Get in touch with us at customercare@packtpub.com for more details.

At www.PacktPub.com, you can also read a collection of free technical articles, sign up for a range of free newsletters and receive exclusive discounts and offers on Packt books and eBooks.

https://www2.packtpub.com/books/subscription/packtlib

Do you need instant solutions to your IT questions? PacktLib is Packt's online digital book library. Here, you can search, access, and read Packt's entire library of books.

Why subscribe?

- Fully searchable across every book published by Packt
- Copy and paste, print, and bookmark content
- On demand and accessible via a web browser

Table of Contents

Preface

Data science and machine learning are some of the top buzzwords in the technical world today. From retail stores to Fortune 500 companies, everyone is working hard to make machine learning give them data-driven insights to grow their businesses. With powerful data manipulation features, machine learning packages, and an active developer community, R empowers users to build sophisticated machine learning systems to solve real-world data problems.

This book takes you on a data-driven journey that starts with the very basics of R and machine learning and gradually builds upon the concepts to work on projects that tackle real-world problems.

What this book covers

Chapter 1, *Getting Started with R and Machine Learning*, acquaints you with the book and helps you reacquaint yourself with R and its basics. This chapter also provides you with a short introduction to machine learning.

Chapter 2, *Let's Help Machines Learn*, dives into machine learning by explaining the concepts that form its base. You are also presented with various types of learning algorithms, along with some real-world examples.

Chapter 3, *Predicting Customer Shopping Trends with Market Basket Analysis*, starts off with our first project, e-commerce product recommendations, predictions, and pattern analysis, using various machine learning techniques. This chapter specifically deals with market basket analysis and association rule mining to detect customer shopping patterns and trends and make product predictions and suggestions using these techniques. These techniques are used widely by retail companies and e-commerce stores such as Target, Macy's, Flipkart, and Amazon for product recommendations.

Chapter 4, Building a Product Recommendation System, covers the second part of our first project on e-commerce product recommendations, predictions, and pattern analysis. This chapter specifically deals with analyzing e-commerce product reviews and ratings by different users, using algorithms and techniques such as user-collaborative filtering to design a recommender system that is production ready.

Chapter 5, Credit Risk Detection and Prediction – Descriptive Analytics, starts off with our second project, applying machine learning to a complex financial scenario where we deal with credit risk detection and prediction. This chapter specifically deals with introducing the main objective, looking at a financial credit dataset for 1,000 people who have applied for loans from a bank. We will use machine learning techniques to detect people who are potential credit risks and may not be able to repay a loan if they take it from the bank, and also predict the same for the future. The chapter will also talk in detail about our dataset, the main challenges when dealing with data, the main features of the dataset, and exploratory and descriptive analytics on the data. It will conclude with the best machine learning techniques suitable for tackling this problem.

Chapter 6, Credit Risk Detection and Prediction – Predictive Analytics, starts from where we left off in the previous chapter about descriptive analytics with looking at using predictive analytics. Here, we specifically deal with using several machine learning algorithms to detect and predict which customers would be potential credit risks and might not be likely to repay a loan to the bank if they take it. This would ultimately help the bank make data-driven decisions as to whether to approve the loan or not. We will be covering several supervised learning algorithms and compare their performance. Different metrics for evaluating the efficiency and accuracy of various machine learning algorithms will also be covered here.

Chapter 7, Social Media Analysis – Analyzing Twitter Data, introduces the world of social media analytics. We begin with an introduction to the world of social media and the process of collecting data through Twitter's APIs. The chapter will walk you through the process of mining useful information from tweets, including visualizing Twitter data with real-world examples, clustering and topic modeling of tweets, the present challenges and complexities, and strategies to address these issues. We show by example how some powerful measures can be computed using Twitter data.

Chapter 8, Sentiment Analysis of Twitter Data, builds upon the knowledge of Twitter APIs to work on a project for analyzing sentiments in tweets. This project presents multiple machine learning algorithms for the classification of tweets based on the sentiments inferred. This chapter will also present these results in a comparative manner and help you understand the workings and difference in results of these algorithms.

What you need for this book

This software applies to all the chapters of the book:

- Windows / Mac OS X / Linux
- R 3.2.0 (or higher)
- RStudio Desktop 0.99 (or higher)

For hardware, there are no specific requirements, since R can run on any PC that has Mac, Linux, or Windows, but a physical memory of minimum 4 GB is preferred to run some of the iterative algorithms smoothly.

Who this book is for

If you are interested in mining useful information from data using state-of-the-art techniques to make data-driven decisions, this is a go-to guide for you. No prior experience with data science is required, although basic knowledge of R is highly desirable. Prior knowledge of machine learning will be helpful but is not necessary.

Conventions

In this book, you will find a number of text styles that distinguish between different kinds of information. Here are some examples of these styles and an explanation of their meaning.

Code words in text, database table names, folder names, filenames, file extensions, pathnames, dummy URLs, user input, and Twitter handles are shown as follows: "We can include other contexts through the use of the `include` directive."

Any command-line input or output is written as follows:

```
# comparing cluster labels with actual iris  species labels.

table(iris$Species, clusters$cluster)
```

New terms and **important words** are shown in bold. Words that you see on the screen, for example, in menus or dialog boxes, appear in the text like this: "From recommendations related to **Who to follow** on Twitter to **Other movies you might enjoy** on Netflix to **Jobs you may be interested in** on LinkedIn, recommender engines are everywhere and not just on e-commerce platforms."

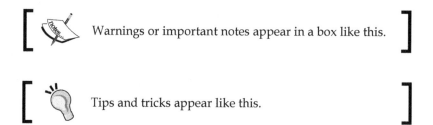

Warnings or important notes appear in a box like this.

Tips and tricks appear like this.

Reader feedback

Feedback from our readers is always welcome. Let us know what you think about this book—what you liked or disliked. Reader feedback is important for us as it helps us develop titles that you will really get the most out of.

To send us general feedback, simply e-mail feedback@packtpub.com, and mention the book's title in the subject of your message.

If there is a topic that you have expertise in and you are interested in either writing or contributing to a book, see our author guide at www.packtpub.com/authors.

Customer support

Now that you are the proud owner of a Packt book, we have a number of things to help you to get the most from your purchase.

Downloading the example code

You can download the example code files for this book from your account at http://www.packtpub.com. If you purchased this book elsewhere, you can visit http://www.packtpub.com/support and register to have the files e-mailed directly to you.

You can download the code files by following these steps:

1. Log in or register to our website using your e-mail address and password.
2. Hover the mouse pointer on the **SUPPORT** tab at the top.
3. Click on **Code Downloads & Errata**.
4. Enter the name of the book in the **Search** box.

5. Select the book for which you're looking to download the code files.

6. Choose from the drop-down menu where you purchased this book from.

7. Click on **Code Download**.

Once the file is downloaded, please make sure that you unzip or extract the folder using the latest version of:

- WinRAR / 7-Zip for Windows
- Zipeg / iZip / UnRarX for Mac
- 7-Zip / PeaZip for Linux

Downloading the color images of this book

We also provide you with a PDF file that has color images of the screenshots/diagrams used in this book. The color images will help you better understand the changes in the output. You can download this file from `https://www.packtpub.com/sites/default/files/downloads/RMachineLearningByExample_ColorImages.pdf`.

Errata

Although we have taken every care to ensure the accuracy of our content, mistakes do happen. If you find a mistake in one of our books — maybe a mistake in the text or the code — we would be grateful if you could report this to us. By doing so, you can save other readers from frustration and help us improve subsequent versions of this book. If you find any errata, please report them by visiting `http://www.packtpub.com/submit-errata`, selecting your book, clicking on the **Errata Submission Form** link, and entering the details of your errata. Once your errata are verified, your submission will be accepted and the errata will be uploaded to our website or added to any list of existing errata under the Errata section of that title.

To view the previously submitted errata, go to `https://www.packtpub.com/books/content/support` and enter the name of the book in the search field. The required information will appear under the **Errata** section.

Piracy

Piracy of copyrighted material on the Internet is an ongoing problem across all media. At Packt, we take the protection of our copyright and licenses very seriously. If you come across any illegal copies of our works in any form on the Internet, please provide us with the location address or website name immediately so that we can pursue a remedy.

Please contact us at copyright@packtpub.com with a link to the suspected pirated material.

We appreciate your help in protecting our authors and our ability to bring you valuable content.

Questions

If you have a problem with any aspect of this book, you can contact us at questions@packtpub.com, and we will do our best to address the problem.

1

Getting Started with R and Machine Learning

This introductory chapter will get you started with the basics of R which include various constructs, useful data structures, loops and vectorization. If you are already an R wizard, you can skim through these sections and dive right into the next part which talks about what machine learning actually represents as a domain and the main areas it encompasses. We will also talk about different machine learning techniques and algorithms used in each area. Finally, we will conclude by looking at some of the most popular machine learning packages in R, some of which we will be using in the subsequent chapters.

If you are a data or machine learning enthusiast, surely you would have heard by now that being a data scientist is referred to as the sexiest job of the 21st century by Harvard Business Review.

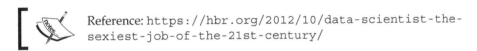

Reference: https://hbr.org/2012/10/data-scientist-the-sexiest-job-of-the-21st-century/

There is a huge demand in the current market for data scientists, primarily because their main job is to gather crucial insights and information from both unstructured and structured data to help their business and organization grow strategically.

Some of you might be wondering how machine learning or R relate to all this! Well, to be a successful data scientist, one of the major tools you need in your toolbox is a powerful language capable of performing complex statistical calculations and working with various types of data and building models which help you get previously unknown insights and R is the perfect language for that! Machine learning forms the foundation of the skills you need to build to become a data analyst or data scientist, this includes using various techniques to build models to get insights from data.

This book will provide you with some of the essential tools you need to be well versed with both R and machine learning by not only looking at concepts but also applying those concepts in real-world examples. Enough talk; now let's get started on our journey into the world of machine learning with R!

In this chapter, we will cover the following aspects:

- Delving into the basics of R
- Understanding the data structures in R
- Working with functions
- Controlling code flow
- Taking further steps with R
- Understanding machine learning basics
- Familiarizing yourself with popular machine learning packages in R

Delving into the basics of R

It is assumed here that you are at least familiar with the basics of R or have worked with R before. Hence, we won't be talking much about downloading and installations. There are plenty of resources on the web which provide a lot of information on this. I recommend that you use RStudio which is an **Integrated Development Environment (IDE)**, which is much better than the base R **Graphical User Interface (GUI)**. You can visit https://www.rstudio.com/ to get more information about it.

For details about the R project, you can visit https://www.r-project.org/ to get an overview of the language. Besides this, R has a vast arsenal of wonderful packages at its disposal and you can view everything related to R and its packages at https://cran.r-project.org/ which contains all the archives.

You must already be familiar with the R interactive interpreter, often called a **Read-Evaluate-Print Loop (REPL)**. This interpreter acts like any command line interface which asks for input and starts with a > character, which indicates that R is waiting for your input. If your input spans multiple lines, like when you are writing a function, you will see a + prompt in each subsequent line, which means that you didn't finish typing the complete expression and R is asking you to provide the rest of the expression.

It is also possible for R to read and execute complete files containing commands and functions which are saved in files with an .R extension. Usually, any big application consists of several .R files. Each file has its own role in the application and is often called as a module. We will be exploring some of the main features and capabilities of R in the following sections.

Using R as a scientific calculator

The most basic constructs in R include variables and arithmetic operators which can be used to perform simple mathematical operations like a calculator or even complex statistical calculations.

```
> 5 + 6
[1] 11
> 3 * 2
[1] 6
> 1 / 0
[1] Inf
```

Remember that everything in R is a vector. Even the output results indicated in the previous code snippet. They have a leading [1] symbol indicating it is a vector of size 1.

You can also assign values to variables and operate on them just like any other programming language.

```
> num <- 6
> num ^ 2
[1] 36
> num
[1] 6      # a variable changes value only on re-assignment
> num <- num ^ 2 * 5 + 10 / 3
> num
[1] 183.3333
```

Operating on vectors

The most basic data structure in R is a vector. Basically, anything in R is a vector, even if it is a single number just like we saw in the earlier example! A vector is basically a sequence or a set of values. We can create vectors using the : operator or the c function which concatenates the values to create a vector.

```
> x <- 1:5
> x
[1] 1 2 3 4 5
> y <- c(6, 7, 8 ,9, 10)
> y
[1]  6  7  8  9 10
> z <- x + y
> z
[1]  7  9 11 13 15
```

You can clearly in the previous code snippet, that we just added two vectors together without using any loop, using just the + operator. This is known as vectorization and we will be discussing more about this later on. Some more operations on vectors are shown next:

```
> c(1,3,5,7,9) * 2
[1]  2  6 10 14 18
> c(1,3,5,7,9) * c(2, 4)
[1]  2 12 10 28 18 # here the second vector gets recycled
```

Output:

```
Warning message:
In c(1, 3, 5, 7, 9) * c(2, 4) :
  longer object length is not a multiple of shorter object length

> factorial(1:5)
[1]   1   2   6  24 120
> exp(2:10)    # exponential function
```

```
[1]      7.389056      20.085537      54.598150      148.413159      403.428793
1096.633158
[7]   2980.957987   8103.083928 22026.465795
> cos(c(0, pi/4))   # cosine function
[1] 1.0000000 0.7071068
> sqrt(c(1, 4, 9, 16))
[1] 1 2 3 4
> sum(1:10)
[1] 55
```

You might be confused with the second operation where we tried to multiply a smaller vector with a bigger vector but we still got a result! If you look closely, R threw a warning also. What happened in this case is, since the two vectors were not equal in size, the smaller vector in this case c(2, 4) got recycled or repeated to become c(2, 4, 2, 4, 2) and then it got multiplied with the first vector c(1, 3, 5, 7 ,9) to give the final result vector, c(2, 12, 10, 28, 18). The other functions mentioned here are standard functions available in base R along with several other functions.

Downloading the example code

You can download the example code files for this book from your account at http://www.packtpub.com. If you purchased this book elsewhere, you can visit http://www.packtpub.com/support and register to have the files e-mailed directly to you.

You can download the code files by following these steps:

- Log in or register to our website using your e-mail address and password.
- Hover the mouse pointer on the **SUPPORT** tab at the top
- Click on **Code Downloads & Errata**
- Enter the name of the book in the **Search** box
- Select the book for which you're looking to download the code files
- Choose from the drop-down menu where you purchased this book from
- Click on **Code Download**

Once the file is downloaded, please make sure that you unzip or extract the folder using the latest version of:

- WinRAR / 7-Zip for Windows
- Zipeg / iZip / UnRarX for Mac
- 7-Zip / PeaZip for Linux

Special values

Since you will be dealing with a lot of messy and dirty data in data analysis and machine learning, it is important to remember some of the special values in R so that you don't get too surprised later on if one of them pops up.

```
> 1 / 0
[1] Inf
> 0 / 0
[1] NaN
> Inf / NaN
[1] NaN
> Inf / Inf
[1] NaN
> log(Inf)
[1] Inf
> Inf + NA
[1] NA
```

The main values which should concern you here are Inf which stands for **Infinity**, NaN which is **Not a Number**, and NA which indicates a value that is missing or **Not Available**. The following code snippet shows some logical tests on these special values and their results. Do remember that TRUE and FALSE are logical data type values, similar to other programming languages.

```
> vec <- c(0, Inf, NaN, NA)
> is.finite(vec)
[1]  TRUE FALSE FALSE FALSE
> is.nan(vec)
[1] FALSE FALSE  TRUE FALSE
> is.na(vec)
[1] FALSE FALSE  TRUE  TRUE
> is.infinite(vec)
[1] FALSE  TRUE FALSE FALSE
```

The functions are pretty self-explanatory from their names. They clearly indicate which values are finite, which are finite and checks for NaN and NA values respectively. Some of these functions are very useful when cleaning dirty data.

Data structures in R

Here we will be looking at the most useful data structures which exist in R and use using them on some fictional examples to get a better grasp on their syntax and constructs. The main data structures which we will be covering here include:

- Vectors
- Arrays and matrices
- Lists
- Data frames

These data structures are used widely inside R as well as by various R packages and functions, including machine learning functions and algorithms which we will be using in the subsequent chapters. So it is essential to know how to use these data structures to work with data efficiently.

Vectors

Just like we mentioned briefly in the previous sections, vectors are the most basic data type inside R. We use vectors to represent anything, be it input or output. We previously saw how we create vectors and apply mathematical operations on them. We will see some more examples here.

Creating vectors

Here we will look at ways to initialize vectors, some of which we had also worked on previously, using operators such as : and functions such as c. In the following code snippet, we will use the seq family of functions to initialize vectors in different ways.

```
> c(2.5:4.5, 6, 7, c(8, 9, 10), c(12:15))
 [1]  2.5  3.5  4.5  6.0  7.0  8.0  9.0 10.0 12.0 13.0 14.0 15.0
> vector("numeric", 5)
[1] 0 0 0 0 0
> vector("logical", 5)
[1] FALSE FALSE FALSE FALSE FALSE
> logical(5)
[1] FALSE FALSE FALSE FALSE FALSE
> # seq is a function which creates sequences
> seq.int(1,10)
```

```
 [1]  1  2  3  4  5  6  7  8  9 10
> seq.int(1,10,2)
[1] 1 3 5 7 9
> seq_len(10)
 [1]  1  2  3  4  5  6  7  8  9 10
```

Indexing and naming vectors

One of the most important operations we can do on vectors involves subsetting and indexing vectors to access specific elements which are often useful when we want to run some code only on specific data points. The following examples show some ways in which we can index and subset vectors:

```
> vec <- c("R", "Python", "Julia", "Haskell", "Java", "Scala")
> vec[1]
[1] "R"
> vec[2:4]
[1] "Python"  "Julia"    "Haskell"
> vec[c(1, 3, 5)]
[1] "R"      "Julia" "Java"
> nums <- c(5, 8, 10, NA, 3, 11)
> nums
[1]  5  8 10 NA  3 11
> which.min(nums)    # index of the minimum element
[1] 5
> which.max(nums)    # index of the maximum element
[1] 6
> nums[which.min(nums)]  # the actual minimum element
[1] 3
> nums[which.max(nums)]  # the actual maximum element
[1] 11
```

Now we look at how we can name vectors. This is basically a nifty feature in R where you can label each element in a vector to make it more readable or easy to interpret. There are two ways this can be done, which are shown in the following examples:

```
> c(first=1, second=2, third=3, fourth=4, fifth=5)
```

Output:

```
first second  third fourth  fifth
    1      2      3      4      5
```

```
> positions <- c(1, 2, 3, 4, 5)
> names(positions)
NULL
> names(positions) <- c("first", "second", "third", "fourth", "fifth")
> positions
```

Output:

```
first second  third fourth  fifth
    1      2      3      4      5
```

```
> names(positions)
[1] "first"  "second" "third"  "fourth" "fifth"
> positions[c("second", "fourth")]
```

Output:

```
second fourth
     2      4
```

Thus, you can see, it becomes really useful to annotate and name vectors sometimes, and we can also subset and slice vectors using element names rather than values.

Arrays and matrices

Vectors are one dimensional data structures, which means that they just have one dimension and we can get the number of elements they have using the `length` property. Do remember that arrays may also have a similar meaning in other programming languages, but in R they have a slightly different meaning. Basically, arrays in R are data structures which hold the data having multiple dimensions. Matrices are just a special case of generic arrays having two dimensions, namely represented by properties `rows` and `columns`. Let us look at some examples in the following code snippets in the accompanying subsection.

Creating arrays and matrices

First we will create an array that has three dimensions. Now it is easy to represent two dimensions in your screen, but to go one dimension higher, there are special ways in which R transforms the data. The following example shows how R fills the data (column first) in each dimension and shows the final output for a 4x3x3 array:

```
> three.dim.array <- array(
+     1:32,      # input data
+     dim = c(4, 3, 3),   # dimensions
+     dimnames = list(    # names of dimensions
+         c("row1", "row2", "row3", "row4"),
+         c("col1", "col2", "col3"),
+         c("first.set", "second.set", "third.set")
+     )
+ )
> three.dim.array
```

Output:

```
, , first.set

      col1 col2 col3
row1     1    5    9
row2     2    6   10
row3     3    7   11
row4     4    8   12

, , second.set

      col1 col2 col3
row1    13   17   21
row2    14   18   22
row3    15   19   23
row4    16   20   24

, , third.set

      col1 col2 col3
row1    25   29    1
row2    26   30    2
row3    27   31    3
row4    28   32    4
```

Like I mentioned earlier, a matrix is just a special case of an array. We can create a matrix using the `matrix` function, shown in detail in the following example. Do note that we use the parameter `byrow` to fill the data row-wise in the matrix instead of R's default column-wise fill in any array or matrix. The `ncol` and `nrow` parameters stand for number of columns and rows respectively.

```
> mat <- matrix(
+     1:24,    # data
+     nrow = 6,  # num of rows
+     ncol = 4,  # num of columns
+     byrow = TRUE,  # fill the elements row-wise
+ )
> mat
```

Output:

```
     [,1] [,2] [,3] [,4]
[1,]    1    2    3    4
[2,]    5    6    7    8
[3,]    9   10   11   12
[4,]   13   14   15   16
[5,]   17   18   19   20
[6,]   21   22   23   24
```

Names and dimensions

Just like we named vectors and accessed element names, will perform similar operations in the following code snippets. You have already seen the use of the `dimnames` parameter in the preceding examples. Let us look at some more examples as follows:

```
> dimnames(three.dim.array)
```

Output:

```
[[1]]
[1] "row1" "row2" "row3" "row4"

[[2]]
[1] "col1" "col2" "col3"

[[3]]
[1] "first.set"  "second.set" "third.set"
```

```
> rownames(three.dim.array)
[1] "row1" "row2" "row3" "row4"
> colnames(three.dim.array)
[1] "col1" "col2" "col3"
> dimnames(mat)
NULL
> rownames(mat)
NULL
> rownames(mat) <- c("r1", "r2", "r3", "r4", "r5", "r6")
> colnames(mat) <- c("c1", "c2", "c3", "c4")
> dimnames(mat)
```

Output:

```
[[1]]
[1] "r1" "r2" "r3" "r4" "r5" "r6"

[[2]]
[1] "c1" "c2" "c3" "c4"

> mat
```

Output:

```
   c1 c2 c3 c4
r1  1  2  3  4
r2  5  6  7  8
r3  9 10 11 12
r4 13 14 15 16
r5 17 18 19 20
r6 21 22 23 24
```

To access details of dimensions related to arrays and matrices, there are special functions. The following examples show the same:

```
> dim(three.dim.array)
[1] 4 3 3
> nrow(three.dim.array)
[1] 4
```

```
> ncol(three.dim.array)
[1] 3
> length(three.dim.array)   # product of dimensions
[1] 36
> dim(mat)
[1] 6 4
> nrow(mat)
[1] 6
> ncol(mat)
[1] 4
> length(mat)
[1] 24
```

Matrix operations

A lot of machine learning and optimization algorithms deal with matrices as their input data. In the following section, we will look at some examples of the most common operations on matrices.

We start by initializing two matrices and then look at ways of combining the two matrices using functions such as c which returns a vector, rbind which combines the matrices by rows, and cbind which does the same by columns.

```
> mat1 <- matrix(
+     1:15,
+     nrow = 5,
+     ncol = 3,
+     byrow = TRUE,
+     dimnames = list(
+         c("M1.r1", "M1.r2", "M1.r3", "M1.r4", "M1.r5")
+         ,c("M1.c1", "M1.c2", "M1.c3")
+     )
+ )
> mat1
```

Output:

```
      M1.c1 M1.c2 M1.c3
M1.r1     1     2     3
M1.r2     4     5     6
M1.r3     7     8     9
M1.r4    10    11    12
M1.r5    13    14    15
```

```
> mat2 <- matrix(
+     16:30,
+     nrow = 5,
+     ncol = 3,
+     byrow = TRUE,
+     dimnames = list(
+         c("M2.r1", "M2.r2", "M2.r3", "M2.r4", "M2.r5"),
+         c("M2.c1", "M2.c2", "M2.c3")
+     )
+ )
> mat2
```

Output:

```
      M2.c1 M2.c2 M2.c3
M2.r1    16    17    18
M2.r2    19    20    21
M2.r3    22    23    24
M2.r4    25    26    27
M2.r5    28    29    30
```

```
> rbind(mat1, mat2)
```

Output:

```
      M1.c1 M1.c2 M1.c3
M1.r1     1     2     3
M1.r2     4     5     6
M1.r3     7     8     9
M1.r4    10    11    12
M1.r5    13    14    15
M2.r1    16    17    18
M2.r2    19    20    21
M2.r3    22    23    24
M2.r4    25    26    27
M2.r5    28    29    30
```

```
> cbind(mat1, mat2)
```

Output:

```
      M1.c1 M1.c2 M1.c3 M2.c1 M2.c2 M2.c3
M1.r1     1     2     3    16    17    18
M1.r2     4     5     6    19    20    21
M1.r3     7     8     9    22    23    24
M1.r4    10    11    12    25    26    27
M1.r5    13    14    15    28    29    30
```

```
> c(mat1, mat2)
```

Output:

```
 [1]  1  4  7 10 13  2  5  8 11 14  3  6  9 12 15 16 19 22 25
[20] 28 17 20 23 26 29 18 21 24 27 30
```

Now we look at some of the important arithmetic operations which can be performed on matrices. Most of them are quite self-explanatory from the following syntax:

```
> mat1 + mat2    # matrix addition
```

```
      M1.c1 M1.c2 M1.c3
M1.r1    17    19    21
M1.r2    23    25    27
M1.r3    29    31    33
M1.r4    35    37    39
M1.r5    41    43    45
```

```
> mat1 * mat2  # element-wise multiplication
```

Output:

```
      M1.c1 M1.c2 M1.c3
M1.r1    16    34    54
M1.r2    76   100   126
M1.r3   154   184   216
M1.r4   250   286   324
M1.r5   364   406   450
```

```
> tmat2 <- t(mat2)  # transpose
> tmat2
```

Output:

```
      M2.r1 M2.r2 M2.r3 M2.r4 M2.r5
M2.c1    16    19    22    25    28
M2.c2    17    20    23    26    29
M2.c3    18    21    24    27    30
```

```
> mat1 %*% tmat2   # matrix inner product
```

Output:

```
      M2.r1 M2.r2 M2.r3 M2.r4 M2.r5
M1.r1   104   122   140   158   176
M1.r2   257   302   347   392   437
M1.r3   410   482   554   626   698
M1.r4   563   662   761   860   959
M1.r5   716   842   968  1094  1220
```

```
> m <- matrix(c(5, -3, 2, 4, 12, -1, 9, 14, 7), nrow = 3, ncol = 3)
> m
```

Output:

```
     [,1] [,2] [,3]
[1,]    5    4    9
[2,]   -3   12   14
[3,]    2   -1    7
```

```
> inv.m <- solve(m)   # matrix inverse
> inv.m
```

Output:

```
            [,1]        [,2]       [,3]
[1,]  0.19718310 -0.07444668 -0.1046278
[2,]  0.09859155  0.03420523 -0.1951710
[3,] -0.04225352  0.02615694  0.1448692
```

```
> round(m %*% inv.m) # matrix * matrix_inverse = identity matrix
```

Output:

```
     [,1] [,2] [,3]
[1,]    1    0    0
[2,]    0    1    0
[3,]    0    0    1
```

The preceding arithmetic operations are just some of the most popular ones amongst the vast number of functions and operators which can be applied to matrices. This becomes useful, especially in areas such as linear optimization.

Lists

Lists are a special case of vectors where each element in the vector can be of a different type of data structure or even simple data types. It is similar to the lists in the Python programming language in some aspects, if you have used it before, where the lists indicate elements which can be of different types and each have a specific index in the list. In R, each element of a list can be as simple as a single element or as complex as a whole matrix, a function, or even a vector of strings.

Creating and indexing lists

We will get started with looking at some common methods to create and initialize lists in the following examples. Besides that, we will also look at how we can access some of these list elements for further computations. Do remember that each element in a list can be a simple primitive data type or even complex data structures or functions.

```
> list.sample <- list(
+       1:5,
+       c("first", "second", "third"),
+       c(TRUE, FALSE, TRUE, TRUE),
+       cos,
+       matrix(1:9, nrow = 3, ncol = 3)
+ )
> list.sample
```

Output:

```
[[1]]
[1] 1 2 3 4 5

[[2]]
[1] "first"  "second" "third"

[[3]]
[1]   TRUE FALSE  TRUE   TRUE

[[4]]
function (x)  .Primitive("cos")

[[5]]
     [,1] [,2] [,3]
[1,]    1    4    7
[2,]    2    5    8
[3,]    3    6    9
```

```
> list.with.names <- list(
+     even.nums = seq.int(2,10,2),
+     odd.nums  = seq.int(1,10,2),
+     languages = c("R", "Python", "Julia", "Java"),
+     cosine.func = cos
+ )
> list.with.names
```

Output:

```
$even.nums
[1]   2   4   6   8 10

$odd.nums
[1] 1 3 5 7 9

$languages
[1] "R"        "Python" "Julia"   "Java"

$cosine.func
function (x)   .Primitive("cos")

> list.with.names$cosine.func
function (x)   .Primitive("cos")
> list.with.names$cosine.func(pi)
[1] -1
>
> list.sample[[4]]
function (x)   .Primitive("cos")
> list.sample[[4]](pi)
[1] -1
>
> list.with.names$odd.nums
[1] 1 3 5 7 9
> list.sample[[1]]
[1] 1 2 3 4 5
> list.sample[[3]]
[1]   TRUE FALSE   TRUE   TRUE
```

You can see from the preceding examples how easy it is to access any element of the list and use it for further computations, such as the `cos` function.

Combining and converting lists

Now we will take a look at how to combine several lists together into one single list in the following examples:

```
> l1 <- list(
+     nums = 1:5,
+     chars = c("a", "b", "c", "d", "e"),
+     cosine = cos
+ )
> l2 <- list(
+     languages = c("R", "Python", "Java"),
+     months = c("Jan", "Feb", "Mar", "Apr"),
+     sine = sin
+ )
> # combining the lists now
> l3 <- c(l1, l2)
> l3
```

Output:

```
$nums
[1] 1 2 3 4 5

$chars
[1] "a" "b" "c" "d" "e"

$cosine
function (x)  .Primitive("cos")

$languages
[1] "R"      "Python" "Java"

$months
[1] "Jan" "Feb" "Mar" "Apr"

$sine
function (x)  .Primitive("sin")
```

It is very easy to convert lists in to vectors and vice versa. The following examples show some common ways we can achieve this:

```
> l1 <- 1:5
> class(l1)
[1] "integer"
> list.l1 <- as.list(l1)
> class(list.l1)
[1] "list"
> list.l1
```

Output:

```
[[1]]
[1] 1

[[2]]
[1] 2

[[3]]
[1] 3

[[4]]
[1] 4

[[5]]
[1] 5

> unlist(list.l1)
[1] 1 2 3 4 5
```

Data frames

Data frames are special data structures which are typically used for storing data tables or data in the form of spreadsheets, where each column indicates a specific attribute or field and the rows consist of specific values for those columns. This data structure is extremely useful in working with datasets which usually have a lot of fields and attributes.

Creating data frames

We can create data frames easily using the `data.frame` function. We will look at some following examples to illustrate the same with some popular superheroes:

```
> df <- data.frame(
+    real.name = c("Bruce Wayne", "Clark Kent", "Slade Wilson", "Tony
Stark", "Steve Rogers"),
+    superhero.name = c("Batman", "Superman", "Deathstroke", "Iron Man",
"Capt. America"),
+    franchise = c("DC", "DC", "DC", "Marvel", "Marvel"),
+    team = c("JLA", "JLA", "Suicide Squad", "Avengers", "Avengers"),
+    origin.year = c(1939, 1938, 1980, 1963, 1941)
+ )
> df
```

Output:

```
    real.name superhero.name franchise          team origin.year
1 Bruce Wayne         Batman        DC           JLA        1939
2  Clark Kent       Superman        DC           JLA        1938
3 Slade Wilson   Deathstroke        DC Suicide Squad        1980
4  Tony Stark       Iron Man    Marvel      Avengers        1963
5 Steve Rogers Capt. America    Marvel      Avengers        1941
```

```
> class(df)
[1] "data.frame"
> str(df)
```

Output:

```
'data.frame':   5 obs. of  5 variables:
 $ real.name     : Factor w/ 5 levels "Bruce Wayne",..: 1 2 3 5 4
 $ superhero.name: Factor w/ 5 levels "Batman","Capt. America",..: 1 5 3 4 2
 $ franchise     : Factor w/ 2 levels "DC","Marvel": 1 1 1 2 2
 $ team          : Factor w/ 3 levels "Avengers","JLA",..: 2 2 3 1 1
 $ origin.year   : num  1939 1938 1980 1963 1941
```

```
> rownames(df)
[1] "1" "2" "3" "4" "5"
> colnames(df)
```

Output:

```
[1] "real.name"     "superhero.name" "franchise"      "team"           "origin.year"
```

```
> dim(df)
```

```
[1] 5 5
```

The `str` function talks in detail about the structure of the data frame where we see details about the data present in each column of the data frame. There are a lot of datasets readily available in R base which you can directly load and start using. One of them is shown next. The `mtcars` dataset has information about various automobiles, which was extracted from the *Motor Trend U.S. Magazine* of 1974.

```
> head(mtcars)    # one of the datasets readily available in R
```

Output:

	mpg	cyl	disp	hp	drat	wt	qsec	vs	am	gear	carb
Mazda RX4	21.0	6	160	110	3.90	2.620	16.46	0	1	4	4
Mazda RX4 Wag	21.0	6	160	110	3.90	2.875	17.02	0	1	4	4
Datsun 710	22.8	4	108	93	3.85	2.320	18.61	1	1	4	1
Hornet 4 Drive	21.4	6	258	110	3.08	3.215	19.44	1	0	3	1
Hornet Sportabout	18.7	8	360	175	3.15	3.440	17.02	0	0	3	2
Valiant	18.1	6	225	105	2.76	3.460	20.22	1	0	3	1

Operating on data frames

There are a lot of operations we can do on data frames, such as merging, combining, slicing, and transposing data frames. We will look at some of the important data frame operations in the following examples.

It is really easy to index and subset specific data inside data frames using simplex indexes and functions such as `subset`.

```
> df[2:4,]
```

Output:

	real.name	superhero.name	franchise	team	origin.year
2	Clark Kent	Superman	DC	JLA	1938
3	Slade Wilson	Deathstroke	DC	Suicide Squad	1980
4	Tony Stark	Iron Man	Marvel	Avengers	1963

```
> df[2:4, 1:2]
```

Output:

```
      real.name superhero.name
2    Clark Kent       Superman
3 Slade Wilson     Deathstroke
4    Tony Stark        Iron Man
```

```
> subset(df, team=="JLA", c(real.name, superhero.name, franchise))
```

Output:

```
      real.name superhero.name franchise
1 Bruce Wayne          Batman        DC
2   Clark Kent        Superman        DC
```

```
> subset(df, team %in% c("Avengers","Suicide Squad"), c(real.name,
superhero.name, franchise))
```

Output:

```
      real.name superhero.name franchise
3 Slade Wilson     Deathstroke        DC
4    Tony Stark        Iron Man    Marvel
5 Steve Rogers  Capt. America    Marvel
```

We will now look at some more complex operations, such as combining and merging data frames.

```
> df1 <- data.frame(
+     id = c('emp001', 'emp003', 'emp007'),
+     name = c('Harvey Dent', 'Dick Grayson', 'James Bond'),
+     alias = c('TwoFace', 'Nightwing', 'Agent 007')
+ )
>
> df2 <- data.frame(
+     id = c('emp001', 'emp003', 'emp007'),
+     location = c('Gotham City', 'Gotham City', 'London'),
+     speciality = c('Split Persona', 'Expert Acrobat', 'Gadget Master')
+ )
> df1
```

Output:

```
       id          name      alias
1 emp001  Harvey Dent     TwoFace
2 emp003 Dick Grayson  Nightwing
3 emp007    James Bond  Agent 007
```

```
> df2
```

Output:

```
       id     location       speciality
1 emp001 Gotham City   Split Persona
2 emp003 Gotham City  Expert Acrobat
3 emp007       London   Gadget Master
```

```
> rbind(df1, df2)    # not possible since column names don't match
Error in match.names(clabs, names(xi)) :
  names do not match previous names
> cbind(df1, df2)
```

Output:

```
       id          name      alias     id    location       speciality
1 emp001  Harvey Dent     TwoFace emp001 Gotham City   Split Persona
2 emp003 Dick Grayson  Nightwing emp003 Gotham City  Expert Acrobat
3 emp007    James Bond  Agent 007 emp007       London   Gadget Master
```

```
> merge(df1, df2, by="id")
```

Output:

```
       id          name      alias     location       speciality
1 emp001  Harvey Dent     TwoFace Gotham City   Split Persona
2 emp003 Dick Grayson  Nightwing Gotham City  Expert Acrobat
3 emp007    James Bond  Agent 007      London   Gadget Master
```

From the preceding operations it is evident that `rbind` and `cbind` work in the same way as we saw previously with arrays and matrices. However, merge lets you merge the data frames in the same way as you join various tables in relational databases.

Working with functions

Next up, we will be looking at functions, which is a technique or methodology to easily structure and modularize your code, specifically lines of code which perform specific tasks, so that you can execute them whenever you need them without writing them again and again. In R, functions are basically treated as just another data type and you can assign functions, manipulate them as and when needed, and also pass them as arguments to other functions. We will be exploring all this in the following section.

Built-in functions

R consists of several functions which are available in the R-base package and, as you install more packages, you get more functionality, which is made available in the form of functions. We will look at a few built-in functions in the following examples:

```
> sqrt(5)
[1] 2.236068
> sqrt(c(1,2,3,4,5,6,7,8,9,10))
[1] 1.000000 1.414214 1.732051 2.000000 2.236068 2.449490 2.645751
[8] 2.828427 3.000000 3.162278
> # aggregating functions
> mean(c(1,2,3,4,5,6,7,8,9,10))
[1] 5.5
> median(c(1,2,3,4,5,6,7,8,9,10))
[1] 5.5
```

You can see from the preceding examples that functions such as mean, median, and sqrt are built-in and can be used anytime when you start R, without loading any other packages or defining the functions explicitly.

User-defined functions

The real power lies in the ability to define your own functions based on different operations and computations you want to perform on the data and making R execute those functions just in the way you intend them to work. Some illustrations are shown as follows:

```
square <- function(data){
  return (data^2)
}
> square(5)
[1] 25
> square(c(1,2,3,4,5))
[1]  1  4  9 16 25
point <- function(xval, yval){
  return (c(x=xval,y=yval))
}
> p1 <- point(5,6)
> p2 <- point(2,3)
>
> p1
x y
5 6
> p2
x y
2 3
```

As we saw in the previous code snippet, we can define functions such as square which computes the square of a single number or even a vector of numbers using the same code. Functions such as point are useful to represent specific entities which represent points in the two-dimensional co-ordinate space. Now we will be looking at how to use the preceding functions together.

Passing functions as arguments

When you define any function, you can also pass other functions to it as arguments if you intend to use them inside your function to perform some complex computations. This reduces the complexity and redundancy of the code. The following example computes the Euclidean distance between two points using the `square` function defined earlier, which is passed as an argument:

```
> # defining the function
euclidean.distance <- function(point1, point2, square.func){
  distance <- sqrt(
                as.integer(
                  square.func(point1['x'] - point2['x'])
                ) +
                as.integer(
                  square.func(point1['y'] - point2['y'])
                )
              )
  return (c(distance=distance))
}
> # executing the function, passing square as argument
> euclidean.distance(point1 = p1, point2 = p2, square.func = square)
distance
4.242641
> euclidean.distance(point1 = p2, point2 = p1, square.func = square)
distance
4.242641
> euclidean.distance(point1 = point(10, 3), point2 = point(-4, 8),
square.func = square)
distance
14.86607
```

Thus, you can see that with functions you can define a specific function once and execute it as many times as you need.

Controlling code flow

This section covers areas related to controlling the execution of your code. Using specific constructs such as `if-else` and `switch`, you can execute code conditionally. Constructs like `for`, `while`, and `repeat`, and `help` in executing the same code multiple times which is also known as looping. We will be exploring all these constructs in the following section.

Working with if, if-else, and ifelse

There are several constructs which help us in executing code conditionally. This is especially useful when we don't want to execute a bunch of statements one after the other sequentially but execute the code only when it meets or does not meet specific conditions. The following examples illustrate the same:

```
> num = 5
> if (num == 5){
+     cat('The number was 5')
+ }
The number was 5

>

> num = 7

>

> if (num == 5){
+     cat('The number was 5')
+ } else{
+     cat('The number was not 5')
+ }
The number was not 5

>

> if (num == 5){
+     cat('The number was 5')
+ } else if (num == 7){
+     cat('The number was 7')
+ } else{
+     cat('No match found')
+ }
```

```
The number was 7
> ifelse(num == 5, "Number was 5", "Number was not 5")
[1] "Number was not 5"
```

Working with switch

The `switch` function is especially useful when you have to match an expression or argument to several conditions and execute only if there is a specific match. This becomes extremely messy when implemented with the `if-else` constructs but is much more elegant with the `switch` function, as we will see next:

```
> switch(
+ "first",
+ first = "1st",
+ second = "2nd",
+ third = "3rd",
+ "No position"
+ )
[1] "1st"
>
> switch(
+ "third",
+ first = "1st",
+ second = "2nd",
+ third = "3rd",
+ "No position"
+ )
[1] "3rd"
> # when no match, default statement executes
> switch(
+ "fifth",
+ first = "1st",
+ second = "2nd",
+ third = "3rd",
+ "No position"
+ )
[1] "No position"
```

Loops

Loops are an excellent way to execute code segments repeatedly when needed. Vectorization constructs are, however, more optimized than loops for working on larger data sets, but we will see that later in this chapter. For now, you should remember that there are three types of loops in R, namely, `for`, `while`, and `repeat`. We will look at all of them in the following examples:

```
> # for loop
> for (i in 1:10){
+     cat(paste(i," "))
+ }
1  2  3  4  5  6  7  8  9  10
>
> sum = 0
> for (i in 1:10){
+     sum <- sum + i
+ }
> sum
[1] 55
>
> # while loop
> count <- 1
> while (count <= 10){
+     cat(paste(count, " "))
+     count <- count + 1
+ }
1  2  3  4  5  6  7  8  9  10
>
> # repeat infinite loop
> count = 1
> repeat{
+     cat(paste(count, " "))
+     if (count >= 10){
+         break  # break off from the infinite loop
+     }
```

```
+       count <- count + 1
+ }
1  2  3  4  5  6  7  8  9  10
```

Advanced constructs

We heard the term **vectorized** earlier when we talked about operating on vectors without using loops. While looping is a great way to iterate through vectors and perform computations, it is not very efficient when we deal with what is known as **Big Data**. In this case, R provides some advanced constructs which we will be looking at in this section. We will be covering the following functions:

- `lapply`: Loops over a list and evaluates a function on each element
- `sapply`: A simplified version of lapply
- `apply`: Evaluates a function on the boundaries or margins of an array
- `tapply`: Evaluates a function over subsets of a vector
- `mapply`: A multivariate version of lapply

lapply and sapply

Like we mentioned earlier, `lapply` takes a list and a function as input and evaluates that function over each element of the list. If the input list is not a list, it is converted into a list using the `as.list` function before the output is returned. It is much faster than a normal loop because the actual looping is done internally using C code. We look at its implementation and an example in the following code snippet:

```
> # lapply function definition
> lapply
function (X, FUN, ...)
{
    FUN <- match.fun(FUN)
    if (!is.vector(X) || is.object(X))
        X <- as.list(X)
    .Internal(lapply(X, FUN))
}
<bytecode: 0x00000000003e4f68>
<environment: namespace:base>
```

```
> # example
> nums <- list(l1=c(1,2,3,4,5,6,7,8,9,10), l2=1000:1020)
> lapply(nums, mean)
```

Output:

```
$l1
[1] 5.5

$l2
[1] 1010
```

Coming to `sapply`, it is similar to `lapply` except that it tries to simplify the results wherever possible. For example, if the final result is such that every element is of length 1, it returns a vector, if the length of every element in the result is the same but more than 1, a matrix is returned, and if it is not able to simplify the results, we get the same result as `lapply`. We illustrate the same with the following example:

```
> data <- list(l1=1:10, l2=runif(10), l3=rnorm(10,2))
> data
```

Output:

```
$l1
 [1]  1  2  3  4  5  6  7  8  9 10

$l2
 [1] 0.3063285 0.3210605 0.2126607 0.4323474 0.7352608
 [6] 0.3211845 0.4266556 0.3350231 0.8402687 0.2214472

$l3
 [1] 3.163047 2.316373 2.928157 1.071683 1.961838 1.714548
 [7] 1.763979 3.798988 1.429736 2.898258

>
> lapply(data, mean)
```

Output:

```
$11
[1] 5.5

$12
[1] 0.4152237

$13
[1] 2.304661

> sapply(data, mean)
```

Output:

```
       11          12          13
5.5000000 0.4152237 2.3046606
```

apply

The `apply` function is used to evaluate a function over the margins or boundaries of an array; for instance, applying aggregate functions on the rows or columns of an array. The `rowSums, rowMeans, colSums,` and `colMeans` functions also use `apply` internally but are much more optimized and useful when operating on large arrays. We will see all the preceding constructs in the following example:

```
> mat <- matrix(rnorm(20), nrow=5, ncol=4)
> mat
```

Output:

```
            [,1]         [,2]        [,3]         [,4]
[1,]  0.1195527   0.7539491  1.04947756 -1.12405275
[2,]  0.1265696  -0.3927123 -0.13780092  0.07646778
[3,]  1.1871906   0.9269384  0.05736586  0.34318494
[4,]  0.6123884   1.7748904 -1.57002544 -0.53468646
[5,]  0.2013425  -1.5749354  0.45371789  0.29642974
```

```
> # row sums

> apply(mat, 1, sum)
```

```
[1]    0.79786959   0.53900665 -2.36486927 -1.28221227   0.06701519
> rowSums(mat)
[1]    0.79786959   0.53900665 -2.36486927 -1.28221227   0.06701519
> # row means
> apply(mat, 1, mean)
[1]    0.1994674   0.1347517 -0.5912173 -0.3205531   0.0167538
> rowMeans(mat)
[1]    0.1994674   0.1347517 -0.5912173 -0.3205531   0.0167538
>
> # col sums
> apply(mat, 2, sum)
[1] -0.6341087   0.3321890 -2.1345245   0.1932540
> colSums(mat)
[1] -0.6341087   0.3321890 -2.1345245   0.1932540
> apply(mat, 2, mean)
[1] -0.12682173   0.06643781 -0.42690489   0.03865079
> colMeans(mat)
[1] -0.12682173   0.06643781 -0.42690489   0.03865079
>
> # row quantiles
> apply(mat, 1, quantile, probs=c(0.25, 0.5, 0.75))
```

Output:

```
          [,1]          [,2]        [,3]         [,4]        [,5]
25% -0.1913486 -0.20152876 0.2717302 -0.79352120 -0.2427270
50%  0.4367509 -0.03066657 0.6350617  0.03885096  0.2488861
75%  0.8278312  0.08899324 0.9920015  0.90301390  0.3357518
```

Thus you can see how easy it is to apply various statistical functions on matrices without using loops at all.

tapply

The function `tapply` is used to evaluate a function over the subsets of any vector. This is similar to applying the GROUP BY construct in SQL if you are familiar with using relational databases. We illustrate the same in the following examples:

```
> data <- c(1:10, rnorm(10,2), runif(10))
> data
```

Output:

```
 [1]  1.00000000  2.00000000  3.00000000  4.00000000  5.00000000
 [6]  6.00000000  7.00000000  8.00000000  9.00000000 10.00000000
[11]  2.23147539  2.21731733  1.83956388  0.03597464  2.91214941
[16]  3.28026069  2.25403785  2.99538891  3.16527292  1.82685914
[21]  0.02740101  0.19610746  0.34837827  0.25190460  0.72999163
[26]  0.47645627  0.61436625  0.80770405  0.92255269  0.86156925
```

```
> groups <- gl(3,10)
> groups
 [1] 1 1 1 1 1 1 1 1 1 1 2 2 2 2 2 2 2 2 2 2 3 3 3 3 3 3 3 3 3 3
Levels: 1 2 3
> tapply(data, groups, mean)
```

Output:

```
        1         2         3
5.5000000 2.2758300 0.5236431
```

```
> tapply(data, groups, mean, simplify = FALSE)
```

Output:

```
$`1`
[1] 5.5

$`2`
[1] 2.27583

$`3`
[1] 0.5236431
```

```
> tapply(data, groups, range)
```

Output:

```
$`1`
[1]    1 10

$`2`
[1]  0.03597464  3.28026069

$`3`
[1]  0.02740101  0.92255269
```

mapply

The `mapply` function is a multivariate version of `lapply` and is used to evaluate a function in parallel over sets of arguments. A simple example is if we have to build a list of vectors using the `rep` function, we have to write it multiple times. However, with `mapply` we can achieve the same in a more elegant way as illustrated next:

```
> list(rep(1,4), rep(2,3), rep(3,2), rep(4,1))
```

Output:

```
[[1]]
[1] 1 1 1 1

[[2]]
[1] 2 2 2

[[3]]
[1] 3 3

[[4]]
[1] 4

> mapply(rep, 1:4, 4:1)
```

Output:

```
[[1]]
[1] 1 1 1 1

[[2]]
[1] 2 2 2

[[3]]
[1] 3 3

[[4]]
[1] 4
```

Next steps with R

Before we dive into machine learning, it will be useful to pause for a moment, take a deep breath, and contemplate on what you have learnt so far. This quick yet detailed refresher of R will help you a lot in the upcoming chapters. However, there are two more things which we must go through quickly. They are how to get help in R and how to work with various packages in R.

Getting help

By now, you must have figured out that there are thousands of functions and constructs in R and it is impossible to remember what each of them actually does and you don't have to either! R provides many intuitive ways to get help regarding any function, package, or data structure. To start with, you can run the help.start() function at the R command prompt, which will start a manual browser. Here you will get detailed information regarding R which includes manuals, references, and other material. The following command shows the contents of help.start() as shown in the screenshot following the command, which you can use to navigate further and get more help:

```
> help.start()
```

If nothing happens, you should open `http://127.0.0.1:31850/doc/html/index.html` yourself.

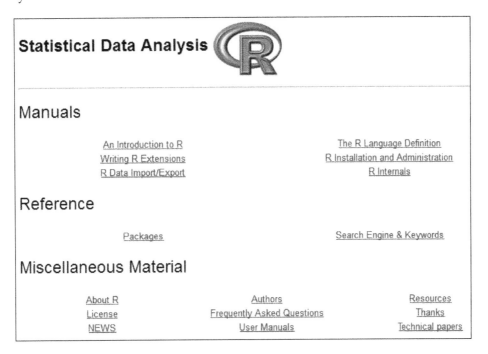

To get help on any particular function or construct in R, if you know the function's name, you can get help using the help function or the `?` operator in combination with the function name. For example, if you want help regarding the `apply` function, just type `help("apply")` or `?apply` to get detailed information regarding the `apply` function. This easy mechanism for getting help in R increases your productivity and makes working with R a pleasant experience. Often, you won't quite remember the exact name of the function you intend to use but you might have a vague idea of what its name might be. R has a help feature for this purpose too, where you can use the `help.search` function or the `??` operator, in combination with the function name. For example, you can use `??apply` to get more information on the apply function.

Handling packages

There are thousands and thousands of packages containing a wide variety of capabilities available on **CRAN (Comprehensive R Archive Network)**, which is a repository hosting all these packages. To download any package from CRAN, all you have to do is run the `install.packages` function passing the package name as a parameter, like `install.packages("caret")`. Once the package is downloaded and installed, you can load it into your current R session using the `library` function. To load the package `caret`, just type `library(caret)` and it should be readily available for use. The `require` function has similar functionality to load a specific package and is used specially inside functions in a similar way by typing `require(caret)` to load the `caret` package. The only difference between `require` and `library` is that, in case the specific package is not found, `library` will show an error but `require` will continue the execution of code without showing any error. However, if there is a dependency call to that package then your code will definitely throw an error.

Machine learning basics

Now that you have refreshed your memory about R, we will be talking about the basics of what machine learning is, how it is used today, and what are the main areas inside machine learning. This section intends to provide an overview into machine learning which will help in paving the way to the next chapter where we will be exploring it in more depth.

Machine learning – what does it really mean?

Machine learning does not have just one distinct textbook definition because it is a field which encompasses and borrows concepts and techniques from several other areas in computer science. It is also taught as an academic course in universities and has recently gained more prominence, with machine learning and data science being widely adopted online, in the form of educational videos, courses, and training. Machine learning is basically an intersection of elements from the fields of computer science, statistics, and mathematics, which uses concepts from artificial intelligence, pattern detection, optimization, and learning theory to develop algorithms and techniques which can learn from and make predictions on data without being explicitly programmed.

The learning here refers to the ability to make computers or machines intelligent based on the data and algorithms which we provide to them so that they start detecting patterns and insights from the provided data. This learning ensures that machines can detect patterns on data fed to it without explicitly programming them every time. The initial data or observations are fed to the machine and the machine learning algorithm works on that data to generate some output which can be a prediction, a hypothesis, or even some numerical result. Based on this output, there can be feedback mechanisms to our machine learning algorithm to improve our results. This whole system forms a machine learning model which can be used directly on completely new data or observations to get results from it without needing to write any separate algorithm again to work on that data.

Machine learning – how is it used in the world?

You might be wondering how on earth some algorithms or code can be used in the real world. It turns out they are used in a wide variety of use-cases in different verticals. Some examples are as follows:

- **Retail**: Machine learning is widely used in the retail and e-commerce vertical where each store wants to outperform its competitors.

    ◦ **Pricing analytics**: Machine learning algorithms are used to compare prices for items across various stores so that a store can sell the item at the most competitive price.

    ◦ **Market basket analysis**: They are used for analysis of customer shopping trends and recommendation of products to buy, which we will be covering in *Chapter 3, Predicting Customer Shopping Trends with Market Basket Analysis*.

    ◦ **Recommendation engines**: They are used to analyze customer purchases, ratings, and satisfaction to recommend products to various users. We will be building some recommendation systems of our own in *Chapter 4, Building a Product Recommendation System*.

- **Advertising**: The advertising industry heavily relies on machine learning to promote and show the right advertisements to consumers for maximum conversion.

    ◦ **Web analytics**: Analyzes website traffic

    ◦ **Churn analytics**: Predicts customer churn rate

- ° **Advertisement click-through prediction**: Used to predict how effective an advertisement would be to consumers such that they click on it to buy the relevant product

- **Healthcare**: Machine learning algorithms are used widely in the healthcare vertical for more effective treatment of patients.
  - ° **Disease detection and prediction**: Used to detect and predict chances of a disease based on the patient's medical history.
  - ° Studying complex structures such as the human brain and DNA to understand the human body's functionality better for more effective treatment.

- Detection and filtering of spam e-mails and messages.

- Predicting election results.

- Fraud detection and prediction. We will be taking a stab at one of the most critical fraud detection problems in *Chapters 5, Credit Risk Detection and Prediction – Descriptive Analytics* and *Chapter 6, Credit Risk Detection and Prediction – Predictive Analytics*.

- Text prediction in a messaging application.

- Self-driving cars, planes, and other vehicles.

- Weather, traffic, and crime activity forecasting and prediction.

- Sentiment and emotion analysis, which we will be covering in *Chapter 8, Sentiment Analysis of Twitter Data*.

The preceding examples just scratch the surface of what machine learning can really do and by now I am sure that you have got a good flavor of the various areas where machine learning is being used extensively.

Types of machine learning algorithms

As we talked about earlier, to make machines learn, you need machine learning algorithms. Machine learning algorithms are a special class of algorithms which work on data and gather insights from it. The idea is to build a model using a combination of data and algorithms which can then be used to work on new data and derive actionable insights.

Each machine learning algorithm depends on what type of data it can work on and what type of problem are we trying to solve. You might be tempted to learn a couple of algorithms and then try to apply them to every problem you face. Do remember that there is no universal machine learning algorithm which fits all problems. The main input to machine learning algorithms is data which consists of features, where each feature can be described as an attribute of the data set, such as your height, weight, and so on if we were dealing with data related to human beings. Machine learning algorithms can be divided into two main areas, namely supervised and unsupervised learning algorithms.

Supervised machine learning algorithms

The supervised learning algorithms are a subset of the family of machine learning algorithms which are mainly used in predictive modeling. A predictive model is basically a model constructed from a machine learning algorithm and features or attributes from training data such that we can predict a value using the other values obtained from the input data. Supervised learning algorithms try to model relationships and dependencies between the target prediction output and the input features such that we can predict the output values for new data based on those relationships which it learned from the previous data sets. The main types of supervised learning algorithms include:

- **Classification algorithms**: These algorithms build predictive models from training data which have features and class labels. These predictive models in-turn use the features learnt from training data on new, previously unseen data to predict their class labels. The output classes are discrete. Types of classification algorithms include decision trees, random forests, support vector machines, and many more. We will be using several of these algorithms in *Chapter 2, Let's Help Machines Learn, Chapter 6, Credit Risk Detection and Prediction – Predictive Analytics*, and *Chapter 8, Sentiment Analysis of Twitter Data*.

- **Regression algorithms**: These algorithms are used to predict output values based on some input features obtained from the data. To do this, the algorithm builds a model based on features and output values of the training data and this model is used to predict values for new data. The output values in this case are continuous and not discrete. Types of regression algorithms include linear regression, multivariate regression, regression trees, and lasso regression, among many others. We explore some of these in *Chapter 2, Let's Help Machines Learn*.

Unsupervised machine learning algorithms

The unsupervised learning algorithms are the family of machine learning algorithms which are mainly used in pattern detection and descriptive modeling. A descriptive model is basically a model constructed from an unsupervised machine learning algorithm and features from input data similar to the supervised learning process. However, there are no output categories or labels here based on which the algorithm can try to model relationships. These algorithms try to use techniques on the input data to mine for rules, detect patterns, and summarize and group the data points which help in deriving meaningful insights and describe the data better to the users. There is no specific concept of training or testing data here since we do not have any specific relationship mapping and we are just trying to get useful insights and descriptions from the data we are trying to analyze. The main types of unsupervised learning algorithms include:

- **Clustering algorithms**: The main objective of these algorithms is to cluster or group input data points into different classes or categories using just the features derived from the input data alone and no other external information. Unlike classification, the output labels are not known beforehand in clustering. There are different approaches to build clustering models, such as by using means, medoids, hierarchies, and many more. Some popular clustering algorithms include k-means, k-medoids, and hierarchical clustering. We will look at some clustering algorithms in *Chapter 2, Let's Help Machines Learn*, and *Chapter 7, Social Media Analysis – Analyzing Twitter Data*.

- **Association rule learning algorithms**: These algorithms are used to mine and extract rules and patterns from data sets. These rules explain relationships between different variables and attributes, and also depict frequent item sets and patterns which occur in the data. These rules in turn help discover useful insights for any business or organization from their huge data repositories. Popular algorithms include Apriori and FP Growth. We will be using some of these in *Chapter 2, Let's Help Machines Learn*, and *Chapter 3, Predicting Customer Shopping Trends with Market Basket Analysis*.

Popular machine learning packages in R

After getting a brief overview of machine learning basics and types of algorithms, you must be getting inquisitive as to how we apply some of these algorithms to solve real world problems using R. It turns out, there are a whole lot of packages in R which are dedicated to just solving machine learning problems. These packages consist of algorithms which are optimized and ready to be used to solve problems. We will list several popular machine learning packages in R, so that you are aware of what tools you might need later on and also feel more familiar with some of these packages when used in the later chapters. Based on usage and functionality, the following R packages are quite popular in solving machine learning problems:

- `caret`: This package (short for classification and regression training) consists of several machine learning algorithms for building predictive models

- `randomForest`: This package deals with implementations of the random forest algorithm for classification and regression

- `rpart`: This package focuses on recursive partitioning and decision trees

- `glmnet`: The main focus of this package is lasso and elastic-net regularized regression models

- `e1071`: This deals with fourier transforms, clustering, support vector machines, and many more supervised and unsupervised algorithms

- `party`: This deals with recursive partitioning

- `arules`: This package is used for association rule learning algorithms

- `recommenderlab`: This is a library to build recommendation engines

- `nnet`: This package enables predictive modeling using neural networks

- `h2o`: It is one of the most popular packages being used in data science these days and offers fast and scalable algorithms including gradient boosting and deep learning

Besides the preceding libraries, there are a ton of other packages out there related to machine learning in R. What matters is choosing the right algorithm and model based on the data and problem in hand.

Summary

In this chapter, we talked briefly about the journey we will take into the world of machine learning and R. We discussed the basics of R and built a strong foundation of the core constructs and data structures used in R. Then we dived into the world of machine learning by looking at some concepts and algorithms, and how it is used in the world to solve problems. Finally, we ended with a quick glance at some of the most popular machine learning packages in R to get us all familiarized with some handy tools for our machine learning toolbox!

In the next chapter, we will be looking in depth about machine learning concepts and algorithms which will help us make the machines learn something!

2

Let's Help Machines Learn

Machine learning, when you first hear it, sounds more like a fancy word from a sci-fi movie than the latest trend in the tech industry. Talk about it to people in general and their responses are either related to being generally curious about the concept or being cautious and fearful about intelligent machines taking over our world in some sort of Terminator-Skynet way.

We live in a digital age and are constantly presented with all sorts of information all the time. As we will see in this and the coming chapters, machine learning is something that loves data. In fact, the recent hype and interest in this field has been fueled by not just the improvements in computing technology but also due to exponential growth in the amount of data being generated every second. The latest numbers stand at around 2.5 quintillion bytes of data every day (that's 2.5 followed by 18 zeroes)!

 Fun Fact: More than 300 hours of video data is uploaded to YouTube every minute
Source: `https://www-01.ibm.com/software/data/bigdata/what-is-big-data.html`

Just take a deep breath and look around. Everything around you is generating data all the time, of all sorts; your phone, your car, the traffic signals, GPS, thermostats, weather systems, social networks, and on and on and on! There is data everywhere and we can do all sorts of interesting things with it and help the systems learn. Well, as fascinating as it sounds, let us start our journey on machine learning. Through this chapter we will cover:

- Understanding machine learning
- Algorithms in machine learning and their application
- Families of algorithms: supervised and unsupervised

Understanding machine learning

Aren't we taught that computer systems have to be programmed to do certain tasks? They may be a million times faster at doing things but they have to be programmed. We have to code each and every step and only then do these systems work and complete a task. Isn't then the very notion of machine learning a very contradictory concept?

In the simplest ways, machine learning refers to a method of teaching the systems to learn to do certain tasks, such as learning a function. As simple as it sounds, it is a bit confusing and difficult to digest. Confusing because our view of the way the systems (computer systems specifically) work and the way we learn are two concepts that hardly intersect. It is even more difficult to digest because learning, though an inherent capability of the human race, is difficult to put in to words, let alone teach to the systems.

Then what is machine learning? Before we even try to answer this question, we need to understand that at a philosophical level it is something more than just a way to program. Machine learning is a lot of things.

There are many ways in which machine learning can be described. Continuing from the high level definition we presented in the previous chapter, let us go through the definition given by Tom Mitchell in 1997:

> *"A computer program is said to learn from experience E with respect to some task T and some performance measure P, if its performance on T, as measured by P, improves with experience E."*

Quick Note about Prof Tom Mitchell

Born in 1951, he is an American computer scientist and professor at Carnegie Mellon University (CMU). He is also the chair of the machine learning department at CMU. He is well known for his contributions in the fields of machine learning, artificial intelligence, and cognitive neuroscience. He is part of various institutions such as the Association for the Advancement of Artificial Intelligence.

Now let us try to make sense out of this concise yet powerful definition with the help of an example. Let us say we want to build a system that predicts the weather. For the current example, the task (T) of the system would be to predict the weather for a certain place. To perform such a task, it needs to rely upon weather information from the past. We shall term it as experience E. Its performance (P) is measured on how well it predicts the weather at any given day. Thus, we can generalize that a system has successfully learned how to predict the weather (or task T) if it gets better at predicting it (or improves its performance P) utilizing the past information (or experience E).

As seen in the preceding example, this definition not only helps us understand machine learning from an engineering point of view, it also gives us tools to quantify the terms. The definition helps us with the fact that learning a particular task involves understanding and processing of the data in the form of experience. It also mentions that if a computer program learns, its performance improves with experience, pretty similar to the way we learn.

Algorithms in machine learning

So far we have developed an abstract understanding of machine learning. We understand the definition of machine learning which states that a task T can be learned by a computer program utilizing data in the form of experience E when its performance P improves with it. We have also seen how machine learning is different from conventional programming paradigms because of the fact that we do not code each and every step, rather we let the program form an understanding of the problem space and help us solve it. It is rather surprising to see such a program work right in front of us.

All along while we learned about the concept of machine learning, we treated this magical computer program as a mysterious black box which learns and solves the problems for us. Now is the time we unravel its enigma and look under the hood and see these magical algorithms in full glory.

We will begin with some of the most commonly and widely used algorithms in machine learning, looking at their intricacies, usage, and a bit of mathematics wherever necessary. Through this chapter, you will be introduced to different families of algorithms. The list is by no means exhaustive and, even though the algorithms will be explained in fair detail, a deep theoretical understanding of each of them is beyond the scope of this book. There is tons of material easily available in the form of books, online courses, blogs, and more.

Perceptron

This is like the `Hello World` algorithm of the machine learning universe. It may be one of the easiest of the lot to understand and use but it is by no means any less powerful.

Published in 1958 by Frank Rosenblatt, the perceptron algorithm gained much attention because of its guarantee to find a separator in a separable data set.

A perceptron is a function (or a simplified neuron to be precise) which takes a vector of real numbers as input and generates a real number as output.

Mathematically, a perceptron can be represented as:

$$y = f\left(w_1 x_1 + w_2 x_2 + \ldots + w_n x_n + b\right) = f\left(w^T x + b\right)$$

Where, `w1`,…, `wn` are weights, `b` is a constant termed as bias, `x1`,…, `xn` are inputs, and `y` is the output of the function `f`, which is called the activation function.

The algorithm is as follows:

1. Initialize weight vector `w` and bias `b` to small random numbers.
2. Calculate the output vector `y` based on the function `f` and vector `x`.
3. Update the weight vector `w` and bias `b` to counter the error.
4. Repeat steps 2 and 3 until there is no error or the error drops below a certain threshold.

The algorithm tries to find a separator which divides the input into two classes by using a labeled data set called the training data set (the training data set corresponds to the experience E as stated in the definition for machine learning in the previous section). The algorithm starts by assigning random weights to the weight vector `w` and the bias `b`. It then processes the input based on the function `f` and gives a vector `y`. This generated output is then compared with the correct output value from the training data set and the updates are made to `w` and `b` respectively. To understand the weight update process, let us consider a point, say `p1`, with a correct output value of `+1`. Now, suppose if the perceptron misclassifies `p1` as `-1`, it updates the weight `w` and bias `b` to move the perceptron by a small amount (movement is restricted by learning rate to prevent sudden jumps) in the direction of `p1` in order to correctly classify it. The algorithm stops when it finds the correct separator or when the error in classifying the inputs drops below a certain user defined threshold.

Now, let us see the algorithm in action with the help of small example.

For the algorithm to work, we need a linearly separable data set. Let us assume the data is generated by the following function:

$$x_2 = x_1 + 1/2$$

Based on the preceding equation, the correct separator will be given as:

$$y = +1, \text{when } x_2 > x_1 + 1/2$$
$$-1 \text{otherwise}$$

Generating an input vector x using uniformly distributed data in R is done as follows:

```
#30 random numbers between -1 and 1 which are uniformly distributed
x1 <- runif(30,-1,1)
x2 <- runif(30,-1,1)
#form the input vector x
x <- cbind(x1,x2)
```

Now that we have the data, we need a function to classify it into one of the two categories.

```
#helper function to calculate distance from hyperplane
calculate_distance = function(x,w,b) {
  sum(x*w) + b
}


#linear classifier
linear_classifier = function(x,w,b) {
distances =apply(x, 1, calculate_distance, w, b)
return(ifelse(distances < 0, -1, +1))
}
```

The helper function, `calculate_distance`, calculates the distance of each point from the separator, while `linear_classifier` classifies each point either as belonging to class -1 or class +1.

The perceptron algorithm then uses the preceding classifier function to find the correct separator using the training data set.

```
#function to calculate 2nd norm
second_norm = function(x) {sqrt(sum(x * x))}


#perceptron training algorithm
perceptron = function(x, y, learning_rate=1) {


w = vector(length = ncol(x)) # initialize w
b = 0 # Initialize b
k = 0 # count iterations


#constant with value greater than distance of furthest point
R = max(apply(x, 1, second_norm))


incorrect = TRUE # flag to identify classifier


#initialize plot
plot(x,cex=0.2)


#loop till correct classifier is not found
while (incorrect ) {


    incorrect =FALSE

  #classify with current weights
    yc <- linear_classifier(x,w,b)
    #Loop over each point in the input x
    for (i in 1:nrow(x)) {
      #update weights if point not classified correctly
      if (y[i] != yc[i]) {
```

```r
        w <- w + learning_rate * y[i]*x[i,]
      b <- b + learning_rate * y[i]*R^2
      k <- k+1


      #currect classifier's components
      # update plot after ever 5 iterations
    if(k%%5 == 0){
        intercept <- - b / w[[2]]
        slope <- - w[[1]] / w[[2]]
        #plot the classifier hyper plane
        abline(intercept,slope,col="red")
        #wait for user input
        cat ("Iteration # ",k,"\n")
        cat ("Press [enter] to continue")
        line <- readline()
     }
    incorrect =TRUE
     }
   }
}


s = second_norm(w)
#scale the classifier with unit vector
return(list(w=w/s,b=b/s,updates=k))
}
```

It's now time to train the perceptron!

```r
#train the perceptron
p <- perceptron(x,Y)
```

The plot will look as follows:

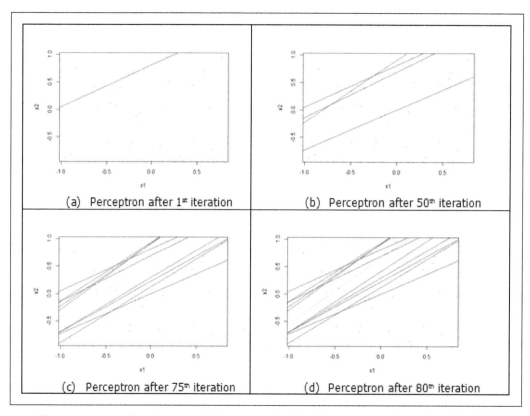

(a) Perceptron after 1ˢᵗ iteration   (b) Perceptron after 50ᵗʰ iteration

(c) Perceptron after 75ᵗʰ iteration   (d) Perceptron after 80ᵗʰ iteration

The perceptron working its way to find the correct classifier. The correct classifier is shown in green

The preceding plots show the perceptron's training state. Each incorrect classifier is shown with a red line. As shown, the perceptron ends after finding the correct classifier marked in green.

A zoomed-in view of the final separator can be seen as follows:

```
#classify based on calculated
y <- linear_classifier(x,p$w,p$b)
```

```
plot(x,cex=0.2)
```

```
#zoom into points near the separator and color code them
#marking data points as + which have y=1 and - for others
```

```
points(subset(x,Y==1),col="black",pch="+",cex=2)
points(subset(x,Y==-1),col="red",pch="-",cex=2)

# compute intercept on y axis of separator
# from w and b
intercept <- - p$b / p$w[[2]]

# compute slope of separator from w
slope <- - p$w[[1]] /p$ w[[2]]

# draw separating boundary
abline(intercept,slope,col="green")
```

The plot looks as shown in the following figure:

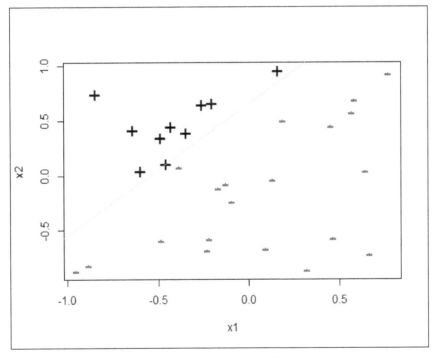

The correct classifier function as found by perceptron

Families of algorithms

There are tons of algorithms in the machine learning universe and more are devised each year. There is tremendous research happening in this space and hence the ever increasing list of algorithms. It is also a fact that the more these algorithms are being used, the more improvements in them are being discovered. Machine learning is one space where industry and academia are running hand in hand.

But, as Spider-Man was told that *with great power comes great responsibility*, the reader should also understand the responsibility at hand. With so many algorithms available, it is necessary to understand what they are and where they fit. It can feel overwhelming and confusing at first but that is when categorizing them into families helps.

Machine learning algorithms can be categorized in many ways. The most common way is to group them into supervised learning algorithms and unsupervised learning algorithms.

Supervised learning algorithms

Supervised learning refers to algorithms which are trained on a predefined data set called the training data set. The training data set is usually a two element tuple consisting of an input element and a desired output element or signal. In general, the input element is a vector. The supervised learning algorithm uses the training data set to produce the desired function. The function so produced (or rather inferred) is then utilized to correctly map new data, better termed as the test data.

An algorithm which has learnt well will be able to correctly determine the outputs for unseen data in a reasonable way. This brings in the concepts of generalization and overfitting.

Briefly, generalization refers to the concept wherein an algorithm generalizes the desired function based upon the (limited) training data to handle unseen data in a correct manner. Overfitting is exactly the opposite concept of generalization, wherein an algorithm infers a function such that it maps exactly to the training data set (including the noise). This may result in huge errors when the function learnt by the algorithm is checked against new/unseen data.

Both generalization and overfitting revolve around the random errors or noise in the input data. While generalization tries to minimize the effect of noise, overfitting does the opposite by fitting in noise as well.

Problems to be solved using supervised methods can be divided into the following steps:

1. **Prepare training data**: Data preparation is the most important step for all machine learning algorithms. Since supervised learning utilizes labeled input data sets (data sets which consist of corresponding outputs for given inputs), this step becomes even more important. This data is usually labeled by human experts or from measurements.

2. **Prepare the model**: The model is the representation of the input data set and the learnt pattern. The model representation is affected by factors such as input features and the learning algorithm itself. The accuracy of the inferred function also depends on how this representation is formed.

3. **Choose an algorithm**: Based on the problem being solved and the input information, an algorithm is then chosen to learn and solve the problem.

4. **Examine and fine tune**: This is an iterative step where the algorithm is run on the input data set and the parameters are fine tuned to achieve the desired level of output. The algorithm is then tested on the test data set to evaluate its performance and measure the error.

Under supervised learning, two major sub categories are:

1. **Regression based machine learning**: Learning algorithms which help us answer quantitative questions such as how many? or how much? The outputs are generally continuous values. More formally, these algorithms predict the output values for unseen/new data based on the training data and the model formed. The output values are continuous in this case. Linear regression, multivariate regression, regression trees, and so on are a few supervised regression algorithms.

2. **Classification based machine learning**: Learning algorithms which help us answer objective questions or yes-or-no predictions. For example, questions such as is this component faulty? or can this tumor cause cancer? More formally, these algorithms predict the class labels for unseen or new data based upon the training data and model formed. **Support Vector Machines (SVM)**, decision trees, random forests, and so on are a few commonly used supervised classification algorithms.

Let us look at some supervised learning algorithms in detail.

Linear regression

Regression, as mentioned previously, helps us answer quantitative questions. Regression has its roots in the statistics domain. Researchers use a linear relationship to predict the output value Y for a given input value X. This linear relationship is called a linear regression or regression line.

Mathematically, linear regression is represented as:

$$y = b_0 + b_1 x$$

Where, b_0 is the intercept or the point where the line crosses the y axis.

b_1 is the slope of the line, that is, the change in y over change in x.

The preceding equation is pretty similar to how a straight line is represented and hence the name linear regression.

Now, how do we decide which line we fit for our input so that it predicts well for unknown data? Well, for this we need an error measure. There can be various error measures; the most commonly used is the **least squares method**.

Before we define the least squares method, we first need to understand the term residual. Residual is simply the deviation of Y from a fitted value. Mathematically:

$$residual_i = y_i - \hat{y}_i$$

Where, $\hat{y}_i$ is the deviated value of y.

The least squares method states that the most optimal fit of a model to data occurs when the sum of the squares of residuals is minimum.

Mathematically:

$$Sum\,of\,Squares\,of\,residual = SS\left(residual_i\right)$$

$$SS\left(residual_i\right) \quad = \sum_{i=1}^{n}\left(y_i - \hat{y}_i\right)^2$$

$$= \sum_{i=1}^{n}\left(y_i - \left(b_0 + b_1 x_i\right)\right)^2$$

We use calculus to minimize the sum of squares for residuals and find the corresponding coefficients.

Now that we understand linear regression, let us take a real world example to see it in action.

Suppose we have data related to the height and weight of school children. The data scientist in you suddenly starts thinking about whether there is any relation between the weights and heights of these children. Formally, could the weight of a child be predicted based upon his/her given height?

To fit in linear regression, the first step is to understand the data and see whether there is a correlation between the two variables (`weight` and `height`). Since in this case we are dealing with just two dimensions, visualizing the data using a scatter plot will help us understand it quickly. This will also enable us to determine if the variables have some linear relationship or not.

Let us prepare our data first and visualize it on a scatter plot along with the correlation coefficient.

```
#Height and weight vectors for 19 children

height <- c(69.1,56.4,65.3,62.8,63,57.3,59.8,62.5,62.5,59.0,51.3,64,56.4,
66.5,72.2,65.0,67.0,57.6,66.6)

weight <- c(113,84,99,103,102,83,85,113,84,99,51,90,77,112,150,128,133,85
,112)

plot(height,weight)
cor(height,weight)
```

Output:

```
[1] 0.8848454
```

The scatter plot looks like this:

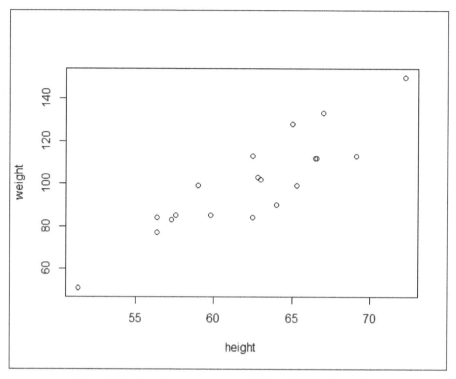

Figure displaying data points across weight and height dimensions

The preceding scatter plot proves that our intuition about weight and height having a linear relationship was correct. This can further be confirmed using the correlation function, which gives us a value of 0.88.

Time to prepare the model for our data set! We use the inbuilt utility lm or the linear model utility to find the coefficients b_0 and b_1.

```
#Fitting the linear model

model <- lm(weight ~ height) # weight = slope*weight + intercept

#get the intercept(b0) and the slope(b1) values
model
```

The output looks like this:

```
Call:
lm(formula = weight ~ height)

Coefficients:
(Intercept)        height
    -143.227         3.905
```

You can experiment a bit more to find out more details calculated by the lm utility using the following commands. We encourage you to go ahead and try these out.

```
#check all attributes calculated by lm
attributes(model)


#getting only the intercept
model$coefficients[1] #or model$coefficients[[1]]


#getting only the slope
model$coefficients[2] #or model$coefficients[[2]]


#checking the residuals
residuals(model)


#predicting the weight for a given height, say 60 inches
model$coefficients[[2]]*50 + model$coefficients[[1]]


#detailed information about the model
summary(model)
```

As the final piece, let us visualize the regression line on our scatter plot itself.

```
#plot data points
 plot(height,weight)


#draw the regression line
abline(model)
```

The scatter plot looks like the following figure:

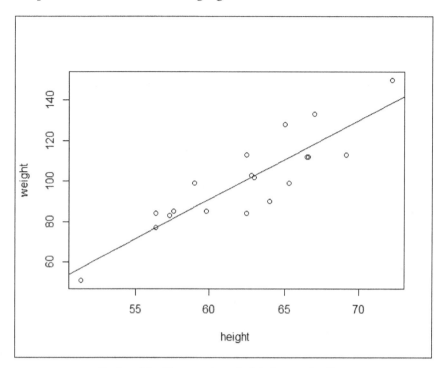

Scatter plot with regression calculated regression line

Thus, we saw how the relationship between two variables can be identified and predictions can be made using a few lines of code. But we are not done yet. There are a couple of caveats which the reader must understand before deciding whether to use linear regression or not.

Linear regression can be used to predict the output values for given inputs, if and only if:

- The scatter plot forms a linear pattern
- The correlation between them is moderate to strong (beyond 0.5 or -0.5)

Cases where only one of the previous two conditions are met can lead to incorrect predictions or altogether invalid models. For example, if we only check the correlation and find it to be strong and skip the step where we look at the scatter plot, then that may lead to invalid predictions as you might have tried to fit a straight line when the data itself is following a curved shape (note that curved data sets can also have high correlation values and hence the mistake).

It is important to remember that **correlation does not imply causation**. In simple words, correlation between two variables does not necessarily imply that one causes the other. There might be a case that cause and effect are indirectly related due to a third variable termed as the cofounding variable. The most common example used to describe this issue is the relationship between shoe size and reading ability. From the survey data (if one existed!) it could be inferred that larger shoe sizes relate to higher reading ability, but this clearly does not mean that large feet cause good reading skills to be developed. It might be rather interesting to note that young children have small feet and have not yet been taught to read. In such a case, the two variables are more accurately correlated with age.

You should now be coming to similar conclusion about the weight to height example we used earlier. Well yes, the earlier example also suffers from similar fallacy, yet it served as an easy to use scenario. Feel free to look around and model cases which do not suffer from this.

Linear regression finds application in the field of finance where it is used for things such as quantification of risks on investments. It is also used widely in the field of economics for trendline analysis and so on.

Apart from linear regression, **logistic regression**, **stepwise regression**, **Multivariate Adaptive Regression Splines** (**MARS**), and others are a few more supervised regression learning algorithms.

K-Nearest Neighbors (KNN)

K-Nearest Neighbors or KNN algorithms are amongst the simplest algorithms from an implementation and understanding point of view. They are yet another type of supervised learning algorithm which helps us classify data.

KNN can be easily described using the quote *like and like strike together – Plato*, that is, similar things are likely have similar properties. KNN utilizes this very concept to label a data point based upon its similarity with respect to its neighbors.

Formally, KNN can be described as the process to classify unlabeled (or unseen) data points by assigning them the class of the most similar labeled data points (or training samples).

KNN is a supervised learning algorithm. Hence, it begins with a training data set of examples which are classified into different classes. The algorithm then picks each data point in the test data set and, based upon a chosen similarity measure, identifies its k nearest neighbors (where k is specified in advance). The data point is then assigned the class of the majority of the k nearest neighbors.

The trick up the KNN's sleeve is the similarity measure. There are various similarity measures available to us. The decision to choose one is based on the complexity of the problem, the type of data, and so on. Euclidean distance is one such measure which is widely used. Euclidean distance is the shortest direct route between two points. Mathematically it is given as:

$$Euclidean-distance(p,q) = \sqrt{\sum_{i=1}^{n}(q_i - p_i)^2}$$

Manhattan distance, Cosine distance, and Minkowski distance are some other types of distance measures which can be used for finding the nearest neighbors.

The next parameter for KNN algorithm is the k in the K-Nearest Neighbors. The value of k determines how well the KNN model generalizes to the test data. The balance between overfitting and underfitting the training data depends upon the value of k. With slight deliberation, it is easy to understand that a large k will minimize the impact of variance caused by noisy data, but at the same time, it will also undermine small but important patterns in the data. This problem is called the **bias-variance tradeoff**.

The optimal value of k, even though hard to determine, lies between the extremes of k=1 to k=total number of training samples. A common practice is to set the value of k equal to the square root of training instances, usually between 3 and 10. Though a common practice, the value of k is dependent on the complexity of the concept to be learned and the number of training examples.

The next step in pursuit of the KNN algorithm is preparation of data. Features used to prepare the input vectors should be on similar scales. The rationale for this step is that the distance formula is dependent on how the features are measured. For example, if certain features have large range of values as compared to others, the distance measurements will then be dominated by such measures. The method of scaling features to a similar scale is called **normalization**. Very much like the distance measure, there are various normalization methods available. One such method is min-max normalization, given mathematically as:

$$x_{new} = \frac{x - \min(x)}{\max(x) - \min(x)}$$

Before we begin with our example to understand KNN, let us outline the steps to be performed to execute KNN:

1. **Collect data and explore data**: We need to collect data relevant to the concept to be learnt. We also need to explore the data to understand various features, know the range of their values, and determine the class labels.

2. **Normalize data**: As discussed previously, KNN's dependence on distance measure makes it very important that we normalize the data to remove any inconsistency or bias in calculations.

3. **Create training and test data sets**: Since it is important to learn a concept and prepare a model which generalizes to acceptable levels for unseen data, we need to prepare training and test data sets. The test data set, even though labeled, is used to determine the accuracy and the ability of the model to generalize the concept learnt. A usual practice is to divide the input sample into two-third and one-third portions for training and test data sets respectively. It is equally important that the two data sets are a good mix of all the class labels and data points, that is both the data sets should be representative subsets of the full data.

4. **Train the model**: Now that we have all the things in place, we can use the training data set, test data set, the labels, and the value of k to train our model and label the data points in the test data set.

5. **Evaluate the model**: The final step is to evaluate the learnt pattern. In this step, we determine how well the algorithm has predicted the class labels of the test data set as compared to their known labels. Usually a confusion matrix is prepared for the same.

Now, let us see KNN in action. The problem at hand is to classify different species of flowers based upon certain features. For this particular example, we will be using the Iris data set. This data set comes built in with the default installation of R.

Collecting and exploring data

Step one is to collect and explore the data. Let us first gather the data.

To check if your system has the required dataset, type in just the name:

```
iris
#this should print the contents of data set onto the console.
```

If you do not have the data set available, no worries! You can download it as follows:

```
#skip these steps if you already have iris on your system
iris <- read.csv(url("http://archive.ics.uci.edu/ml/machine-learning-
databases/iris/iris.data"), header = FALSE)


#assign proper headers
names(iris) <- c("Sepal.Length", "Sepal.Width", "Petal.Length", "Petal.
Width", "Species")
```

Now that we have the data, it is time to explore and understand it. For exploring the data set and its attributes, we use the following commands:

```
#to view top few rows of data
head(iris)
```

Output:

```
  Sepal.Length Sepal.Width Petal.Length Petal.Width     Species
1          5.1         3.5          1.4         0.2 Iris-setosa
2          4.9         3.0          1.4         0.2 Iris-setosa
3          4.7         3.2          1.3         0.2 Iris-setosa
4          4.6         3.1          1.5         0.2 Iris-setosa
5          5.0         3.6          1.4         0.2 Iris-setosa
6          5.4         3.9          1.7         0.4 Iris-setosa
```

```
#to view data types, sample values, categorical values, etc
str(iris)
```

Output:

```
'data.frame':   150 obs. of  5 variables:
 $ Sepal.Length: num  5.1 4.9 4.7 4.6 5 5.4 4.6 5 4.4 4.9 ...
 $ Sepal.Width : num  3.5 3 3.2 3.1 3.6 3.9 3.4 3.4 2.9 3.1 ...
 $ Petal.Length: num  1.4 1.4 1.3 1.5 1.4 1.7 1.4 1.5 1.4 1.5 ...
 $ Petal.Width : num  0.2 0.2 0.2 0.2 0.2 0.4 0.3 0.2 0.2 0.1 ...
 $ Species     : Factor w/ 3 levels "Iris-setosa",..: 1 1 1 1 1 1 1 1 1 1 ...
```

```
#detailed view of the data set
summary(iris)
```

Output:

```
 Sepal.Length    Sepal.Width     Petal.Length    Petal.Width             Species
Min.    :4.300  Min.    :2.000  Min.    :1.000  Min.    :0.100  Iris-setosa    :50
1st Qu.:5.100   1st Qu.:2.800   1st Qu.:1.600   1st Qu.:0.300   Iris-versicolor:50
Median :5.800   Median :3.000   Median :4.350   Median :1.300   Iris-virginica :50
Mean    :5.843  Mean    :3.054  Mean    :3.759  Mean    :1.199
3rd Qu.:6.400   3rd Qu.:3.300   3rd Qu.:5.100   3rd Qu.:1.800
Max.    :7.900  Max.    :4.400  Max.    :6.900  Max.    :2.500
```

The summary command helps us understand the data in a better way. It clearly shows different attributes along with min, max, median, and other such statistics. These help us in the coming steps where we might have to scale or normalize the data or features.

During step one is where we usually label our input data. Since our current data set is already labeled, we can skip this step for this example problem. Let us visually see how the species are spread. We take help of the famous scatter plot again, but this time we use a package called ggvis.

You can install ggvis as:

```
install.packages("ggvis")
```

For visualizing petal widths and lengths for all 3 species, we use the following code snippet:

```
#load the package
library(ggvis)


#plot the species
iris %>% ggvis(~Petal.Length, ~Petal.Width, fill = ~factor(Species)) %>%
layer_points()
```

The ggvis package is an interactive graphics package in R. It follows a unique way of expressing inputs to generate visualizations. The preceding snippet of code uses the pipe operator, %>%, to pass input data to ggvis and again uses the pipe operator to pass on the output to layer_points for final plotting. The ~ operator signifies to ggvis that Petal.Length is a variable in the input dataset (iris). Read more about ggvis at http://ggvis.rstudio.com/ggvis-basics.html.

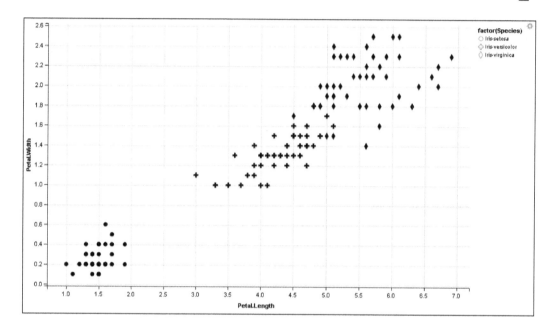

The preceding plot clearly shows that there is a high correlation between petal widths and lengths for **Iris-setosa** flowers, while it is a little less for the other two species.

 Try visualizing sepal width versus sepal length as well and see if you can spot any correlation.

Normalizing data

The next step is to normalize the data so that all the features are on the same scale. As seen from the data exploration step, the values of all the attributes are more or less in a comparable range. But, for the sake of this example, let us write a min-max normalization function:

```
#normalization function

min_max_normalizer <- function(x)
{
num <- x - min(x)
denom <- max(x) - min(x)
return (num/denom)
}
```

Remember, normalization does not alter the data, it simply scales it. Therefore, even though our data does not require normalization, doing so will not cause any harm.

Note

In the following steps, we will be using un-normalized data for clarity of output.

```
#normalizing iris data set
normalized_iris <- as.data.frame(lapply(iris[1:4], min_max_normalizer))

#viewing normalized data
summary(normalized_iris)
```

The following is a summary of the normalized data frame:

```
  Sepal.Length        Sepal.Width         Petal.Length        Petal.Width
 Min.   :0.0000     Min.   :0.0000      Min.   :0.0000      Min.   :0.00000
 1st Qu.:0.2222     1st Qu.:0.3333      1st Qu.:0.1017      1st Qu.:0.08333
 Median :0.4167     Median :0.4167      Median :0.5678      Median :0.50000
 Mean   :0.4287     Mean   :0.4392      Mean   :0.4676      Mean   :0.45778
 3rd Qu.:0.5833     3rd Qu.:0.5417      3rd Qu.:0.6949      3rd Qu.:0.70833
 Max.   :1.0000     Max.   :1.0000      Max.   :1.0000      Max.   :1.00000
```

Creating training and test data sets

Now that we have our data normalized, we can divide it into training and test data sets. We will follow the usual two-third one-third rule of splitting the data into two. As mentioned earlier, both data sets should be representative of the whole data and hence we need to pick proper samples. We will utilize R's `sample()` function to prepare our samples.

```
#checking the data constituency
table(iris$Species)
```

Output:

```
    Iris-setosa Iris-versicolor  Iris-virginica
             50              50              50
```

```
#set seed for randomization
set.seed(1234)
```

```
# setting the training-test split to 67% and 33% respectively
random_samples <- sample(2, nrow(iris), replace=TRUE, prob=c(0.67, 0.33))
```

```
# training data set
iris.training <- iris[
random_samples ==1, 1:4]
```

```
#training labels
iris.trainLabels <- iris[
random_samples ==1, 5]
```

```
# test data set
iris.test <- iris[
random_samples ==2, 1:4]
```

```
#testing labels
iris.testLabels <- iris[
random_samples ==2, 5]
```

Learning from data/training the model

Once we have the data ready in our training and test data sets, we can proceed to the next step and learn from the data using KNN. The KNN implementation in R is present in the class library. The KNN function takes the following inputs:

- `train`: The data frame containing the training data.
- `test`: The data frame containing the test data.
- `class`: A vector containing the class labels. Also called the factor vector.
- `k`: The value of k-nearest neighbors.

For the current case, let us assume the value of k to be 3. Odd numbers are usually good at breaking ties. KNN is executed as:

```
#setting library
library(class)


#executing knn for k=3
iris_model <- knn(train = iris.training, test = iris.test, cl = iris.
trainLabels, k=3)


#summary of the model learnt
iris_model
```

Output:

```
[1] Iris-setosa     Iris-setosa     Iris-setosa     Iris-setosa
[5] Iris-setosa     Iris-setosa     Iris-setosa     Iris-setosa
[9] Iris-setosa     Iris-setosa     Iris-setosa     Iris-setosa
[13] Iris-versicolor Iris-versicolor Iris-versicolor Iris-versicolor
[17] Iris-versicolor Iris-versicolor Iris-versicolor Iris-versicolor
[21] Iris-versicolor Iris-versicolor Iris-versicolor Iris-versicolor
[25] Iris-virginica  Iris-virginica  Iris-virginica  Iris-virginica
[29] Iris-versicolor Iris-virginica  Iris-virginica  Iris-virginica
[33] Iris-virginica  Iris-virginica  Iris-virginica  Iris-virginica
[37] Iris-virginica  Iris-virginica  Iris-virginica  Iris-virginica
Levels: Iris-setosa Iris-versicolor Iris-virginica
```

A quick scan of the output shows everything correct except one versicolor label amongst virginica's. Though this one was easy to spot, there are better ways to evaluate the model.

Evaluating the model

This brings us to the last step where we evaluate the model. We do this by preparing a confusion matrix or a cross table which helps us understand how the predicted labels are with respect to the known labels of the test data. R provides us with yet another utility function called `CrossTable()` which is present in the `gmodels` library. Let us see the output:

```
#setting library
library(gmodels)


#Preparing cross table
CrossTable(x = iris.testLabels, y = iris_model, prop.chisq=FALSE)
```

Output:

```
   Cell Contents
|-------------------------|
|                       N |
|         N / Row Total   |
|         N / Col Total   |
|       N / Table Total   |
|-------------------------|


Total Observations in Table:  40
```

iris.testLabels	iris_model Iris-setosa	Iris-versicolor	Iris-virginica	Row Total
Iris-setosa	12 1.000 1.000 0.300	0 0.000 0.000 0.000	0 0.000 0.000 0.000	12 0.300
Iris-versicolor	0 0.000 0.000 0.000	12 1.000 0.923 0.300	0 0.000 0.000 0.000	12 0.300
Iris-virginica	0 0.000 0.000 0.000	1 0.062 0.077 0.025	15 0.938 1.000 0.375	16 0.400
Column Total	12 0.300	13 0.325	15 0.375	40

From the preceding output we can conclude that the model has labeled one instance of virginica as versicolor while all the other test data points have been correctly labeled. This also helps us infer that the choice of k=3 was indeed good enough. We urge the reader to try the same example with different values of k and see the change in results.

KNN is a simple yet powerful algorithm which makes no assumptions about the underlying data distribution and hence can be used in cases where relationships between features and classes are complex or difficult to understand.

On the downside, KNN is a resource intensive algorithm as it requires a large amount of memory to process the data. Dependency on distance measures and missing data requires additional processing which is another overhead with this algorithm.

Despite its limitations, KNN is used in a number of real life applications such as for text mining, predicting heart attacks, predicting cancer and so on. KNN also finds application in the field of finance and agriculture as well.

Decision trees, random forests, and support vector machines are some of the most popular and widely used supervised classification algorithms.

Unsupervised learning algorithms

Unsupervised learning refers to algorithms which learn a concept(s) on their own. Now that we are familiar with the concept of supervised learning, let us utilize our knowledge to understand unsupervised learning.

Unlike supervised learning algorithms, which require a labeled input training data set, unsupervised learning algorithms are tasked with finding relationships and patterns in the data without any labeled training data set. These algorithms process the input data to mine for rules, detect patterns, summarize and group the data points which helps in deriving meaningful insights, and describing the data to the users. In the case of unsupervised learning algorithms, there is no concept of training and test data sets. Rather, as mentioned before, input data is analyzed and used to derive patterns and relationships.

Similar to supervised learning, unsupervised learning algorithms can also be divided into two main categories:

- **Association rule based machine learning**: These algorithms mine the input data to identify patterns and rules. The rules explain interesting relationships between the variables in the data set to depict frequent itemsets and patterns which occur in the data. These rules in turn help discover useful insights for any business or organization from their huge data repositories. Popular algorithms include Apriori and FP-Growth.

- **Clustering based machine learning**: Similar to supervised learning based classification algorithms, the main objective of these algorithms is to cluster or group the input data points into different classes or categories using just features derived from the input data alone and no other external information. Unlike classification, the output labels are not known beforehand in clustering. Some popular clustering algorithms include k-means, k-medoids, and hierarchical clustering.

Let us look at some unsupervised learning algorithms.

Apriori algorithm

This algorithm which took the world by storm was proposed by Agarwal and Srikant in 1993. The algorithm is designed to handle transactional data, where each transaction is a set of items, or itemset. The algorithm in short identifies the item sets which are subsets of at least C transactions in the data set.

Formally, let T be a set of items and D be a set of transactions, where each transaction T is a subset of T. Mathematically:

$$T = \{i_1, i_2, \ldots i_n\}$$
$$\text{and } T \subseteq_T$$

Then an association rule is an implication of the form X → Y, where a transaction T contains X as a subset of T and:

$$X \subseteq_T$$
$$Y \subseteq_T$$
$$X \cap Y = \phi$$

The implication X → Y holds true in the transaction set D with a confidence factor c if c% of the transactions in D that contain X also contain Y. The association rule X → Y is said to have a support factor of s if s% of transactions in D contain X ∪ Y. Hence, given a set of transactions D, the task of identifying association rules implies generating all such rules that have confidence and support greater than a user defined thresholds called `minsup` (for minimum support threshold) and `minconf` (for minimum confidence threshold).

Broadly, the algorithm works in two steps. The first one being identification of the itemsets whose occurrence exceeds a predefined threshold. Such itemsets are called **Frequent Itemsets**. The second step is to generate association rules from the identified frequent itemsets which satisfy the constraints of minimum confidence and support.

The same two steps can be explained better using the following pseudo-code:

$$\text{Apriori}\left(T,\varepsilon\right)$$

$$L_1 \leftarrow \{large\,1-itemsets\}$$

$$k \leftarrow 2$$

$$\textbf{while } L_{k-1} \neq \theta$$

$$C_k \leftarrow \{a\cup\{b\}\,|\,a \in L_{k-1} \wedge b \notin a\} - \{c\,|\,\{s\,|\,s \subseteq c \wedge |s| = k-1\} \not\subset L_{k-1}\}$$

$$\textbf{for transactions } t \in T$$

$$C_t \leftarrow \{c\,|\,c \in C_k \wedge c \subseteq t\}$$

$$\textbf{for candidates } c \in C_t$$

$$count\left[c\right] \leftarrow count\left[c\right] + 1$$

$$L_k \leftarrow \{c\,|\,c \in C_k \wedge count\left[c\right] \geq \varepsilon\}$$

$$k \leftarrow k+1$$

$$\textbf{return} \bigcup_k L_k$$

Now let us see the algorithm in action. The data set in consideration is the UCI machine learning repository's `Adult` data set. The data set contains census data with attributes such as gender, age, marital status, native country, and occupation, along with economic attributes such as work class, income, and so on. We will use this data set to identify if there are association rules between census information and the income of the person.

The Apriori algorithm is present in the `arules` library and the data set in consideration is named `Adult`. It is also available with default R installation.

```
# setting the apriori library
library(arules)


# loading data
data("Adult");
```

Time to explore our data set and see a few sample records:

```
# summary of data set
summary(Adult);


# Sample 5 records
inspect(Adult[0:5]);
```

We get to know that the data set contains some `48k` transactions with 115 columns. We also get information regarding the distribution of itemsets based on their sizes. The `inspect` function gives us a peek into sample transactions and the values each of the columns hold.

Now, let us build some relationships:

```
# executing apriori with support=50% confidence =80%
rules <- apriori(Adult, parameter=list(support=0.5, confidence=0.8,target
="rules"));


# view a summary
summary(rules);


#view top 3 rules
as(head(sort(rules, by = c("confidence", "support")), n=3), "data.frame")
```

The Apriori algorithm uses the `Adult` data set as input to identify rules and patterns in the transactional data. On viewing the summary, we can see that the algorithm successfully identified `84` rules meeting the support and confidence constraints of `50%` and `80%` respectively. Now that we have identified the rules, let us see what they are:

```
> as(head(sort(rules, by = c("confidence", "support")), n=3), "data.frame")
                                                        rules  support confidence      lift
7                         {hours-per-week=Full-time} => {capital-loss=None} 0.5606650  0.9582531 1.005219
15                                    {workclass=Private} => {capital-loss=None} 0.6639982  0.9564974 1.003377
50 {workclass=Private,native-country=United-States} => {capital-loss=None} 0.5897179  0.9554818 1.002312
```

The rules are of the form x→ y where x is the lhs or left-hand side and y is the rhs or right-hand side. The preceding image displays corresponding confidence and support values as well. From the output we can infer that if people are working full time then their chances of facing capital loss is almost none (confidence factor 95.8%). Another rule helps us infer that people who work for a private employer also have close to no chance of facing a capital loss. Such rules can be used in preparing policies or schemes for social welfare, economic reforms, and so on.

Apart from Apriori, there are other association rule mining algorithms such as FP Growth, ECLAT, and many others which have been used for various applications over the years.

K-Means

In the world of unsupervised clustering algorithms, the most simple and widely used algorithm is K-Means. As we have seen recently, unsupervised learning algorithms process the input data without any prior labels or training to come up with patterns and relationships. Clustering algorithms in particular help us cluster or partition the data points.

By definition, clustering refers to the task of grouping objects into groups such that elements of a group are more similar to each other than those in other groups. K-Means does the same in an unsupervised manner.

Mathematically, given a set of n observations {x1, x2, ..., xn}, where each observation is a d dimensional vector, the algorithm tries to partition these n observations into k (≤ n) sets by minimizing an objective function.

As with the other algorithms, there can be different objective functions. For the sake of simplicity, we will use the most widely used function called the **with-in cluster sum of squares** or **WCSS function**.

$$Set\ of\ n\ observations: \left\{ x_1, x_2, \ldots x_n \right\}$$

$$Set\ S\ of\ partitions: S = \left\{ S_1, S_2 \ldots S_k \right\}$$

$$Objective\ is\ to\ minimize\ the\ with-in\ cluster\ sum\ of\ squares:$$

$$\arg\min_{s} \sum_{x=1}^{k} \sum_{x\varepsilon S_i} \| X - \mu_i \|$$

Here μ_i is the mean of points in the partition S_i.

The algorithm follows a simple two step iterative process, where the first step is called the assignment step, followed by the update step.

- Initialize by setting the means for k partitions: m1, m2...mk
- Until the mean does not change or the change is lower than a certain threshold:
  1. **Assignment step**: Assign each observation to a partition for which the with-in cluster sum of squares value is minimum, that is, assign the observation to a partition whose mean is closest to the observation.
  2. **Update step**: For i in 1 to k, update each mean mi based on all the observations in that partition.

The algorithm can use different initialization methods. The most common ones are Forgy and Random Partition methods. I encourage you to read more on these. Also, apart from the input data set, the algorithm requires the value of k, that is the number of clusters to be formed. The optimal value may depend on various factors and is generally decided based on the use case.

Let us see the algorithm in action.

We will again use the Iris flower data set which we already used for the KNN algorithm. For KNN we already had the species labeled and then tried to learn and classify the data points in the test data set into correct classes.

With K-Means, we also aim to achieve the same partitioning of the data but without any labeled training data set (or supervision).

```
# prepare a copy of iris data set
kmean_iris <- iris


#Erase/ Nullify species labels
kmean_iris$Species <- NULL


#apply k-means with k=3
(clusters <- kmeans(kmean_iris, 3))
```

Now that we have the output from k-means, let us see how well it has partitioned the various species. Remember, k-means does not have partition labels and simply groups the data points.

```
# comparing cluster labels with actual iris  species labels.
table(iris$Species, clusters$cluster)
```

Output:

```
              1  2  3
Iris-setosa   0 50  0
Iris-versicolor 2  0 48
Iris-virginica 36  0 14
```

The output shows that the species setosa matches cluster label 2, versicolor matches label 3, and so on. Visually, it is easy to make out how the data points are clustered:

```
# plot the clustered points along sepal length and width
plot(kmean_iris[c("Sepal.Length", "Sepal.Width")],
col=clusters$cluster,pch = c(15,16,17)[as.numeric(clusters$cluster)])

points(clusters$centers[,c("Sepal.Length", "Sepal.Width")], col=1:3,
pch=8, cex=2)
```

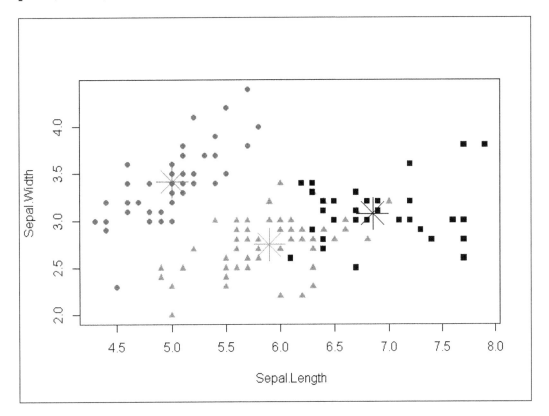

K-Means finds wide usage in areas like computer graphics for color quantization; it is combined with other algorithms and used for natural language processing, computer vision, and so on.

There are different variations of k-means (R itself provides three different variations). Apart from k-means, other unsupervised clustering algorithms are k-medoids, hierarchical clustering, and others.

Summary

Through this chapter, we formally defined the concept of machine learning. We talked about how a machine learning algorithm actually learns a concept. We touched upon various other concepts such as generalization, overfitting, training, testing, frequent itemsets, and so on. We also learnt about the families of machine learning algorithms. We went through different machine learning algorithms to understand the magic under the hood, along with their areas of application.

With this knowledge we are ready to solve some real world problems and save the world.

The coming few chapters build on the concepts in this chapter to solve specific problems and use cases. Get ready for some action!

3
Predicting Customer Shopping Trends with Market Basket Analysis

After the previous *Chapter 2, Let's Help Machine Learn*, you now know how to make machines learn from observations and data points so that they can find out interesting patterns, trends, and make predictions. In this chapter, we will be dealing with one of the complex problems faced by retailers, stores, and e-commerce marketplaces today. With the advent of modern technology and innovations, shopping has become a relatively pleasant and enjoyable experience which we can enjoy from the comfort of our home, without even venturing to an actual store, using the web or dedicated apps which provide shopping facilities. With a humongous number of retailers, stores, marketplaces, and sellers, competition is pretty stiff, and to attract customers, they have to use all the data they can gather from consumers about their personal traits and shopping patterns, and use machine learning techniques to try and make shopping experiences as personalized as possible based on each customer.

You might be wondering how machine learning can help in making shopping experiences personalized for each user! The answer lies in two things: data and algorithms. Using a combination of both of these, retailers are able to figure out what are the most trending items that the consumers buy, the likes and dislikes of the customers, the peak times when the sales go up and come down, the trending combination of products which people tend to buy, and the product reviews and prices which are being offered by other retailers for the same products. Retailers have their own data science teams which aggregate this data and apply various machine learning algorithms which are used to analyze the trending products and build recommender engines which predict what the customers are most likely to buy, and give recommendations to the customers based on their interests and shopping history.

In this chapter, we will be focusing on product based recommendations where the algorithms focus on customer shopping transactional data, where we observe common patterns of product combinations bought by the customers, to detect and predict what products customers are most likely to buy and what they have bought in the past. The main techniques we will be focusing on in this chapter are as follows:

- Product contingency matrix evaluation
- Frequent itemsets generation
- Association rule mining

Trend analysis using association rules and pattern mining however have their own limitations. They do not provide a more personalized shopping experience for each customer based on attributes like their interests, products they have bought and rated. We will be looking at that in the subsequent chapter where we focus on algorithms such as user-based collaborative filtering, which takes into account both product based and user based features when building recommender engines.

What is most interesting is that all the retailers and e-commerce marketplaces, such as Staples, Macy's, Target, Amazon, Flipkart, Alibaba, Rakuten, Lazada, and many many others, have their own data science teams, which solve a wide variety of problems including the one we discussed earlier. They make use of all the data generated from customer shopping transactions, product stocks, deliveries, SLAs, reviews, advertisements, click-through rates, bounce rates, pricing data, and many other sources. They process this data and feed it into their machine learning algorithm based engines to generate data driven insights to increase sales and profits for the business. Now this is definitely one domain which is hot in the market right now. Let's now look further into some of the machine learning techniques and algorithms which help them in making such great data driven decisions!

Detecting and predicting trends

In this section, we will talk about what exactly we mean by trends and how the retailers detect and predict these trends. Basically, a trend in the retail context can be defined as a specific pattern or behavior which occurs over a period of time. This may involve a product or a combination of products being sold out in a very short period of time or even the reverse. A simple example would be a best-selling smartphone being prebooked and out of stock before even hitting the shelves on any e-commerce marketplace, or a combination of products like the classic beer and diapers combination which is frequently found in shopping baskets or carts of customers!

How can we even start analyzing shopping carts or start to detect and predict shopping trends. Like I mentioned earlier, we can achieve this with a combination of the right data and algorithms. Let's assume that we are heading a large retail chain. First we will have to keep track of each and every transaction which is taking place from our stores and website. We will need to gather data points relevant to the items being purchased, stockouts, combinations of items purchased together, and customer transactions to begin with.

Once we have this data, we can start processing, normalizing, and aggregating this data to machine readable formats, which can be easily operated on and fed to machine learning algorithms for product recommendations based on the shopping trends. We can achieve this by using the right data structures and constructs which we learned back in *Chapter 1, Getting Started with R and Machine Learning*. There are several machine learning algorithms which help us in analyzing the shopping transactional data and recommending products based on the shopping trends. The main paradigm under which these algorithms fall is popularly known as **market basket analysis**. Interestingly, these algorithms use statistical and machine learning concepts such as probability, support, confidence, lift, pattern detection, and many more to determine what are the items being bought together frequently, which helps us in analyzing shopping transactions and detecting and predicting trends. This ultimately helps us in making product recommendations for the customers and also making business decisions wisely, if we were running a retail chain! Do note that the only data we will be using in both these algorithms is pure shopping transactions based data.

Before we start diving into building algorithms to analyze the shopping carts and transactions, let us first see what market basket analysis actually means and the concepts associated with it. This will come in handy later on, when we implement machine learning algorithms using some of these concepts to solve real world problems.

Market basket analysis

Market basket analysis consists of some modeling techniques which are typically used by retailers and e-commerce marketplaces to analyze shopping carts and transactions to find out what customers buy the most, what kind of items they buy, what the peak season is for specific items to be sold the most, and so on. We will be focusing on item based transactional patterns in this chapter for detecting and predicting what items people are buying and are most likely to buy. Let us first look at the formal definition of market basket analysis and then we will look at core concepts, metrics, and techniques tied to it. Finally, we will conclude with how to actually use these results to make data driven decisions.

What does market basket analysis actually mean?

Market basket analysis typically encompasses several modeling techniques based upon the simple principle that while shopping if you buy a certain group of items (also known as an itemset in machine learning lingo), you are likely to buy an other specific item or items along with that itemset. We analyze human shopping patterns and apply statistical techniques to generate frequent itemsets. These itemsets contain combination of items that people are most likely to buy together, based on past shopping history.

A simple example of an itemset would be people buying beer and diapers frequently at the market. The itemset can be depicted as { beer, diapers }. A frequent itemset is indicated by an itemset which occurs more frequently than usual and is specified by a metric known as support, which we will be talking about later on. Hence, from the preceding example you can say that if I buy beer, I am also most likely to buy diapers, and recommend that product to me. We can also build item association rules on top of these itemsets by analyzing shopping purchases. An example association rule can be denoted by using itemsets using the notation, { beer, diapers } -> { milk } which would indicate that if I am buying beer and diapers together, I am most likely to also purchase milk along with that!

Core concepts and definitions

Now that you know what market basket analysis actually does, let us look at some definitions and concepts which are widely used in the algorithms and techniques.

Transactional datasets indicate databases or datasets where the customer's shopping transactions are recorded daily/weekly and consist of various items bought together by the customers. We will take an example transactional dataset which we will also be using later on in the chapter for our algorithms. Consider the following dataset, which you can also get from the shopping_transaction_log.csv file for this chapter. The data is represented in the following figure:

⊿	A	B	C	D
1	beer	diapers	bread	
2	diapers	eggs		
3	diapers	beer		
4	beer	diapers	eggs	
5	beer	diapers		
6	diapers	milk		
7	milk	bread		
8	diapers	beer	milk	bread
9	beer	diapers	milk	

Each cell in the preceding dataset is also defined as an item. Items are also denoted by the symbol In where n denotes the `n-th` item number, and examples are enclosed in curly braces in formal definitions and when building algorithm pseudocode or doing some computations by hand. For example, cell combination `(1, A)` indicates item I1 whose value is depicted as { `beer` }.

Itemsets are defined as sets or groups of items which were bought together in any shopping transaction. Hence, these items are said to co-occur based on the transactions. We will denote itemsets as ISn where *n* denotes the `n-th` itemset number. The itemset values will will be enclosed in curly braces. Each row in the preceding dataset denotes a particular transaction and the combination of items form the itemsets. The itemset IS1 is depicted by { `beer, diapers, bread` }.

Association rules or just rules are statements which have a **left-hand side** (**LHS**) and a **right-hand side** (**RHS**), and indicate that if we have the items on the LHS for purchase, we are likely to be interested in purchasing the RHS items too. This signifies that the itemsets are associated with each other. They are denoted as ISx → ISy, which means that if I have itemset x in my shopping cart, I will also be interested in purchasing itemset y along with it. An example rule can be { `beer` } → { `diapers` } which indicates that if I have beer in my cart, there is a chance I will buy diapers too! We will now see some metrics which determine how to measure frequent itemsets and the strength of the association rules.

The **frequency** of an itemset is basically the number of times a particular itemset occurs in the list of all transactions. Do note that the itemset can be a subset of a larger itemset in the transactions and still be counted because the subset denotes that the itemset containing the specific set of items was bought along with some other products. We can denote it as `f(ISn)`, where `ISn` is a particular itemset and function `f( )` gives us the frequency of that itemset in the whole transactional based dataset. Taking our previous dataset, `f(IS{beer, diapers})` is six, which indicates `IS{beer, diapers}` has been purchased six times in total out of all the transactional data in our dataset.

The **support** of an itemset is defined as the fraction of transactions in our transactional dataset which consists of that particular itemset. Basically, it means the number of times that itemset was purchased divided by the total number of transactions in the dataset. It can be denoted as $S(IS_n) = \dfrac{f(IS_n)}{count\left(\sum_{i=1}^{n} IS_i\right)}$, where `S( )` denotes the support of the itemset `ISn`. Taking our preceding example, `S(IS{beer, diapers})` is $\dfrac{6}{9}$ which gives us `66.67%`. The support for an association rule is similar and can be depicted as $S(IS_x \rightarrow IS_y) = \dfrac{f(IS_x \cup IS_y)}{count\left(\sum_{i=1}^{n} IS_i\right)}$, where we use the intersection operator to see the frequency of both the itemsets occurring together in the transactional dataset. The support for the rule we defined earlier, `S(IS{beer} → IS{diapers})`, is once again $\dfrac{6}{9}$ or `66.67%` because the itemset combining beer and diapers occurs six times in total, as we saw earlier. When evaluating results from association rules or frequent itemsets, the higher the support, the better it is. Support is more about measuring the quality of rules detecting what has already happened from the past transactions.

The **confidence** of an association rule is defined as the probability or likelihood that, for a new transaction containing itemset in the LHS of the rule, the transaction also contains the itemset on the RHS of the rule. The confidence for a rule can be depicted as $C\left(IS_x \rightarrow IS_y\right) = \dfrac{S\left(IS_x \cup IS_y\right)}{S\left(IS_x\right)}$, where C( ) denotes the confidence of the rule. Do note that since calculation of support involves dividing itemset frequency by the total number of transactions in the denominator, the RHS of the preceding equation ultimately reduces to getting the frequency of the itemsets for both the numerator and denominator. Thus we get $C\left(IS_x \rightarrow IS_y\right) = \dfrac{f\left(IS_x \cup IS_y\right)}{f\left(IS_x\right)}$ as the reduced formula for getting confidence. The confidence for our earlier rule

C(IS{beer} → IS{diapers}) is $\dfrac{6}{6}$ or 100%, which means the probability of buying diapers, if I have beer in my shopping basket, is a hundred percent! That is pretty high and if you go back to the dataset, you can see that it is true because for every transaction involving beer, we can see diapers associated with it. Thus, you can see that making predictions and recommendations is not rocket science but just simple applied math and statistical methods on top of data. Remember that confidence is more about detecting the quality of rules predicting what can happen in the future based on the past transactional data.

The **lift** of an association rule is defined as the ratio of the support of the combination of two itemsets on the LHS and RHS together divided by the product of the support of each of the itemsets. The lift for a rule can be depicted as

$$L\left(IS_x \to IS_y\right) = \frac{S\left(IS_x \cup IS_y\right)}{S\left(IS_x\right) \times S\left(IS_y\right)}$$, where `L( )` denotes the lift of the rule. For our example rule, `L(IS{beer} → IS{diapers})` is, $\dfrac{S\left(IS_{\{beer\}} \cup IS_{\{diapers\}}\right)}{S\left(IS_{\{beer\}}\right) \times S\left(IS_{\{diapers\}}\right)}$ which evaluates to $\dfrac{6 \div 9}{\left(6 \div 9\right) \times \left(8 \div 9\right)}$ giving us the value of `1.125` which is pretty decent! The lift of a rule in general is another metric to evaluate the quality of the rule. If the lift is `> 1` then it indicates that the presence of the itemset in the LHS is responsible for the increase in probability that the customer is also going to buy the itemset on the RHS. This is another very important way to determine itemset associations and which items influence people to buy other items, because if the lift has a value `= 1`, it means that the itemsets on the LHS and RHS are independent and buying one itemset will not affect the customer to buy the other itemset. If the lift is `< 1`, it indicates that if the customer has an itemset on the LHS then the probability of buying the itemset on the RHS is relatively low.

Techniques used for analysis

If you have been overwhelmed by all the mathematical information in the previous section, just relax and take a deep breath! You do not need to remember everything because most of the time, the algorithms will compute everything for you! The thing where you need to be good at is using these techniques and algorithms in the right way and interpreting the results to filter out what is necessary and useful. The earlier mentioned concepts will help you when you start implementing and applying the techniques later on, which we will briefly describe in this section. We will mainly be talking about three techniques which we will be exploring in this chapter.

Evaluation of a product contingency matrix is the simplest approach to start with, which is more of a global trend capturing mechanism and shows the top most products that are being bought together in a contingency matrix. The R package `arules`, which we will be using later on, has a nice function called **crossTable** which helps in cross-tabulating the joint occurrences across pairs of items into a contingency matrix. We will use this matrix to predict which products the customers would most likely buy with some other product from the matrix.

Frequent itemset generation takes off from where product contingency matrix stops, because it has a severe limitation of not being able to deal with pairs of products at any point in time. Hence, to get into itemsets which can have any number of products and detect patterns from there, we will be building our own frequent itemset generator using machine learning! Using this, we will be able to get frequent itemsets with specific support values indicating the sets of items likely to be purchased together, and hence forming the basis of recommending products to the customers.

Finally, we will be implementing association rule mining using the wonderful Apriori algorithm which uses frequent itemsets as a part of its rule generation process. You have already seen a demo of this in the *Chapter 2, Let's Help Machines Learn*. However, this time we will be using its full-fledged capabilities to view the association rules between product itemsets, evaluating the quality of the rules using the metrics we discussed earlier, and also using these rules to make trend predictions and recommendations for products in shopping transactions.

Making data driven decisions

You now know what market basket analysis is, what techniques are used for it, and what results they give us. Remember that the output of market basket analysis is a set of items or products which co-occur frequently in transactions. Now this can happen because of strong support, confidence, and lift which boost its association and the customers tend to buy them, or it could also be because the retailer has placed the items together or side by side in the store or website. However, do remember that strong associations do not always happen just by chance and that is what the retailers are always trying to find out using the techniques we talked about earlier to boost sales.

The following are some crucial data driven decisions which the retailers usually tend to take based on the results obtained from market basket analysis:

- Frequent itemsets containing pairs of products such as diapers and beer should be typically placed side by side in the store, which would give customers easy access and they would tend to buy them more.

- Frequent itemsets which have a large number of distinct items or product counts should be placed in a specific category or theme for the itemset, such as special grocery combos or baby products. Discounts offered on the whole itemset attracts more customers.

- Association rules having a long list of items in the itemset or products obtained from frequent itemsets or contingency matrices can be shown as product suggestions and recommendations to the customers, in specific product pages associated with the itemsets, when they browse the shopping or e-commerce website. Care should be taken that the lift of these rules be greater than 1 at least, like we discussed earlier.

- Recommendation systems, targeted advertising, and marketing everything can be built upon the results obtained from market basket analysis.

These decisions if made at the right place and right time can help the retailers immensely in boosting their sales and making good profits.

Now that we have a solid grasp of what market basket analysis actually does and how it works, we will start by building a simple algorithm for our first technique, where we make product recommendations using a product contingency matrix based on top trending products purchased in a supermarket, and then move on to building more sophisticated analyzers and recommenders using powerful machine learning capabilities of the R language.

Evaluating a product contingency matrix

We will be doing a couple of things here. First, we will analyze a small toy dataset belonging to a supermarket, by using a product contingency matrix of product pair purchases based on their frequency. Then we will move on to contingency matrices based on other metrics such as support, lift, and so on by using another dataset.

The data for our first matrix consists of the six most popular products sold at the supermarket and also the number of times each product was sold by itself and in combination with the other products. We have the data in the form of a data table captured in a csv file, as you can see in the following figure:

	A	B	C	D	E	F	G
1	Items	milk	bread	butter	beer	wine	diapers
2	milk	10000	8758	5241	300	215	753
3	bread	8758	9562	8865	427	322	353
4	butter	5241	8865	11753	310	447	114
5	beer	300	427	310	12985	10115	9173
6	wine	215	322	447	10115	7825	228
7	diapers	753	353	114	9173	228	18105

To analyze this data, we first need to understand what it depicts. Basically, each cell value denotes the number of times that product combination was sold. Thus, the cell combination (1, A) denotes the product combination (milk, milk), which is basically the number of times milk was bought. Another example is the cell combination (4, C) which is analogous to cell combination (3, D) which indicates the number of times bread was bought along with butter. This is also often known as a contingency matrix and in our case it is a product contingency matrix since it deals with product data. Let us follow our standard machine learning pipeline of getting the data, analyzing it, running it on our algorithm, and getting the intended results.

Getting the data

Here, we will first load the dataset into memory from the disk using the following code snippet. Remember to have the top_supermarket_transactions.csv file in the same directory from which you run the following code snippet, which is also available in the file named ch3_product contingency matrix.R along with this book.

```
> # reading in the dataset
> data <- read.csv("supermarket_transactions.csv")
>
> # assigning row names to be same as column names
> # to build the contingency matrix
> row.names(data) <- data[[1]]
> data <- subset(data, select = c(-1))
>
```

```
> ## viewing the contingency matrix
> cat("Products Transactions Contingency Matrix")
Products Transactions Contingency Matrix
> data
```

Output:

```
           milk bread butter  beer  wine diapers
milk      10000  8758   5241   300   215     753
bread      8758  9562   8865   427   322     353
butter     5241  8865  11753   310   447     114
beer        300   427    310 12985 10115    9173
wine        215   322    447 10115  7825     228
diapers     753   353    114  9173   228   18105
```

Analyzing and visualizing the data

Here, we will do some exploratory analysis of the dataset to see what kind of story the data tells us. For that, we will first look at the transactions related to buying milk and bread in the following code snippet:

```
> ## Analyzing and visualizing the data
> # Frequency of products bought with milk
> data['milk', ]
      milk bread butter beer wine diapers
milk 10000  8758   5241  300  215     753
>
> # Sorting to get top products bought with milk
> sort(data['milk', ], decreasing = TRUE)
      milk bread butter diapers beer wine
milk 10000  8758   5241     753  300  215
>
> # Frequency of products bought with bread
> data['bread', ]
       milk bread butter beer wine diapers
bread  8758  9562   8865  427  322     353
>
> # Sorting to get top products bought with bread
```

```
> sort(data['bread', ], decreasing = TRUE)
     bread butter milk beer diapers wine
bread 9562   8865 8758  427     353  322
```

Thus, you can see that just by sorting the data columns we are able to see the top products which were bought in combination with bread or with milk. When recommending top products to buy from the matrix, we will remove the product from the recommendation list if that product is in the shopping cart already, because, if I buy bread, it makes no sense to recommend bread to me. Now, we will visualize the complete dataset using a mosaic plot. Do note that the product combinations which were bought very frequently will have high frequency values and will be indicated by a significant area in the mosaic plot.

```
> # Visualizing the data
> mosaicplot(as.matrix(data),
+            color=TRUE,
+            title(main="Products Contingency Mosaic Plot"),
+            las=2
+            )
```

The code generates the following mosaic plot where we apply a gradient using the color parameter and specify that axis labels be at right angles to the axis using the las parameter to make a cleaner plot.

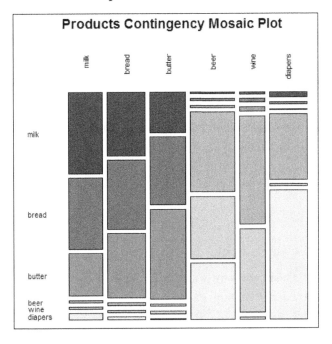

From the preceding plot you can note that it is now very easy to see which products were bought a large number of times in combination with another product. Ignoring the same product row and column values, we can easily deduce that product combinations such as beer and diapers were bought very frequently!

The background story about our beer – diapers combination was actually discovered by Walmart sometime back when they analyzed customer transactional data to find that, on Fridays, young American dads tend to buy beer and diapers together. They would celebrate the weekend with their friends but, having fathered an offspring, they also carried out essential duties of taking care of their children's needs. In fact, Walmart placed beer and diapers side by side in stores and their sales went up significantly! This is the power of analytics and machine learning which enables us to find out unknown and unexpected patterns.

Global recommendations

Now we will recommend products based on the product chosen by a customer in his shopping cart. Do note that we mention this as global recommendations because these product recommendations are neither based on association rules or frequent itemsets that we will be exploring after this. They are purely based on the global product contingency matrix of product pair purchase counts. The following code snippet enables us to recommend the top two suggested products for each item from the matrix:

```
## Global Recommendations
cat("Recommendations based on global products contingency matrix")
items <- names(data)
for (item in items){
  cat(paste("Top 2 recommended items to buy with", item, "are: "))
   item.data <- subset(data[item,], select=names(data)[!names(data) %in%
item])
  cat(names(item.data[order(item.data, decreasing = TRUE)][c(1,2)]))
  cat("\n")
}
```

This gives us the following output:

```
Top 2 recommended items to buy with milk are: bread butter
Top 2 recommended items to buy with bread are: butter milk
Top 2 recommended items to buy with butter are: bread milk
```

```
Top 2 recommended items to buy with beer are: wine diapers
Top 2 recommended items to buy with wine are: beer butter
Top 2 recommended items to buy with diapers are: beer milk
```

Thus you can see that, based on the product pair purchases from the contingency matrix, we get the top two products which people would tend to buy, based on the global trends captured in that matrix. Now we will look at some more ways to generate more advanced contingency matrices based on some other metrics.

Advanced contingency matrices

Until now we have just used product contingency matrices based on product purchase frequencies. We will now look at creating some more contingency matrices using metrics such as support and lift, which we talked about earlier, since they are better indicators for items which have a probability of being purchased together by customers when shopping. For this we will be using the package `arules` available in the **Comprehensive R Archive Network (CRAN)** repositories. You can download it if not present using the `install.packages('arules')` command. Once it is installed, we will look at a standard grocery based transactional log database and build the contingency matrices using the standard machine learning methodology that we used in the previous chapters to work on any dataset or problem.

First, we will start by loading the required package and the data into our workspace and looking at what the transactional data looks like:

```
> # loading the required package
> library(arules)
>
> # getting and loading the data
> data(Groceries)
>
> # inspecting the first 3 transactions
> inspect(Groceries[1:3])
  items
1 {citrus fruit,semi-finished bread,margarine,ready soups}
2 {tropical fruit,yogurt,coffee}
3 {whole milk}
```

Each preceding transaction is a set of products which were purchased together, just as we had discussed in the previous sections. We will now build several contingency matrices on different matrices and view the top five product pairs which customers would be interested in buying together. The following code snippet shows us a count based product contingency matrix:

```
> # count based product contingency matrix
> ct <- crossTable(Groceries, measure="count", sort=TRUE)
> ct[1:5, 1:5]
```

Output:

	whole milk	other vegetables	rolls/buns	soda	yogurt
whole milk	2513	736	557	394	551
other vegetables	736	1903	419	322	427
rolls/buns	557	419	1809	377	338
soda	394	322	377	1715	269
yogurt	551	427	338	269	1372

Here we see a similar matrix to what we had worked with earlier. Now we will create a support based product contingency matrix:

```
> # support based product contingency matrix
> ct <- crossTable(Groceries, measure="support", sort=TRUE)
> ct[1:5, 1:5]
```

Output:

	whole milk	other vegetables	rolls/buns	soda	yogurt
whole milk	0.25551601	0.07483477	0.05663447	0.04006101	0.05602440
other vegetables	0.07483477	0.19349263	0.04260295	0.03274021	0.04341637
rolls/buns	0.05663447	0.04260295	0.18393493	0.03833249	0.03436706
soda	0.04006101	0.03274021	0.03833249	0.17437722	0.02735130
yogurt	0.05602440	0.04341637	0.03436706	0.02735130	0.13950178

Finally, we look at another matrix based on the metric lift which we discussed earlier. If you remember, the higher the value of lift, if greater than 1, the stronger the chance of both products being bought together by customers.

```
> # lift based product contingency matrix
> ct <- crossTable(Groceries, measure="lift", sort=TRUE)
> ct[1:5, 1:5]
```

Output:

```
                whole milk other vegetables rolls/buns      soda   yogurt
whole milk              NA         1.5136341   1.205032 0.8991124 1.571735
other vegetables 1.5136341                NA   1.197047 0.9703476 1.608457
rolls/buns       1.2050318         1.1970465         NA 1.1951242 1.339363
soda             0.8991124         0.9703476   1.195124        NA 1.124368
yogurt           1.5717351         1.6084566   1.339363 1.1243678       NA
```

From the preceding matrix, you can get such insights as that people tend to buy yoghurt and whole milk together, or that soda and whole milk do not really go together since it has a lift value less than 1. These kinds of insights help in planning product placement in stores and shopping websites for better sales and recommendations.

However, some of the main issues with this model are as follows:

- High number of products leads to a huge matrix which is difficult to work with since it needs more time and space to process.

- Can detect pairs of items in frequent itemsets only for recommendations. It is possible to find out combinations of more than two items from this model but that needs additional logic related to set theory.

- Faces the cold start problem, typically known in recommender engines, which happens when a new product is launched and we cannot predict recommendations or how it will sell in the market since our historical data does not have any information associated with it.

Frequent itemset generation

We will now look at a better technique to find patterns and detect frequently bought products. For this, we will be using the frequent itemset generation technique. We will be implementing this algorithm from scratch because, even though when we solve any machine learning or optimization problem we usually use readymade machine learning algorithms out of the box which are optimized and available in various R packages, one of the main objectives of this book is to make sure we understand what exactly goes on behind the scenes of a machine learning algorithm. Thus, we will see how we can build some of these algorithms ourselves using the principles of mathematics, statistics, and logic.

Getting started

The data we will be using for this is the `shopping_transaction_log.csv` dataset which we used to explain the concepts of market basket analysis at the beginning of the chapter. The code we will be using for this section is available in the `ch3_frequent` itemset `generation.R` file. We will first go through all the functions and then define the main function which utilizes all the helper functions to define a workflow for frequent itemset generation.

We will start by loading some library dependencies and utility functions:

```
## load library dependencies
library(dplyr)  # manipulating data frames
library(gridExtra)  # output clean formatted tables


## Utility function: Appends vectors to a list
list.append <- function (mylist, ...){
  mylist <- c(mylist, list(...))
  return(mylist)
}
```

Data retrieval and transformation

Next, we will define the functions for getting the data and transforming it into the required format of a data frame consisting of products and purchase frequency. We also have a function to prune this data frame if we want to remove products below a certain purchase frequency threshold.

```
## Step 1: Function to read the dataset into memory from file
get_transaction_dataset <- function(filename){
  df <- read.csv(filename, header = FALSE)
  dataset <- list()
  for (index in seq(nrow(df))){
    transaction.set <- as.vector(unlist(df[index,]))
    transaction.set <- transaction.set[transaction.set != ""]
    dataset <- list.append(dataset, transaction.set)
  }
```

```
  return(dataset)
}


## Step 2: Function to convert dataset into a data frame
get_item_freq_table <- function(dataset){
  item.freq.table <- unlist(dataset) %>% table %>% data.frame
  return (item.freq.table)
}


## Step 3: Function to prune items based on minimum frequency
##         as specified by the user.
##         Here min freq <- item.min.freq
prune_item_freq_table <- function(item.freq.table, item.min.freq){
  pruned.item.table <- item.freq.table[item.freq.table$Freq >=
                                       item.min.freq,]

  return (pruned.item.table)
}
```

Building an itemset association matrix

Now, we will implement three functions to help us build the itemset association matrix. We start with building the first function, which returns us different unique itemset combinations from the list of items in our transactional dataset based on the number of items in each itemset passed as a parameter. This helps us in getting itemsets of a particular count.

```
## Step 4: Function to get possible itemset combinations where
##         each itemset has n number of items where n is specified ##
by the user. Here n <- num.items
get_associated_itemset_combinations <- function(pruned.item.table,
                                                num.items){
  itemset.associations <- c()
  itemset.association.matrix <- combn(pruned.item.table$.,
                                      num.items)
  for (index in seq(ncol(itemset.association.matrix))){
    itemset.associations <- c(itemset.associations,
                      paste(itemset.association.matrix[,index],
                              collapse = ", ")
```

```
                              )
  }
  itemset.associations <- unique(itemset.associations)
  return (itemset.associations)
}
```

The following function builds a frequency contingency table showing the occurrence of each itemset in each transaction from the dataset. This forms the basis of getting the data for building our frequent itemsets. The itemset association matrix shows on a high level the occurrence of the different unique itemsets generated in the previous function per transaction in our dataset.

```
## Step 5: Function to build an itemset association matrix where ##
we see a contingency table showing itemset association
##            occurrence in each transaction of the dataset
build_itemset_association_matrix <- function(dataset,
                                    itemset.association.labels,
                                    itemset.combination.nums) {
  itemset.transaction.labels <- sapply(dataset, paste,
                                    collapse=", ")
  itemset.associations <- lapply(itemset.association.labels,
                          function(itemset){
                            unlist(strsplit(itemset, ", ",
                                        fixed = TRUE)
                            )
                          }
                        )
  # building the itemset association matrix
  association.vector <- c()
  for (itemset.association in itemset.associations){
    association.vector <- c(association.vector,
            unlist(
              lapply(dataset,
                    function(dataitem,
                              num.items=itemset.combination.nums){
                      m <- match(dataitem, itemset.association)
                      m <- length(m[!is.na(m)])
                      if (m == num.items){
```

```
                              1
                           }else{
                              NA
                           }
                        }
                     )
                  )
            )
      }


      itemset.association.matrix <- matrix(association.vector,
                                        nrow = length(dataset))
      itemset.association.labels <- sapply(itemset.association.labels,
                                        function(item) {
                                           paste0('{', paste(item,
                                             collapse = ', '), '}')
                                        }
                                     )


      itemset.transaction.labels <- sapply(dataset,
                                        function(itemset){
                                           paste0('{', paste(itemset,
                                             collapse = ', '), '}')
                                        }
                                     )
      colnames(itemset.association.matrix) <- itemset.association.labels
      rownames(itemset.association.matrix) <- itemset.transaction.labels


      return (itemset.association.matrix)
}
```

Once we have the itemset association matrix, we use it in the following function, to sum up these individual itemset occurrences to get the total occurrence of each itemset in the whole dataset:

```
## Step 6: Function to generate total occurrences of each itemset
##         in the transactional dataset based on data from the
##         association matrix
```

```
get_frequent_itemset_details <- function(itemset.association.matrix){
  frequent.itemsets.table <- apply(itemset.association.matrix,
                                    2, sum, na.rm=TRUE)
  return (frequent.itemsets.table)
}
```

Creating a frequent itemsets generation workflow

Finally, we will define the function which will utilize all the previous functions to create a workflow for generating the frequent itemsets. The main parameters we will be taking here include `data.file.path` which contains the location of the dataset, `itemset.combination.nums` which denotes the number of items which should be in each itemset, `item.min.freq` which denotes the minimum purchase count threshold of each item, and `minsup` which tells us the minimum support for the generated frequent itemsets.

```
## Step 7: Function containing entire workflow to generate
##          frequent itemsets
frequent.itemsets.generator <- function(data.file.path,
                                         itemset.combination.nums=2,
                                         item.min.freq=2, minsup=0.2){
  # get the dataset
  dataset <- get_transaction_dataset(data.file.path)

  # convert data into item frequency table
  item.freq.table <- get_item_freq_table(dataset)
  pruned.item.table <- prune_item_freq_table(item.freq.table,
                                             item.min.freq)

  # get itemset associations
  itemset.association.labels <- get_associated_itemset_
combinations(pruned.item.table,
                                     itemset.combination.nums)
  itemset.association.matrix <- build_itemset_association_matrix(dataset,
                                     itemset.association.labels,
```

```
                              itemset.combination.nums)


  # generate frequent itemsets
  frequent.itemsets.table <- get_frequent_itemset_details(itemset.
association.matrix)
  frequent.itemsets.table <- sort(frequent.itemsets.table[frequent.
itemsets.table > 0],

                              decreasing = TRUE)


  frequent.itemsets.names <- names(frequent.itemsets.table)
  frequent.itemsets.frequencies <- as.vector(frequent.itemsets.table)
  frequent.itemsets.support <- round((frequent.itemsets.frequencies *
100) / length(dataset),

                              digits=2)


  frequent.itemsets <- data.frame(Itemset=frequent.itemsets.names,
                        Frequency=frequent.itemsets.frequencies,
                        Support=frequent.itemsets.support)
  # apply minimum support cutoff to get frequent itemsets
  minsup.percentage <- minsup * 100
  frequent.itemsets <- subset(frequent.itemsets,
  frequent.itemsets['Support'] >= minsup.percentage)
  frequent.itemsets.support <- sapply(frequent.itemsets.support,
                              function(value){
                                 paste0(value,'%')
                              }
                        )


  # printing to console
  cat("\nItem Association Matrix\n")
  print(itemset.association.matrix)
  cat("\n\n")
  cat("\nValid Frequent Itemsets with Frequency and Support\n")
  print(frequent.itemsets)


  # displaying frequent itemsets as a pretty table
```

```
  if (names(dev.cur()) != "null device"){
    dev.off()
  }
  grid.table(frequent.itemsets)
}
```

Detecting shopping trends

Now it's time to test our algorithm! We will first generate all the frequent itemsets that have two items where each item has been purchased at least three times in the overall dataset and have a minimum support of at least 20%. To do this, you will have to fire up the following function in the R console. Do remember to load all the previous functions in memory first.

```
> frequent.itemsets.generator(
          data.file.path='shopping_transaction_log.csv',
          itemset.combination.nums=2, item.min.freq=3, minsup=0.2)
```

We get the following itemset contingency matrix, which is used to generate the frequent itemsets. The left side rows indicate the transactions and each column represents an itemset.

```
Item Association Matrix
                              {beer, bread} {beer, diapers} {beer, milk} {bread, diapers} {bread, milk} {diapers, milk}
{beer, diapers, bread}            1               1             NA              1               NA             NA
{diapers, eggs}                  NA              NA             NA             NA               NA             NA
{diapers, beer}                  NA               1             NA             NA               NA             NA
{beer, diapers, eggs}            NA               1             NA             NA               NA             NA
{beer, diapers}                  NA               1             NA             NA               NA             NA
{diapers, milk}                  NA              NA             NA             NA               NA              1
{milk, bread}                    NA              NA             NA             NA                1             NA
{diapers, beer, milk, bread}      1               1              1              1                1              1
{beer, diapers, milk}            NA               1              1             NA               NA              1
```

The final frequent itemsets will be shown both in the console and in the plot section in the form of a pretty table, as follows:

	Itemset	Frequency	Support
1	{beer, diapers}	6	66.67
2	{diapers, milk}	3	33.33
3	{beer, bread}	2	22.22
4	{beer, milk}	2	22.22
5	{bread, diapers}	2	22.22
6	{bread, milk}	2	22.22

Thus, you can clearly see that the itemset {beer, diapers} is our most frequent itemset with a support of approximately 67%, which has occurred six times in total in our dataset, and the association matrix shows you the exact transactions where it has occurred. Thus, this function detects a trend of people buying beer and diapers or diapers and milk more frequently, and thus we can recommend people the same when they are shopping. We will also take a look at the frequent itemsets containing three items next:

```
> frequent.itemsets.generator(
        data.file.path='shopping_transaction_log.csv',
        itemset.combination.nums=3, item.min.freq=1, minsup=0.2)
```

This gives us the following table showing the frequent itemsets with their necessary statistics:

	Itemset	Frequency	Support
1	{beer, bread, diapers}	2	22.22
2	{beer, diapers, milk}	2	22.22

Thus we see that we get two frequent itemsets with support greater than 20%. Of course remember that this is a small dataset and the bigger the dataset you have containing purchase transactions, the more patterns you will get with stronger support.

We have successfully built an algorithm for generating frequent itemsets! You can use this same algorithm on new datasets to generate more and more frequent itemsets and then we can start recommending products for people to purchase as soon as we see them buying one or more items from any of the frequent itemsets. A simple example would be if we see people buying beer, we can recommend diapers and milk to them since that shopping trend was detected by our algorithm in the frequent itemsets earlier.

Association rule mining

We will now be implementing the final technique in market basket analysis for finding out association rules between itemsets to detect and predict product purchase patterns which can be used for product recommendations and suggestions. We will be notably using the Apriori algorithm from the `arules` package which uses an implementation for generating frequent itemsets first, which we discussed earlier. Once it has the frequent itemsets, the algorithm generates necessary rules based on parameters such as support, confidence, and lift. We will also show how you can visualize and interact with these rules using the `arulesViz` package. The code for this implementation is in the `ch3_association` rule `mining.R` file which you can directly load and follow the book.

Loading dependencies and data

We will first load the necessary package and data dependencies. Do note that we will be using the `Groceries` dataset which we discussed earlier in the section dealing with advanced contingency matrices.

```
> ## loading package dependencies
> library(arules) # apriori algorithm
> library(arulesViz)  # visualize association rules
>
> ## loading dataset
> data(Groceries)
```

Exploratory analysis

We will do some basic exploratory analysis on our dataset here, to see what kind of data we are dealing with and what products are the most popular among the customers.

```
> ## exploring the data
> inspect(Groceries[1:3])
  items
1 {citrus fruit,semi-finished bread,margarine,ready soups}
2 {tropical fruit,yogurt,coffee}
3 {whole milk}
> # viewing the top ten purchased products
> sort(itemFrequency(Groceries, type="absolute"),
+                    decreasing = TRUE)[1:10]
```

Output:

```
    whole milk other vegetables     rolls/buns          soda          yogurt
         2513               1903           1809          1715            1372
bottled water  root vegetables  tropical fruit  shopping bags         sausage
         1087               1072           1032           969             924
```

```
> # visualizing the top ten purchased products
> itemFrequencyPlot(Groceries,topN=10,type="absolute")
```

The preceding code snippet renders the following bar plot, which tells us the top ten most purchased products, which gives us a preliminary idea of what the customers buy the most when they purchase grocery items. It looks like people usually buy essential items such as milk and vegetables the most!

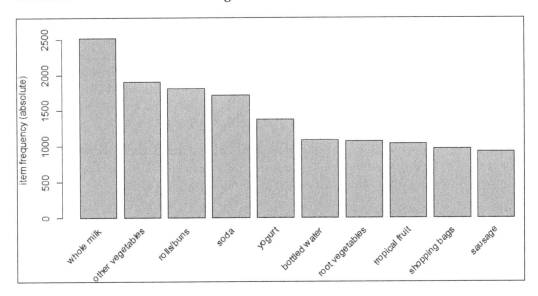

Detecting and predicting shopping trends

We will be generating association rules now using the Apriori algorithm, which we talked about earlier, to detect shopping trends so that we can predict what customers might buy in the future and even recommend it to them. We will start off with a normal workflow for generating association rules:

```
> # normal workflow
> metric.params <- list(supp=0.001, conf=0.5)
> rules <- apriori(Groceries, parameter = metric.params)
> inspect(rules[1:5])
```

Output:

```
    lhs                         rhs            support      confidence lift
1 {honey}                   => {whole milk}  0.001118454  0.7333333  2.870009
2 {tidbits}                 => {rolls/buns}  0.001220132  0.5217391  2.836542
3 {cocoa drinks}            => {whole milk}  0.001321810  0.5909091  2.312611
4 {pudding powder}          => {whole milk}  0.001321810  0.5652174  2.212062
5 {cooking chocolate}       => {whole milk}  0.001321810  0.5200000  2.035097
```

The way to interpret these rules is that you observe the items on the LHS and the items on the RHS, and conclude that if a customer has the item(s) from the LHS in his shopping cart, there is a chance of him also buying the item(s) on the RHS. This chance can be quantified using the metrics which are present in the remaining columns. We have discussed the significance of these metrics in the concepts of market basket analysis. From the previous rules, we can say that there is a 73.3% confidence that if a customer buys honey, he will also buy whole milk. From the previous rules, we see a trend that items such as honey, cocoa, pudding, and cooking chocolate all need milk as an essential ingredient, which might explain why people tend to buy that together with these products and we can recommend that to the customers. Feel free to tune the parameters for lift, support, and confidence to extract more rules from the dataset to get more and more patterns!

Often the rules generated by the Apriori algorithm have duplicate association rules which need to be removed before we examine the set of rules. You can do the same using the following utility function on the generated rules:

```
# pruning duplicate rules
prune.dup.rules <- function(rules){
  rule.subset.matrix <- is.subset(rules, rules)
  rule.subset.matrix[lower.tri(rule.subset.matrix, diag=T)] <- NA
  dup.rules <- colSums(rule.subset.matrix, na.rm=T) >= 1
  pruned.rules <- rules[!dup.rules]
  return(pruned.rules)
}
```

There are also ways to sort rules by specific metrics to see the rules with the best quality. We will look at the best rules using the previous metric parameter values sorted by the best confidence values.

```
# sorting rules based on metrics
rules <- sort(rules, by="confidence", decreasing=TRUE)
rules <- prune.dup.rules(rules)
inspect(rules[1:5])
```

Output:

```
      lhs                                                   rhs              support      confidence lift
113   {rice,sugar}                                       => {whole milk} 0.001220132 1          3.913649
258   {canned fish,hygiene articles}                     => {whole milk} 0.001118454 1          3.913649
1487  {root vegetables,butter,rice}                      => {whole milk} 0.001016777 1          3.913649
1646  {root vegetables,whipped/sour cream,flour}         => {whole milk} 0.001728521 1          3.913649
1670  {butter,soft cheese,domestic eggs}                 => {whole milk} 0.001016777 1          3.913649
```

We see itemsets in the previous rules like { rice, sugar }, which have a strong tendency to be purchased along with { whole milk }. The confidence values are pretty high (and they should be since we sorted them!) of 100% and the lift is also greater than 1, indicating a positive association between the itemsets. Do note that in large datasets, the support values may not be very high and that is perfectly normal because we are searching some specific patterns in the whole transaction dataset which may not even cover 1% of the total transactions present due to the varied type of transactions. However, it is extremely important for us to detect these patterns to make informed decisions about predicting what products might get sold together and recommending them to the customers. We will next look at another example of showing the best quality rules sorted by lift:

```
> rules<-sort(rules, by="lift", decreasing=TRUE)

> rules <- prune.dup.rules(rules)

> inspect(rules[1:5])
```

Output:

```
     lhs                                          rhs                  support      confidence lift
53   {Instant food products,soda}              => {hamburger meat} 0.001220132 0.6315789 18.99565
37   {soda,popcorn}                            => {salty snack}    0.001220132 0.6315789 16.69779
444  {flour,baking powder}                     => {sugar}          0.001016777 0.5555556 16.40807
327  {ham,processed cheese}                    => {white bread}    0.001931876 0.6333333 15.04549
330  {processed cheese,domestic eggs}          => {white bread}    0.001118454 0.5238095 12.44364
```

We see that these rules have really high lift and good confidence too making them items which customers would tend to buy together the most!

We will now look at detecting specific shopping patterns which we discussed earlier. One way to do this is to target specific items and generate association rules containing those items explicitly. The first way is to predict what items the customers might have in their shopping cart if they have bought an item on the RHS of association rules. We do this by specifying the item explicitly as shown next and analyze the transactional dataset:

```
> # finding itemsets which lead to buying of an item on RHS

> metric.params <- list(supp=0.001,conf=0.5, minlen=2)
```

```
> rules<-apriori(data=Groceries, parameter=metric.params,
+                    appearance = list(default="lhs",rhs="soda"),
+                    control = list(verbose=F))
> rules <- prune.dup.rules(rules)
> rules<-sort(rules, decreasing=TRUE, by="confidence")
> inspect(rules[1:5])
```

Output:

```
   lhs                                    rhs      support     confidence lift
12 {coffee,misc. beverages}           => {soda} 0.001016777 0.7692308   4.411303
37 {sausage,bottled water,bottled beer} => {soda} 0.001118454 0.7333333   4.205442
29 {sausage,white bread,shopping bags} => {soda} 0.001016777 0.6666667   3.823129
34 {rolls/buns,bottled water,chocolate} => {soda} 0.001321810 0.6500000   3.727551
13 {pastry,misc. beverages}           => {soda} 0.001220132 0.6315789   3.621912
```

It is interesting to note that people tend to buy beverages together, such as coffee, water, beer, and other miscellaneous beverages along with soda from the previous rules. Thus you can see that it is quite easy to predict when the users might buy soda using these rules and take action accordingly.

We can also predict what items the users are going to buy if they have already put some specific items in their shopping cart, by explicitly setting specific itemset values on the LHS of the association rules using the following technique:

```
# finding items which are bought when we have an itemset on LHS
metric.params <- list(supp=0.001, conf = 0.3, minlen=2)
rules<-apriori(data=Groceries, parameter=metric.params,
               appearance = list(default="rhs",
                                  lhs=c("yogurt", "sugar")),
               control=list(verbose=F))
#rules <- prune.dup.rules(rules)
rules<-sort(rules, decreasing=TRUE,by="confidence")
inspect(rules[1:5])
```

Output:

```
   lhs               rhs                 support     confidence lift
8 {yogurt,sugar} => {whole milk}       0.003660397 0.5294118  2.071932
2 {sugar}        => {whole milk}       0.015048297 0.4444444  1.739400
7 {yogurt,sugar} => {other vegetables} 0.002846975 0.4117647  2.128064
4 {yogurt}       => {whole milk}       0.056024403 0.4016035  1.571735
1 {sugar}        => {other vegetables} 0.010777834 0.3183183  1.645119
```

You can clearly see from the previous rules that people tend to buy milk if they have yogurt and sugar in their shopping cart together or individually. Thus, by targeting specific itemsets, you can offer specific product based recommendations to the customers.

Visualizing association rules

There is an excellent package, `arulesViz` which provides an interactive way to visualize the association rules and interact with them. Following is a sample visualization for the preceding association rules:

```
> ## visualizing rules
> plot(rules, method="graph", interactive=TRUE, shading=TRUE)
```

The preceding code snippet generates the following visualization which aids us in understanding the association rules even better. We have kept the itemsets on the LHS on the left-side of the visualization indicated by the vertices yogurt and sugar. We can see items on the RHS which have a probability to be bought if we buy any of the items on the LHS or both together. For example, people tend to buy whole milk if they have yogurt as well as sugar in their shopping cart, or either one of them.

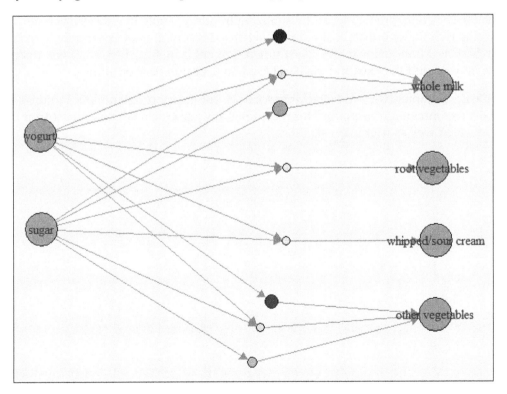

This visualization generated by `arulesViz` is completely interactive and you can play around with the vertices and edges, and place the itemsets according to your desire to find more and more trends and patterns from various rules.

This concludes our discussion on the main techniques which are being used in market basket analysis to detect and predict trends from shopping transaction logs and take actions accordingly from the derived insights.

Summary

In this chapter, we covered a lot of ground! We started with a discussion about how trends are detected and predicted in the retail vertical. Then we dived into what market basket analysis really means and the core concepts, mathematical formulae underlying the algorithms, and the critical metrics which are used to evaluate the results obtained from the algorithms, notably, support, confidence, and lift. We also discussed the most popular techniques used for analysis, including contingency matrix evaluation, frequent itemset generation, and association rule mining. Next, we talked about how to make data driven decisions using market basket analysis. Finally, we implemented our own algorithms and also used some of the popular libraries in R, such as `arules`, to apply these techniques to some real world transactional data for detecting, predicting, and visualizing trends. Do note that these machine learning techniques only talk about product based recommendations purely based on purchase and transactional logs. The human element is missing here since we don't take into account the likes and dislikes based on user purchase or ratings.

In the next chapter, we will be tackling some of these very problems and building robust recommendation engines for recommending products taking into account products as well as user interests.

4

Building a Product
Recommendation System

The digital world has made everything available at the click of a button. With everything going the online way, online shopping or e-commerce has become a big thing. From groceries to electronics to even cars, everything is available at the Amazon, Flipkart, and eBay of the world. This ever expanding digital market is just the right place for data science to show its magic.

The online revolution of e-commerce has not only empowered the customers, it has also overwhelmed them with too many choices. Choices are not only in terms of products or categories but also between different e-commerce platforms. Being an ecommerce company in this highly competitive market can be really difficult. Standing out is a challenge and that is where data yet again comes to the rescue.

As we saw in *Chapter 3, Predicting Customer Shopping Trends with Market Basket Analysis*, purchase patterns can provide a lot of insights about shopping behaviors. We utilized such data to find association rules to not only help the customers quickly find the right products but also help the retailers increase revenues (see *Chapter 3, Predicting Customer Shopping Trends with Market Basket Analysis*). For association rules, the granularity lies at the transaction level. They use transactions as a central entity and hence do not provide user specific insights.

In this chapter as well, we will continue our project work in the e-commerce domain. Here we will tackle the problem of personalization. We will use machine learning algorithms to provide user specific recommendations.

Through this chapter we will learn about:

- Recommendation systems and their types
- Issues with recommendation systems

- Collaborative filters
- Building a recommendation system from scratch based on matrix factorization
- Utilizing highly optimized R packages to build a production ready recommendation engine and evaluate its recommendations

Throughout this chapter we will use the terms **recommender engines** and **recommendation systems** interchangeably.

Understanding recommendation systems

Every individual in unique, the way we do things is what defines us uniquely. We eat, walk, talk, and even shop in a very unique way. Since the focus of this chapter is e-commerce, we will focus mostly on our shopping behaviors. We will utilize each customer's unique behavior to provide a personalized shopping experience.

To accomplish the task of providing a personalized shopping experience, we need a system to understand and model our customers. Recommendation engines are the systems which learn about customer preferences, choices, and so on, to recommend new products which are closer to what the user might have purchased themselves, thus providing a personalized experience. The options presented by such systems would have a high probability of the customer purchasing them.

Let us try to formally define a recommendation system.

Recommendation systems (or **recommender engines**) are a class of information filtering systems which analyze the input data to predict preferences of a user as they might have done for themselves.

Unlike information filtering systems which remove or filter information, recommender engines add or re-arrange the information flowing towards the user, which is more relevant to the current context.

Recommender engines are not a new concept. They have existed long before the internet was there. They existed in the form of our friends and family who used to recommend us things to buy because they understood our choices. These were and still are a sort of **offline-recommender engines**. The web is full of **online-recommender engines**. From recommendation related to **Who to follow** on Twitter to **Other movies you might enjoy** on Netflix to **Jobs you may be interested in** on LinkedIn, recommender engines are everywhere and not just on e-commerce platforms.

Now that we have understood what a recommendation engine is, let us look at their different types:

- **User-based recommender engines**: As the name suggests, these systems have the user as the central entity. The activities, preferences, or behavior of the users are analyzed to predict what they might like depending upon their similarity with other such users. They are also termed as User Based Collaborative Filters in general due to extensive use of collaborative filters specifically for such recommender engines.

- **Content-based recommender engines**: As the name suggests, these engines have the content or the items as the central entities. These items are analyzed to extract features; also the user profiles are built to map user preferences to the type of items. The engines then use this information to predict items which are similar to the ones the users have liked in the past. Such recommender engines are also known as **item-based collaborative filters** and have their roots in information retrieval theory.

- **Hybrid recommender engines**: These systems take the best of both worlds to improve upon the prediction results. The two pure types can be used simultaneously and then their results can be combined; they can be used by adding collaborative filtering capabilities to content based systems or even by unifying both the approaches into a single model. Multiple studies have been conducted to demonstrate that hybrid approaches are better than the simple ones. Hybrid recommendation engines are also better at tackling the problems which haunt recommender engines in general.

Before we dive deep into the intricacies of these algorithms, let us see the issues that affect the recommender systems.

Issues with recommendation systems

Recommender engines are affected mainly by the following two issues:

- **The sparsity problem**: Recommender engines work upon user preferences (or ratings for different items, depending upon the application) to predict or recommend products. Usually the ratings are given on some chosen scale but the user may choose not to rate certain items which he/she hasn't bought or looked at. For such cases, the rating is blank or zero. Hence, the ratings matrix R has elements of the form:

$r_{ij} = k$, if user has rated the item; where $k = 1$ to n

    0, otherwise

For any real world application, such as an e-commerce platform, the size of such a ratings matrix is huge due to the large number of users and items available on the platform. Even though a lot of user related information is gathered on such a platform, the ratings matrix itself might still be pretty sparse, that is the matrix might have a many elements as blanks (or zeroes). This problem in general is termed the **sparsity problem**. The sparsity problem renders the recommender engine's predictions ineffective as the algorithms are not able to infer the correlations correctly due to blanks or missing ratings. In the worst cases, the algorithm may term two users as un-correlated when actually they have highly similar preferences. The sparsity problem usually affects collaborative filtering algorithms.

- **The cold start problem**: A special case of the sparsity problem is the cold start issue. As mentioned previously, when the ratings matrix contains sparsely populated elements (or ratings), the recommender engine fails to return valid recommendations. The cold start problem occurs in two particular cases. Firstly, assume a user has newly been added to the system. In this case, the row representing the user would contain zeroes (mostly). Recommending items to such a user is virtually impossible due to unavailability of information related to his/her preferences. The second scenario is when an item is newly added to the system. Since the newly added item will not have any ratings by the users, recommending such an item would be difficult for the recommender system. Hence, these two scenarios represent what is termed the cold start problem. Very much like the sparsity problem, the cold start problem also plagues collaborative filters.

Collaborative filters

Recommendation systems and collaborative filters share a long history. From the early days of primitive recommender engines which utilized specific categorizations with hard-coded results, to current sophisticated recommender engines on various e-commerce platforms, recommender engines have made use of collaborative filters throughout. They are not only easy to understand but are equally simple to implement. Let us take this opportunity to learn more about collaborative filters before we dive into implementation details.

Fun Fact

Recommender engines surely outdate any known e-commerce platform! Grundy, a virtual librarian, was developed in 1979. It was a system for recommending books to users. It modeled the users based upon certain pre-defined stereotypes and recommended books from a known list for each such category.

Core concepts and definitions

Collaborative filters (denoted as **CF** henceforth) and recommender engines in general use certain terms and definitions to formally define and tackle the problem.

The problem domain of recommender engines revolves around the users and the items they are interested in. A **user** is anybody who interacts with the system and performs certain actions on the **item** (say purchases or views it). Similarly, a **rating** defines a user's preference for an item in consideration. Generally, this trio is represented as a (user, item, rating) tuple. Since the ratings quantify a user's preference, the ratings can themselves be defined in different ways depending upon the application. Applications define ratings as integer-valued scales ranging from say *0-5*, while others may define a real-valued scale. Some applications might use binary scales with values such as *Like/Dislike* or *Purchased/Not-Purchased*. Thus, each application makes use of a rating scale to suit its user's preferences.

Now that we know the key players involved, the next step is the representation of these core-concepts mathematically. A tuple of (user, item, rating) is usually represented in the form of a sparse matrix called a **ratings matrix**. Each user is represented by a row while the columns denote the items. Each element of this ratings matrix refers to the rating or preference of the user for an item. The ratings matrix is a **sparse matrix** since not all the items would be rated by every user and hence such unrated items would contain nulls or blank values. A ratings matrix using a 0-5 scale (unrated/missing ratings are denoted by ?) looks like the following matrix showing the preference of three users for different laptop models:

	Dell Inspiron	Mac Book Air	Acer Aspire	Alienware MX101	Mac Book Pro	Dell Vostro
User 1	?	5	2	?	4	1
User 2	4	?	3	?	1	4
User 3	3	?	?	5	4	3

A sample ratings matrix

A recommender engine is tasked to perform two main operations: **predict** and **recommend**. The prediction operation works upon a given user and item to determine the user's likely preference for the item in consideration. For the ratings matrix (like the one shown earlier), prediction is like identification of the missing values (represented by ? in the previous example).

The recommendation operation comes after the predictions have been done. Given a user, the recommendation operation generates a list of top N items based on the user's preferences.

 Note that the user in consideration for the predict and recommend tasks is termed the **active-user** in the context of recommender engines.

The collaborative filtering algorithm

Collaborative filters are a popular set of algorithms heavily used across applications. As we know, collaborative filters utilize the behaviour of similar users to predict and recommend items for the active user. These algorithms work on a simple assumption that similar users showcase similar behaviours. More formally, the algorithm assumes that the preferences or ratings of the other users in the system can be utilized to provide reasonable predictions for the active user.

Neighbour-based collaborative filtering, also known as **user-user collaborative filtering** or **kNN collaborative filtering**, is one of the earliest and most widely used algorithms from the family of collaborative filters. The kNN collaborative filter is based on the core assumption of similar behaviour amongst users with similar preferences. This algorithm makes use of similarity measures (discussed in *Chapter 2, Let's Help Machines Learn*) to predict and recommend items for the active user. The algorithm follows a two-step approach of first computing the predictions followed by the recommendations. The three main components of this algorithm are discussed next.

Predictions

The first step of kNN CF is to make use of the ratings matrix (usually denoted as R) to calculate predictions. Since we are concerned about user-user CF, the neighbourhood of active user (the user in consideration), denoted as u, is to be taken into account.

Let U be the set of all available users in the system and N denote the required neighbourhood where $N \subseteq U$. The algorithm then uses a similarity measure, say s, to compute the neighbours of u. Once N (the neighborhood of u) has been identified, the ratings of the neighbouring users are aggregated to compute u's preference for the current item. The most common measure to aggregate preferences is to use the **weighted average** of N neighboring users.

Mathematically, the active user u's predicted preference for item i, denoted as p_{ui} is given as:

$$p_{ui} = \overline{r}_u + \frac{\sum_{u' \in N} s(u, u')(r_{u'i} - \overline{r}_u)}{\sum_{u' \in N} |s(u, u')|}$$

Where:

- $\overline{r}_u$ is the active user u's mean rating

- $s(u, u')$ is the similarity measure between the active user u and the neighbouring user u'

In the preceding equation, we subtract the mean of the active user's rating $\overline{r}_u$ from the neighbouring user's mean rating to remove the rating bias of the users (some users give extremely high or low ratings and thus they may bias the overall predicted rating). A biased recommender engine might prevent better user-product matches in favour of popular or against not so popular ones. We can further improve the predictions by normalizing the user's ratings by using standard deviation to control the rating spread across the mean. To keep things simple, we will use the equation as mentioned previously. The following image depicts the nearest neighbours for an active user:

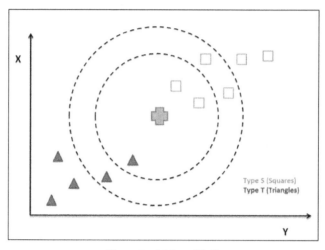

Nearest neighbors ($K=3$)

The question now arises that why only weighted average was used to predict the ratings and what the optimal number of neighbours (N) is. The reason behind using weighted average is that it is one of the measures which helps in generating consistent results. Different systems over the years have used various methods, such as *multivariate regressions* (the BellCore system for video recommendations), *unweighted averages* (Ringo for music recommendations), and so on, but weighted average performs pretty well in practice.

 For more information, have a look at W. Hill, L. Stead, M. Rosenstein, and G. Furnas, *Recommending and evaluating choices in a virtual community of use*, in ACM CHI '95, pp. 194–201, ACM Press/Addison-Wesley Publishing Co., 1995.

Coming onto the second question of the optimal number of neighbours, this is something very application dependent. We saw in *Chapter 2, Let's Help Machines Learn*, how the number of neighbours can change the outcome of an algorithm (see *K-Nearest Neighbors (KNN)*), similarly the value of N can affect the outcome of a recommender engine. In general, limiting the number of neighbouring users helps in reducing the noise by removing users with low correlation to the active user. But then again, the value of N is application dependent and requires due diligence at the data scientist's end.

Recommendations

Once predictions have been done for the *active user*, a recommendation list can be generated by ordering the items by predicted rank. This recommendation list may be further fine-tuned by applying certain minimal thresholds and other user specific characteristics, such as preferences for color, size, price sensitivity, and so on. Thus, this step generates a list of probable items which the user is more likely to buy based on his/her personal preferences. We will cover more on this in the coming section, *Building a recommender engine*.

Similarity

A similarity measure is an important component of our collaborative filtering based recommender engine algorithm. There are various similarity measures available for use. The most common amongst them is the **cosine similarity** measure. This approach represents each user as an n dimensional vector of ratings and similarity is measured by calculating the cosine distance between two such user vectors.

Mathematically, cosine similarity is given as:

$$s(u,v) = \frac{r_u.r_v}{\|r_u\|_2 \|r_v\|_2}$$

Where, $\|r_u\|_2$ and $\|r_v\|_2$ are the **L2** or **Euclidean norms** for each of the rating vectors.

Pearson correlation and **Spearman rank correlation** are a couple of statistical similarity measures which are also used widely.

Now that we understand the basics of collaborative filters and general concepts, we are ready to get our hands dirty with implementation details. Let us start with building the recommender system, brick-by-brick!

Building a recommender engine

As discussed in the previous section, collaborative filtering is a simple yet very effective approach for predicting and recommending items to users. If we look closely, the algorithms work on input data, which is nothing but a matrix representation of the user ratings for different products.

Bringing in a mathematical perspective into the picture, **matrix factorization** is a technique to manipulate matrices and identify latent or hidden features from the data represented in the matrix. Building on the same concept, let us use matrix factorization as the basis for predicting ratings for items which the user has not yet rated.

Matrix factorization

Matrix factorization refers to the identification of two or more matrices such that when these matrices are multiplied we get the original matrix. Matrix factorization, as mentioned earlier, can be used to discover latent features between two different kinds of entities. We will understand and use the concepts of matrix factorization as we go along preparing our recommender engine for our e-commerce platform.

As our aim for the current project is to personalize the shopping experience and recommend product ratings for an e-commerce platform, our input data contains user ratings for various products on the website. We process the input data and transform it into a matrix representation for analyzing it using matrix factorization. The input data looks like this:

	iPhone.4	iPhone.5S	Nexus.5	Moto.X	Moto.G	Nexus.6	One.Plus.One
1	5	5	1	0	0	0	1
2	1	1	4	0	4	5	0
3	1	0	4	0	0	4	5
4	0	1	4	0	0	5	4
5	5	5	0	0	1	0	1
6	1	0	4	0	0	5	4
7	1	1	0	5	4	4	0
8	0	5	1	0	1	0	1

User ratings matrix

As you can see, the input data is a matrix with each row representing a particular user's rating for different items represented in the columns. For the current case, the columns representing items are different mobile phones such as iPhone 4, iPhone 5s, Nexus 5, and so on. Each row contains ratings for each of these mobile phones as given by eight different users. The ratings range from 1 to 5 with 1 being the lowest and 5 being the highest. A rating of 0 represents unrated items or missing rating.

The task of our recommender engine will be to predict the correct rating for the missing ones in the input matrix. We could then use the predicted ratings to recommend items most desired by the user.

The premise here is that two users would rate a product similarly if they like similar features of the product or item. Since our current data is related to user ratings for different mobile phones, people might rate the phones based on their hardware configuration, price, OS, and so on. Hence, matrix factorization tries to identify these latent features to predict ratings for a certain user and a certain product.

While trying to identify these latent features, we proceed with the basic assumption that the number of such features is less than the total number of items in consideration. This assumption makes sense because if this was the case, then each user would have a specific feature associated with him/her (and similarly for the product). This would in turn make recommendations futile as none of the users would be interested in items rated by other users (which is not usually the case).

Now let us get into the mathematical details of matrix factorization and our recommender engine.

Since we are dealing with user ratings for different products, let us assume U to be a matrix representing user preferences and similarly a matrix P represents the products for which we have the ratings. Then the ratings matrix R will be defined as

$$R = U \times P^T \left(\text{we take transpose of } P \text{ as } P^T \text{for matrix multiplication} \right)$$

$$\text{where,} |R| = |U| \times |P|$$

Assuming the process helps us identify K latent features, our aim is to find two matrices X and Y such that their product (matrix multiplication) approximates R.

$$X = |U| \times K \ matrix$$
$$Y = |P| \times K \ matrix$$

Where, X is a user related matrix which represents the associations between the users and the latent features. Y, on the other hand, is the product related matrix which represents the associations between the products and the latent features.

The task of predicting the rating $\hat{r}_{ij}$ of a product p_j by a user u_i is done by calculating the dot product of the vectors corresponding to p_j (vector Y, that is the user) and u_i (vector X, that is the product).

$$\hat{r}_{ij} = x_i^T \cdot y_i$$

$$= \sum_{k=1}^{K} x_{ik} \cdot y_{kj}$$

Now, to find the matrices X and Y, we utilize a technique called **gradient descent**. Gradient descent, in simple terms, tries to find the local minimum of a function; it is an optimization technique. We use gradient descent in the current context to iteratively minimize the difference between the predicted ratings and the actual ratings. To begin with, we randomly initialize the matrices X and Y and then calculate how different their product is from the actual ratings matrix R.

The difference between the predicted and the actual values is what is termed the **error**. For our problem, we will consider the **squared error,** which is calculated as:

$$e_{ij}^2 = \left(r_{ij} - \hat{r}_{ij} \right)^2$$

$$= \left(r_{ij} - \sum_{k=1}^{K} x_{ik} \cdot y_{kj} \right)^2$$

Where, r_{ij} is the actual rating by user i for product j and $\hat{r}_{ij}$ is the predicted value of the same.

To minimize the error, we need to find the correct direction or gradient to change our values to. To obtain the gradient for each of the variables x and y, we differentiate them separately as:

$$\frac{\partial \varepsilon_{ij}^2}{\partial x_{ik}} = -2\left(r_{ij} - \hat{r}_{ij}\right) \cdot y_{kj}$$

$$= -2e_{ij} y_{kj}$$

$$\frac{\partial \varepsilon_{ij}^2}{\partial y_{ik}} = -2\left(r_{ij} - \hat{r}_{ij}\right) \cdot x_{ik}$$

$$= -2e_{ij} x_{ik}$$

Hence, the equations to find x_{ik} and y_{kj} can be given as:

$$x_{ik}' = x_{ik} + \alpha \frac{\partial e_{ij}^2}{\partial x_{ik}}$$

$$= x_{ik} + 2\alpha e_{ij} y_{kj}$$

$$y_{kj}' = y_{kj} + \alpha \frac{\partial e_{ij}^2}{\partial y_{ik}}$$

$$= y_{kj} + 2\alpha e_{ij} x_{ik}$$

Where α is the constant to denote the **rate of descent** or the rate of approaching the minima (also known as the learning rate). The value of α defines the size of steps we take in either direction to reach the minima. Large values may lead to oscillations as we may overshoot the minima every time. Usual practice is to select very small values for α, of the order 10^{-4}. x_{ik}' and y_{kj}' are the updated values of x_{ik} and y_{kj} after each iteration of gradient descent.

As seen in *Chapter 2, Let's Help Machines Learn*, machine learning algorithms can suffer from overfitting. To avoid overfitting, along with controlling extreme or large values in the matrices X and Y, we introduce the concept of regularization. Formally, **regularization** refers to the process of introducing additional information in order to prevent overfitting. Regularization penalizes models with extreme values.

To prevent overfitting in our case, we introduce the regularization constant called β. With the introduction of β, the equations are updated as follows:

$$e_{ij}^2 = \left(r_{ij} - \sum_{k=1}^{K} x_{ik} \cdot y_{kj} \right)^2 + \frac{\beta}{2} \sum_{k=1}^{K} \left(\| X \|^2 + \| Y \|^2 \right)$$

Also,

$$x'_{ik} = x_{ik} + \alpha \frac{\partial e_{ik}^2}{\partial x_{ik}}$$

$$= x_{ik} + 2\alpha e_{ij} y_{kj} - \beta x_{ik}$$

$$y'_{kj} = y_{kj} + \alpha \frac{\partial e_{ij}^2}{\partial y_{ik}}$$

$$= y_{kj} + 2\alpha e_{ij} x_{ik} - \beta y_{kj}$$

As we already have the ratings matrix R and we use it to determine how far our predicted values are from the actual, matrix factorization turns into a supervised learning problem. For this supervised problem, just as we saw in *Chapter 2, Let's Help Machines Learn*, we use some of the rows as our training samples. Let S be our training set with elements being tuples of the form (u_i, p_j, r_{ij}). Thus, our task is to minimize the error (e_{ij}) for every tuple (u_i, p_j, r_{ij}) ∈ in training set S.

The overall error (say E) can be calculated as:

$$E = \sum \left(u_i, p_j, r_{ij} \right) \in S\, e_{ij}$$

$$= \sum \left(u_i, p_j, r_{ij} \right) \in S \left(r_{ij} - \sum_{k=1}^{K} x_{ik} y_{kj} \right)^2$$

Implementation

Now that we have looked into the mathematics of matrix factorization, let us convert the algorithm into code and prepare a recommender engine for the mobile phone ratings input data set discussed earlier.

As shown in the *Matrix factorization* section, the input dataset is a matrix with each row representing a user's rating for the products mentioned as columns. The ratings range from 1 to 5 with 0 representing the missing values.

To transform our algorithm into working code, we need to compute and complete the following tasks:

- Load the input data and transform it into ratings matrix representation
- Prepare a matrix factorization based recommendation model
- Predict and recommend products to the users
- Interpret and evaluate the model

Loading and transforming input data into matrix representation is simple. As seen earlier, R provides us with easy to use utility functions for the same.

```
# load raw ratings from csv
raw_ratings <- read.csv(<file_name>)


# convert columnar data to sparse ratings matrix
ratings_matrix <- data.matrix(raw_ratings)
```

Now that we have our data loaded into an R matrix, we proceed and prepare the user-latent features matrix X and item-latent features matrix Y. We initialize both from uniform distributions using the runif function.

```
# number of rows in ratings
rows <- nrow(ratings_matrix)


# number of columns in ratings matrix
columns <- ncol(ratings_matrix)


# latent features
K <- 2


# User-Feature Matrix
```

```
X <- matrix(runif(rows*K), nrow=rows, byrow=TRUE)


# Item-Feature Matrix
Y <- matrix(runif(columns*K), nrow=columns, byrow=TRUE)
```

The major component is the matrix factorization function itself. Let us split the task into two, calculation of the gradient and subsequently the overall error.

The calculation of the gradient involves the ratings matrix R and the two factor matrices X and Y, along with the constants α and β. Since we are dealing with matrix manipulations (specifically, multiplication), we transpose Y before we begin with any further calculations. The following lines of code convert the algorithm discussed previously into R syntax. All variables follow naming convention similar to the algorithm for ease of understanding.

```
for (i in seq(nrow(ratings_matrix))){


    for (j in seq(length(ratings_matrix[i, ]))){

      if (ratings_matrix[i, j] > 0){

        # error
        eij = ratings_matrix[i, j] - as.numeric(X[i, ] %*% Y[, j])


      # gradient calculation

        for (k in seq(K)){
          X[i, k] = X[i, k] + alpha * (2 * eij * Y[k, j]/
          - beta * X[i, k])

          Y[k, j] = Y[k, j] + alpha * (2 * eij * X[i, k]/
          - beta * Y[k, j])
        }
      }
    }
}
```

The next part of the algorithm is to calculate the overall error; we again use similar variable names for consistency:

```
# Overall Squared Error Calculation


e = 0


for (i in seq(nrow(ratings_matrix))){

  for (j in seq(length(ratings_matrix[i, ]))){

    if (ratings_matrix[i, j] > 0){

      e = e + (ratings_matrix[i, j] - /
          as.numeric(X[i, ] %*% Y[, j]))^2

      for (k in seq(K)){
        e = e + (beta/2) * (X[i, k]^2 + Y[k, j]^2)
      }
    }
  }
}
```

As a final piece, we iterate over these calculations multiple times to mitigate the risks of cold start and sparsity. We term the variable controlling multiple starts as **epoch**. We also terminate the calculations once the overall error drops below a certain threshold.

Moreover, as we had initialized x and y from uniform distributions, the predicted values would be real numbers. We round the final output before returning the predicted matrix.

Note that this is a very simplistic implementation and a lot of complexity has been kept out for ease of understanding. Hence, this may result in the predicted matrix containing values greater than 5. For the current scenario, it is safe to assume the values above the max scale of 5 are equivalent to 5 (and similarly for values less than 0). We encourage the reader to fine tune the code to handle such cases.

Setting α to 0.0002, β to 0.02, K (that is, latent features) to 2, and epoch to 1000, let us see a sample run of our code with overall error threshold set to 0.001:

```
# load raw ratings from csv
raw_ratings <- read.csv("product_ratings.csv")


# convert columnar data to sparse ratings matrix
ratings_matrix <- data.matrix(raw_ratings)



# number of rows in ratings
rows <- nrow(ratings_matrix)


# number of columns in ratings matrix
columns <- ncol(ratings_matrix)


# latent features
K <- 2


# User-Feature Matrix
X <- matrix(runif(rows*K), nrow=rows, byrow=TRUE)


# Item-Feature Matrix
Y <- matrix(runif(columns*K), nrow=columns, byrow=TRUE)


# iterations
epoch <- 10000


# rate of descent
alpha <- 0.0002


# regularization constant
beta <- 0.02



pred.matrix <- mf_based_ucf(ratings_matrix, X, Y, K, epoch = epoch)
```

```
# setting column names
colnames(pred.matrix)<-
c("iPhone.4","iPhone.5s","Nexus.5","Moto.X","Moto.G","Nexus.6",/
"One.Plus.One")
```

The preceding lines of code utilize the functions explained earlier to prepare the recommendation model. The predicted ratings or the output matrix looks like the following:

	iPhone.4	iPhone.5s	Nexus.5	Moto.X	Moto.G	Nexus.6	One.Plus.One
1	4.97	4.99	1.00	3.41	1.01	2.05	0.99
2	1.06	0.99	4.03	5.58	4.20	4.74	4.38
3	0.87	0.80	3.97	5.43	4.14	4.64	4.32
4	1.13	1.06	3.97	5.53	4.14	4.69	4.31
5	4.97	4.99	1.00	3.41	1.00	2.05	0.99
6	1.06	1.00	3.97	5.51	4.14	4.68	4.32
7	1.01	0.95	3.58	4.98	3.73	4.22	3.88
8	4.94	4.96	1.00	3.39	1.00	2.04	0.99

Predicted ratings matrix

Result interpretation

Let us do a quick visual inspection to see how good or bad our predictions have been. Consider users 1 and 3 as our training samples. From the input dataset, we can clearly see that user 1 has given high ratings to iPhones while user 3 has done the same for Android based phones. The following side by side comparison shows that our algorithm has predicted values close enough to the actual values:

iPhone.4	5	iPhone.5s	4.99
iPhone.5S	5	iPhone.4	4.97
Nexus.5	1	Moto.X	3.41
Moto.X	0	Nexus.6	2.05
Moto.G	0	Moto.G	1.01
Nexus.6	0	Nexus.5	1.00
One.Plus.One	1	One.Plus.One	0.99
(a) Actual Ratings		(b) Predicted Ratings	

Ratings by user 1

Let us see the ratings of user 3 in the following screenshot:

iPhone.4	1	iPhone.4	0.87
iPhone.5S	0	iPhone.5s	0.80
Nexus.5	4	Nexus.5	3.97
Moto.X	0	Moto.X	5.43
Moto.G	0	Moto.G	4.14
Nexus.6	4	Nexus.6	4.64
One.Plus.One	5	One.Plus.One	4.32
(a) Actual Ratings		(b) Predicted Ratings	

Ratings by user 3

Now that we have our ratings matrix with updated values, we are ready to recommend products to users. It is common sense to show only the products which the user hasn't rated yet. The right set of recommendations will also enable the seller to pitch the products which have high probability of being purchased by the user.

The usual practice is to return a list of the top N items from the unrated list of products for each user. The user in consideration is usually termed the **active-user**. Let us consider user 6 as our active-user. This user has only rated Nexus 6, One Plus One, Nexus 5, and iPhone4 in that order of rating, that is Nexus 6 was highly rated and iPhone4 was rated the least. Getting a list of the *Top 2* recommended phones for such a customer using our algorithm would result in Moto X and Moto G (very rightly indeed, do you see why?).

Thus, we built a recommender engine smart enough to recommend the right mobile phones to an Android fanboy and saved the world from yet another catastrophe!

Data to the rescue!

This simple implementation of a recommender engine using matrix factorization gave us a flavor of how such a system actually works. Next, let us get into some real world action using recommender engines.

Production ready recommender engines

In this chapter so far, we have learnt about recommender engines in detail and even developed one from scratch (using matrix factorization). Through all this, it is clearly evident how widespread the application of such systems is.

E-commerce websites (or for that fact, any popular technology platform) out there today have tones of content to offer. Not only that, but the number of users is also huge. In such a scenario, where thousands of users are browsing/buying stuff simultaneously across the globe, providing recommendations to them is a task in itself. To complicate things even further, a good user experience (response times, for example) can create a big difference between two competitors. These are live examples of production systems handling millions of customers day in and day out.

Fun Fact

Amazon.com is one of the biggest names in the e-commerce space with 244 million active customers. Imagine the amount of data being processed to provide recommendations to such a huge customer base browsing through millions of products!

Source: `http://www.amazon.com/b?ie=UTF8&node=8445211011`

In order to provide a seamless capability for use in such platforms, we need highly optimized libraries and hardware. For a recommender engine to handle thousands of users simultaneously every second, R has a robust and reliable framework called the **recommenderlab**.

Recommenderlab is a widely used R extension designed to provide a robust foundation for recommender engines. The focus of this library is to provide efficient handling of data, availability of standard algorithms and evaluation capabilities. In this section, we will be using recommenderlab to handle a considerably larger data set for recommending items to users. We will also use the evaluation functions from recommenderlab to see how good or bad our recommendation system is. These capabilities will help us build a production ready recommender system similar (or at least closer) to what many online applications such as Amazon or Netflix use.

The dataset used in this section contains ratings for 100 items as rated by 5000 users. The data has been anonymized and the product names have been replaced by product IDs. The rating scale used is 0 to 5 with 1 being the worst, 5 being the best, and 0 representing unrated items or missing ratings.

To build a recommender engine using recommenderlab for a production ready system, the following steps are to be performed:

1. Extract, transform, and analyze the data.
2. Prepare a recommendation model and generate recommendations.
3. Evaluate the recommendation model.

We will look at all these steps in the following subsections.

Extract, transform, and analyze

As in case of any data intensive (particularly machine learning) application, the first and foremost step is to get the data, understand/explore it, and then transform it into the format required by the algorithm deemed fit for the current application. For our recommender engine using the recommenderlab package, we will first load the data from a csv file described in the previous section and then explore it using various R functions.

```
# Load recommenderlab library
library("recommenderlab")


# Read dataset from csv file
raw_data <- read.csv("product_ratings_data.csv")


# Create rating matrix from data
ratings_matrix<- as(raw_data, "realRatingMatrix")


#view transformed data
image(ratings_matrix[1:6,1:10])
```

The preceding section of code loads the recommenderlab package and then uses the standard utility function to read the `product_ratings_data.csv` file. For exploratory as well as further steps, we need the data to be transformed into the user-item ratings matrix format (as described in the *Core concepts and definitions* section).

The `as(<data>,<type>)` utility converts `csv` into the required ratings matrix format.

The `csv` file contains data in the format shown in the following screenshot. Each row contains a user's rating for a specific product. The column headers are self explanatory.

	UserID	Product	Ratings
1	u10005	prod_5	0
2	u10005	prod_7	0
3	u10005	prod_8	1
4	u10005	prod_13	0
5	u10005	prod_15	1
6	u10005	prod_16	0

Product ratings data

The `realRatingMatrix` conversion transforms the data into a matrix as shown in the following image. The users are depicted as rows while the columns represent the products. Ratings are represented using a gradient scale where white represents missing/unrated rating while black denotes a rating of 5/best.

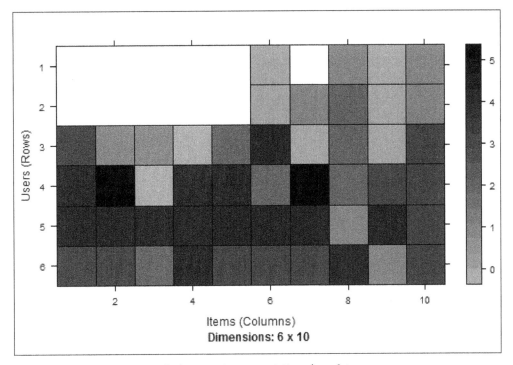

Ratings matrix representation of our data

Now that we have the data in our environment, let us explore some of its characteristics and see if we can decipher some key patterns.

First of all, we extract a representative sample from our main data set (refer to the screenshot *Product ratings data*) and analyze it for:

- Average rating score for our user population
- Spread/distribution of item ratings across the user population
- Number of items rated per user

The following lines of code help us explore our data set sample and analyze the points mentioned previously:

```
# Extract a sample from ratings matrix
sample_ratings <-sample(ratings_matrix,1000)


# Get the mean product ratings as given by first user
rowMeans(sample_ratings[1,])



# Get distribution of item ratings
hist(getRatings(sample_ratings), breaks=100,/
    xlab = "Product Ratings",main = " Histogram of Product Ratings")


# Get distribution of normalized item ratings
hist(getRatings(normalize(sample_ratings)),breaks=100,/
            xlab = "Normalized Product Ratings",main = /
                " Histogram of Normalized Product Ratings")


# Number of items rated per user
hist(rowCounts(sample_ratings),breaks=50,/
    xlab = "Number of Products",main =/
    " Histogram of Product Count Distribution")
```

We extract a sample of 1,000 users from our dataset for exploration purposes. The mean of product ratings as given by the first row in our user-rating sample is 2.055. This tells us that this user either hasn't seen/rated many products or he usually rates the products pretty low. To get a better idea of how the users rate products, we generate a histogram of item rating distribution. This distribution peaks around the middle, that is, 3. The histogram is shown next:

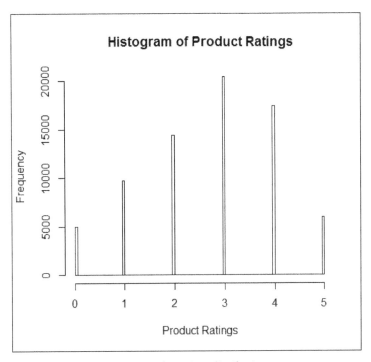

Histogram for ratings distribution

The histogram shows that the ratings are normally distributed around the mean with low counts for products with very high or very low ratings.

Finally, we check the spread of the number of products rated by the users. We prepare a histogram which shows this spread:

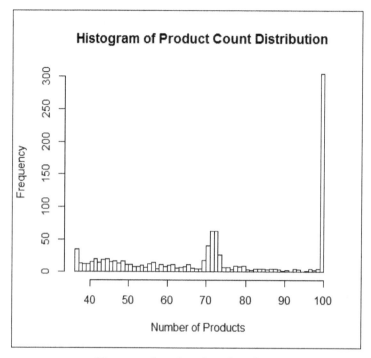

Histogram of number of rated products

The preceding histogram shows that there are many users who have rated 70 or more products, as well as there are many users who have rated all 100 products.

The exploration step helps us get an idea of how our data is. We also get an idea about the way the users generally rate the products and how many products are being rated.

Model preparation and prediction

We have the data in our R environment which has been transformed into the ratings matrix format. In this section, we are interested in preparing a recommender engine based on user-based collaborative filtering. We will be using similar terminology as described in the previous sections. Recommenderlab provides straight-forward utilities to learn and prepare a model for building recommender engines.

We prepare our model based upon a sample of just 1,000 users. This way, we can use this model to predict the missing ratings for the rest of the users in our ratings matrix. The following lines of code utilize the first thousand rows for learning the model:

```
# Create 'User Based collaborative filtering' model
ubcf_recommender <- Recommender(ratings_matrix[1:1000],"UBCF")
```

"UBCF" in the preceding code signifies user-based collaborative filtering. Recommenderlab also provides other algorithms, such as **IBCF** or **Item-Based Collaborative Filtering**, **PCA** or **Principal Component Analysis**, and others as well.

After preparing the model, we use it to predict the ratings for our 1,010[th] and 1,011[th] users in the system. Recommenderlab also requires us to mention the number of items to be recommended to the users (in the order of preference of course). For the current case, we mention 5 as the number of items to be recommended.

```
# Predict list of product which can be recommended to given users
recommendations <- predict(ubcf_recommender,/
                ratings_matrix[1010:1011], n=5)


# show recommendation in form of the list
as(recommendations, "list")
```

The preceding lines of code generate two lists, one for each of the users. Each element in these lists is a product for recommendation. The model predicted that, for user 1,010, product prod_93 should be recommended as the top most product followed by prod_79, and so on.

```
# output generated by the model
[[1]]
[1] "prod_93" "prod_79" "prod_80" "prod_83" "prod_89"


[[2]]
[1] "prod_80" "prod_85" "prod_87" "prod_75" "prod_79"
```

Recommenderlab is a robust platform which is optimized to handle large datasets. With a few lines of code, we were able to load the data, learn a model, and even recommend products to the users in virtually no time. Compare this with the basic recommender engine we developed using matrix factorization which involved many lines of code (when compared to recommenderlab) apart from the obvious difference in performance.

Model evaluation

We have successfully prepared a model and used it for predicting and recommending products to the users in our system. But what do we know about the accuracy of our model? To evaluate the prepared model, recommenderlab has handy and easy to use utilities. Since we need to evaluate our model, we need to split it into training and test data sets. Also, recommenderlab requires us to mention the number of items to be used for testing (it uses the rest for computing the error).

For the current case, we will use 500 users to prepare an evaluation model. The model will be based on a 90-10 training-testing dataset split with 15 items used for test sets.

```
# Evaluation scheme
eval_scheme <- evaluationScheme(ratings_matrix[1:500],/
                    method="split",train=0.9,given=15)


# View the evaluation scheme
eval_scheme


# Training model
training_recommender <- Recommender(getData(eval_scheme,/
                    "train"), "UBCF")


# Preditions on the test dataset
test_rating <- predict(training_recommender,/
            getData(eval_scheme, "known"), type="ratings")


#Error
error <- calcPredictionAccuracy(test_rating,/
                getData(eval_scheme, "unknown"))


error
```

We use the evaluation scheme to train our model based on the *UBCF* algorithm. The prepared model from the training dataset is used to predict ratings for the given items. We finally use the method `calcPredictionAccuracy` to calculate the error in predicting the ratings between known and unknown components of the test set. For our case, we get an output as follows:

```
     RMSE        MSE        MAE
1.1628422 1.3522021 0.9099283
```

The generated output mentions the values for **RMSE** or root mean squared error, **MSE** or mean squared error, and **MAE** or mean absolute error. For RMSE in particular, the values deviate from the correct values by `1.162` (note that the values might deviate slightly across runs due to various factors such as sampling, iterations, and so on). This evaluation will make more sense when the outcomes are compared from different CF algorithms.

To evaluate UBCF, we use IBCF as comparison. The following few lines of code help us prepare an IBCF based model and test the ratings, which can then be compared using the `calcPredictionAccuracy` utility:

```
# Training model using IBCF
training_recommender_2 <- Recommender(getData(eval_scheme,/
                                "train"), "IBCF")


# Preditions on the test dataset
test_rating_2 <- predict(training_recommender_2,/
                getData(eval_scheme, "known"),/
              type="ratings")


error_compare <- rbind(calcPredictionAccuracy(test_rating,/
              getData(eval_scheme, "unknown")),/
                calcPredictionAccuracy(test_rating_2,/
              getData(eval_scheme, "unknown")))


rownames(error_compare) <- c("User Based CF","Item Based CF")
```

The comparative output shows that UBCF outperforms IBCF with lower values of RMSE, MSE, and MAE.

```
                  RMSE       MSE        MAE
User Based CF 1.162842 1.352202 0.9099283
Item Based CF 1.221485 1.492025 0.9324538
```

Similarly, we can use the other algorithms available in recommenderlab to test/evaluate our models. We encourage the user to try out a few more and see which algorithm has the least error in predicted ratings.

Summary

In this chapter, we continued our pursuit of using machine learning in the field of e-commerce to enhance sales and overall user experience. The previous chapter had discussed recommendations based on transactional logs; in this chapter, we accounted for the human factor and looked into the recommendation engines based on user behavior.

We started off by understanding what recommendation systems and their classifications into user-based, content-based, and hybrid recommender systems. We touched on the problems associated with recommender engines in general. Then we dived deep into the specifics of collaborative filters and discussed the math around prediction and similarity measures. After getting our basics straight, we moved onto building a recommender engine of our own from scratch. We utilized matrix factorization to build a recommender engine step by step using a small dummy dataset. We then moved onto building a production ready recommender engine using R's popular library called recommenderlab. We used user-based CF as our core algorithm to build a recommendation model on a bigger dataset containing ratings for 100 products by 5,000 users. We closed our discussion by evaluating our recommendation model using recommenderlab's utility methods.

The next couple of chapters will move from e-commerce to the financial domain and utilize machine learning for some more interesting use cases.

5
Credit Risk Detection and Prediction – Descriptive Analytics

In the last two chapters, you saw some interesting problems revolving around the retail and e-commerce domains. You now know how to detect and predict shopping trends from shopping patterns as well as how to build recommendation systems. If you remember from *Chapter 1*, *Getting started with R and Machine Learning* that the applications of machine learning are diverse, we can apply the same concepts and techniques to solve a wide variety of problems in the real world. We will be tackling a completely new problem here, but hold on to what you have learnt because several concepts you learnt previously will come in handy soon!

In the next couple of chapters, we will be tackling a new problem related to the financial domain. We will be looking at the bank customers of a particular German bank who could be credit risks for the bank, based on some data that has been previously collected. We will perform descriptive and exploratory analysis on this data to highlight different potential features in the dataset and also look at their relationship with credit risk. In the next step, we will be building predictive models using machine learning algorithms and these data features to detect and predict customers who could be potential credit risks. You may remember that the two main things that we need to do this analysis to remain unchanged are data and algorithms.

You might be surprised to know that risk analysis is one of the top most focus areas of financial organizations including in banks, investment firms, insurance firms, and brokerage firms. Each of these organizations often has dedicated teams for solving problems revolving around risk analysis. Some examples of risk which are frequently analyzed include credit risk, sales risk, fraud related risks, and many more.

In this chapter, we will be focusing on the following topics:

- Descriptive analytics of our credit risk dataset
- Domain knowledge of the credit risk problem
- Detailed analysis of dataset features
- Exploratory analysis of the data
- Visualizations on various data features
- Statistical tests to determine feature significance

Always remember that domain knowledge is essential before solving any machine learning problem because otherwise we will end up applying random algorithms and techniques blindly which may not give the right results.

Types of analytics

Before we start tackling our next challenge, it will be useful to get an idea of the different types of analytics which broadly encompass the data science domain. We use a variety of data mining and machine learning techniques to solve different data problems. However, depending on the mechanism of the technique and its end result, we can broadly classify analytics into four different types which are explained next:

- **Descriptive analytics**: This is what we use when we have some data to analyze. We start with looking at the different attributes of the data, extract meaningful features, and use statistics and visualizations to understand what has already happened. The main aim of descriptive analytics is to get a broad idea of what kind of data we are dealing with and summarize what has happened in the past. Above almost 80% of all analytics in businesses today are descriptive.
- **Diagnostic analytics**: This is sometimes clubbed together with descriptive analytics. Here the main objective is to delve deeper into the data to find specific patterns and answer questions such as why did this occur. Usually, it involves root-cause analysis to come to the root of why something happened and what were the main factors involved in doing during its occurrence. Sometimes techniques such as regression modeling help in achieving this.

- **Predictive analytics**: This is the final step in any analytics pipeline. Once you have built consistent and stable predictive models with a good flow of clean data for predictions, you can build systems which utilize this and start prescribing actions which you might take to improve your business. Do remember that predictive modeling can only predict what might happen in the future because all models are probabilistic in nature and nothing is 100 percent certain.

- **Prescriptive analytics**: This is the final step in any analytics pipeline if you are in the stage that you have built consistent predictive models with a good flow of clean data such that you are able to predict what might happen in the future. Then you can build systems which utilize this and start prescribing actions which you might take to improve your business. Do remember that you need working predictive models with good data and an excellent feedback mechanism to achieve this.

Most organizations do a lot of descriptive analytics and some amount of predictive analytics. However, it is really difficult to implement prescriptive analytics due to the ever changing business conditions and data streams and problems associated with that, the most common one being data sanitization issues. We will be touching upon descriptive analytics in this chapter before moving on to predictive analytics in the next chapter to solve our problem related to credit risk analytics.

Our next challenge

We have dealt with some interesting applications of machine learning in the e-commerce domain in the last couple of chapters. For the next two chapters, our big challenge will be in the financial domain. We will be using data analysis and machine learning techniques to analyze financial data from a German bank. This data will contain a lot of information regarding customers of that bank. We will be analyzing that data in two stages which include descriptive and predictive analytics.

- **Descriptive**: Here we will look closely at the data and its various attributes. We will perform descriptive analysis and visualizations to see the kind of features we are dealing with and how they might be related to credit risk. The data we will be dealing with here consists of labeled data already and we will be able to see how many customers were credit risks and how many weren't. We will also look closely at each feature in the data and understand its significance which will be useful in the next step.

- **Predictive**: Here we will focus more on the machine learning algorithms used in predictive modeling to build predictive models using the data we have already acquired in the previous step. We will be using various machine learning algorithms and testing the accuracy of the models when predicting if a customer could be a potential credit risk. We will be using labeled data to train the model and then test the models on several data instances, comparing our predicted result with the actual result to see how well our models perform.

The significance of predicting credit risks is quite useful for financial organizations, such as banks that have to often deal with loan applications from their customers. They have to then make the decision to approve or deny the loan based on information they have about the customer. If they have a robust machine learning system built in place which can analyze the data about the customer and say which customers might be credit risks, then they can prevent losses to their business by not approving loans to such customers.

What is credit risk?

We have been using this term **credit risk** since the start of this chapter and many of you might be wondering what exactly does this mean, even though you might have guessed it after reading the previous section. Here, we will be explaining this term clearly so that you will have no problem in understanding the data and its features in the subsequent sections when we will be analyzing the data.

The standard definition of credit risk is the risk of defaulting on a debt which takes place due to the borrower failing to make the required debt payments in time. This risk is taken by the lender since the lender incurs losses of both the principal amount as well as the interest on it.

In our case, we will be dealing with a bank which acts as the financial organization giving out loans to customers who apply for them. Hence, customers who might default on the loan payment would be credit risks for the bank. By analyzing customer data and applying machine learning algorithms on it, the bank will be able to predict in advance which customers might be potential credit risks. This will help in risk mitigation and in minimizing losses by not giving away loans to customers who could be credit risks for the bank.

Getting the data

The first step in our data analysis pipeline is to get the dataset. We have actually cleaned the data and provided meaningful names to the data attributes and you can check that out by opening the german_credit_dataset.csv file. You can also get the actual dataset from the source which is from the Department of Statistics, University of Munich through the following URL: http://www.statistik.lmu.de/service/datenarchiv/kredit/kredit_e.html.

You can download the data and then run the following commands by firing up R in the same directory with the data file, to get a feel of the data we will be dealing with in the following sections:

```
> # load in the data and attach the data frame
> credit.df <- read.csv("german_credit_dataset.csv", header = TRUE, sep =
",")
> # class should be data.frame
> class(credit.df)
[1] "data.frame"
>
> # get a quick peek at the data
> head(credit.df)
```

The following figure shows the first six rows of the data. Each column indicates an attribute of the dataset. We will be focusing on each attribute in more detail later.

	credit.rating	account.balance	credit.duration.months	previous.credit.payment.status
1	1	1	18	4
2	1	1	9	4
3	1	2	12	2
4	1	1	12	4
5	1	1	12	4
6	1	1	10	4

	credit.purpose	credit.amount	savings	employment.duration	installment.rate
1	2	1049	1	2	4
2	0	2799	1	3	2
3	9	841	2	4	2
4	0	2122	1	3	3
5	0	2171	1	3	4
6	0	2241	1	2	1

	marital.status	guarantor	residence.duration	current.assets	age	other.credits
1	2	1	4	2	21	3
2	3	1	2	1	36	3
3	2	1	4	1	23	3
4	3	1	2	1	39	3
5	3	1	4	2	38	1
6	3	1	3	1	48	3

	apartment.type	bank.credits	occupation	dependents	telephone	foreign.worker
1	1	1	3	1	1	1
2	1	2	3	2	1	1
3	1	1	2	1	1	1
4	1	2	2	2	1	2
5	2	2	2	1	1	2
6	1	2	2	2	1	2

To get detailed information about the dataset and its attributes, you can use the following code snippet:

```
> # get dataset detailed info
> str(credit.df)
```

The preceding code will enable you to get a quick look at the total number of data points you are dealing with, which includes the number of records, the number of attributes, and the detailed information about each attribute including things such as the attribute name, type, and some samples of attribute values, as you can see in the following screenshot. Using this, we can get a good idea about the different attributes and their data types so that we know what transformations to apply on them and what statistical methods to use during descriptive analytics.

```
'data.frame':    1000 obs. of  21 variables:
 $ credit.rating                 : int  1 1 1 1 1 1 1 1 1 1 ...
 $ account.balance               : int  1 1 2 1 1 1 1 1 4 2 ...
 $ credit.duration.months        : int  18 9 12 12 12 10 8 6 18 24 ...
 $ previous.credit.payment.status: int  4 4 2 4 4 4 4 4 4 2 ...
 $ credit.purpose                : int  2 0 9 0 0 0 0 0 3 3 ...
 $ credit.amount                 : int  1049 2799 841 2122 2171 2241 3398..
 $ savings                       : int  1 1 2 1 1 1 1 1 1 3 ...
 $ employment.duration           : int  2 3 4 3 3 2 4 2 1 1 ...
 $ installment.rate              : int  4 2 2 3 4 1 1 2 4 1 ...
 $ marital.status                : int  2 3 2 3 3 3 3 3 2 2 ...
 $ guarantor                     : int  1 1 1 1 1 1 1 1 1 1 ...
 $ residence.duration            : int  4 2 4 2 4 3 4 4 4 4 ...
 $ current.assets                : int  2 1 1 1 2 1 1 1 3 4 ...
 $ age                           : int  21 36 23 39 38 48 39 40 65 23 ...
 $ other.credits                 : int  3 3 3 3 1 3 3 3 3 3 ...
 $ apartment.type                : int  1 1 1 1 2 1 2 2 2 1 ...
 $ bank.credits                  : int  1 2 1 2 2 2 2 1 2 1 ...
 $ occupation                    : int  3 3 2 2 2 2 2 2 1 1 ...
 $ dependents                    : int  1 2 1 2 1 2 1 2 1 1 ...
 $ telephone                     : int  1 1 1 1 1 1 1 1 1 1 ...
 $ foreign.worker                : int  1 1 1 2 2 2 2 2 1 1 ...
```

From the preceding output, you can see that our dataset has a total of 1000 records, where each record deals with data points pertaining to one bank customer. Each record has various data points or attributes describing the data and we have a total of 21 attributes for each record. The data type and sample values for each attribute are also shown in the previous image.

 Do note that by default R has assigned the `int` datatype to the variables based on their values but we will be changing some of that in our data preprocessing phase based on their actual semantics.

Data preprocessing

In this section, we will be focusing on data preprocessing which includes data cleaning, transformation, and normalizations if required. Basically, we perform operations to get the data ready before we start performing any analysis on it.

Dealing with missing values

There will be situations when the data you are dealing with will have missing values, which are often represented as NA in R. There are several ways to detect them and we will show you a couple of ways next. Note that there are several ways in which you can do this.

```
> # check if data frame contains NA values
> sum(is.na(credit.df))
[1] 0
>
> # check if total records reduced after removing rows with NA
> # values
> sum(complete.cases(credit.df))
[1] 1000
```

The is.na function is really useful as it helps in finding out if any element has an NA value in the dataset. There is another way of doing the same by using the complete. cases function, which essentially returns a logical vector saying whether the rows are complete and if they have any NA values. You can check if the total records count has decreased compared to the original dataset as then you will know that you have some missing values in the dataset. Fortunately, in our case, we do not have any missing values. However, in the future if you are dealing with missing values, there are various ways to deal with that. Some of them include removing the rows with missing values by using functions such as complete.cases, or filling them up with a value which could be the most frequent value or the mean, and so on. This is also known as missing value imputation and it depends on the variable attribute and the domain you are dealing with. Hence, we won't be focusing too much in this area here.

Datatype conversions

We had mentioned earlier that by default all the attributes of the dataset had been declared as `int`, which is a numeric type by R, but it is not so in this case and we have to change that based on the variable semantics and values. If you have taken a basic course on statistics, you might know that usually we deal with two types of variables:

- **Numeric variables**: The values of these variables carry some mathematical meaning. This means that you can carry out mathematical operations on them, such as addition, subtraction, and so on. Some examples can be a person's age, weight, and so on.

- **Categorical variables**: The values of these variables do not have any mathematical significance and you cannot perform any mathematical operations on them. Each value in this variable belongs to a specific class or category. Some examples can be a person's gender, job, and so on.

Since all the variables in our dataset have been converted to numeric by default, we will only need to convert the categorical variables from numeric data types to factors, which is a nice way to represent categorical variables in R.

The numeric variables in our dataset include `credit.duration.months`, `credit.amount`, and age and we will not need to perform any conversions. However, the remaining 18 variables are all categorical and we will be using the following utility function to convert their data types:

```
# data transformation
to.factors <- function(df, variables){
  for (variable in variables){
    df[[variable]] <- as.factor(df[[variable]])
  }
  return(df)
}
```

This function will be used on our existing data frame `credit.df` as follows for transforming the variable data types:

```
> # select variables for data transformation
> categorical.vars <- c('credit.rating', 'account.balance',
+                        'previous.credit.payment.status',
+                        'credit.purpose', 'savings',
+                        'employment.duration', 'installment.rate',
+                        'marital.status', 'guarantor',
```

```
+                   'residence.duration', 'current.assets',
+                   'other.credits', 'apartment.type',
+                   'bank.credits', 'occupation',
+                   'dependents', 'telephone',
+                   'foreign.worker')
>
> # transform data types
> credit.df <- to.factors(df = credit.df,
+                         variables=categorical.vars)
>
> # verify transformation in data frame details
> str(credit.df)
```

Now we can see the attribute details in the data frame with the transformed data types for the selected categorical variables in the following output. You will notice that out of the 21 variables/attributes of the dataset, 18 of them have been successfully transformed into categorical variables.

```
'data.frame':   1000 obs. of  21 variables:
 $ credit.rating                  : Factor w/ 2 levels "0","1": 2 2 2 2 2 2 2 2 2 ...
 $ account.balance                : Factor w/ 4 levels "1","2","3","4": 1 1 2 1 1 1 1 1 4 2 ...
 $ credit.duration.months         : int  18 9 12 12 12 10 8 6 18 24 ...
 $ previous.credit.payment.status : Factor w/ 5 levels "0","1","2","3",..: 5 5 3 5 5 5 5 5 5 3 ...
 $ credit.purpose                 : Factor w/ 10 levels "0","1","2","3",..: 3 1 9 1 1 1 1 1 4 4 ...
 $ credit.amount                  : int  1049 2799 841 2122 2171 2241 3398 1361 1098 3758 ...
 $ savings                        : Factor w/ 5 levels "1","2","3","4",..: 1 1 2 1 1 1 1 1 1 3 ...
 $ employment.duration            : Factor w/ 5 levels "1","2","3","4",..: 2 3 4 3 3 2 4 2 1 1 ...
 $ installment.rate               : Factor w/ 4 levels "1","2","3","4": 4 2 2 3 4 1 1 2 4 1 ...
 $ marital.status                 : Factor w/ 4 levels "1","2","3","4": 2 3 2 3 3 3 3 3 2 2 ...
 $ guarantor                      : Factor w/ 3 levels "1","2","3": 1 1 1 1 1 1 1 1 1 1 ...
 $ residence.duration             : Factor w/ 4 levels "1","2","3","4": 4 2 4 2 4 3 4 4 4 4 ...
 $ current.assets                 : Factor w/ 4 levels "1","2","3","4": 2 1 1 1 2 1 1 1 3 4 ...
 $ age                            : int  21 36 23 39 38 48 39 40 65 23 ...
 $ other.credits                  : Factor w/ 3 levels "1","2","3": 3 3 3 3 1 3 3 3 3 3 ...
 $ apartment.type                 : Factor w/ 3 levels "1","2","3": 1 1 1 1 2 1 2 2 2 1 ...
 $ bank.credits                   : Factor w/ 4 levels "1","2","3","4": 1 2 1 2 2 2 2 1 2 1 ...
 $ occupation                     : Factor w/ 4 levels "1","2","3","4": 3 3 2 2 2 2 2 2 1 1 ...
 $ dependents                     : Factor w/ 2 levels "1","2": 1 2 1 2 1 2 1 2 1 1 ...
 $ telephone                      : Factor w/ 2 levels "1","2": 1 1 1 1 1 1 1 1 1 1 ...
 $ foreign.worker                 : Factor w/ 2 levels "1","2": 1 1 1 2 2 2 2 2 1 1 ...
```

This brings an end to the data preprocessing step and we will now dive into analyzing our dataset.

 Do note that several of our dataset attributes/features have a lot of classes or categories and we will need to do some more data transformations and feature engineering in the analysis phase to prevent overfitting of our predictive models, which we shall discuss later.

Data analysis and transformation

Now that we have processed our data, it is ready for analysis. We will be carrying out descriptive and exploratory analysis in this section, as mentioned earlier. We will analyze the different dataset attributes and talk about their significance, semantics, and relationship with the credit risk attribute. We will be using statistical functions, contingency tables, and visualizations to depict all of this.

Besides this, we will also be doing data transformation for some of the features in our dataset, namely the categorical variables. We will be doing this to combine the category classes which have similar semantics and remove the classes having very less proportion by merging them with a similar class. Some reasons for doing this include preventing the overfitting of our predictive models, which we will be building in *Chapter 6, Credit Risk Detection and Prediction – Predictive Analytics*, linking semantically similar classes together and also because modeling techniques like logistic regression do not handle categorical variables with a large number of classes very well. We will analyze each feature/variable in the dataset first and then perform any transformations if necessary.

Building analysis utilities

Before we begin our analysis, we will be developing some utility functions which we will be using to analyze the dataset features. Do note that all the utility functions are defined in a separate .R file called descriptive_analytics_utils.R. You can load all the functions in memory or in any other R script file by using the command source('descriptive_analytics_utils.R') and then start using them. We will be talking about these utility functions now.

We will now talk about the various packages we have used. We have used some packages such as pastecs and gmodels for getting summary statistics of features and for building contingency tables. The packages gridExtra and ggplot2 have been used for grid layouts and building visualizations respectively. If you do not have them installed, you can use the install.packages command to install them. Next, load the packages as shown in the following code snippet:

```
# load dependencies
library(gridExtra) # grid layouts
library(pastecs) # details summary stats
library(ggplot2) # visualizations
library(gmodels) # build contingency tables
```

Now that we have all the required dependencies, we will first implement a function to get summary statistics about the numerical variables. The following code snippet achieves the same. If you see, we have made use of the `stat.desc` and `summary` functions for getting detailed and condensed summary statistics about the variable. The conventions for independent variables and dependent variables are denoted by `indep.var` and `dep.var` in the code segments that follow and in other functions later on.

```
# summary statistics
get.numeric.variable.stats <- function(indep.var, detailed=FALSE){
  options(scipen=100)
  options(digits=2)
  if (detailed){
    var.stats <- stat.desc(indep.var)
  }else{
    var.stats <- summary(indep.var)
  }

  df <- data.frame(round(as.numeric(var.stats),2))
  colnames(df) <- deparse(substitute(indep.var))
  rownames(df) <- names(var.stats)

  if (names(dev.cur()) != "null device"){
    dev.off()
  }
  grid.table(t(df))
}
```

Next, we will build some functions for visualizing the numeric variables. We will be doing that by using `histograms\density` plots and `box plots` to depict the attribute distributions.

```
# visualizations
# histograms\density
visualize.distribution <- function(indep.var){
  pl1 <- qplot(indep.var, geom="histogram",
               fill=I('gray'), binwidth=5,
               col=I('black'))+ theme_bw()
  pl2 <- qplot(age, geom="density",
```

```
              fill=I('gray'), binwidth=5,
              col=I('black'))+ theme_bw()


  grid.arrange(pl1,pl2, ncol=2)
}


# box plots
visualize.boxplot <- function(indep.var, dep.var){
  pl1 <- qplot(factor(0),indep.var, geom="boxplot",
              xlab = deparse(substitute(indep.var)),
              ylab="values") + theme_bw()
  pl2 <- qplot(dep.var,indep.var,geom="boxplot",
              xlab = deparse(substitute(dep.var)),
              ylab = deparse(substitute(indep.var))) + theme_bw()


  grid.arrange(pl1,pl2, ncol=2)
}
```

We have used the `qplot` function from the `ggplot2` package for building the visualizations which we will be seeing in action soon. Now we will be shifting our focus to `categorical variables`. We will start with building a function to get summary statistics of any `categorical variable`.

```
# summary statistics
get.categorical.variable.stats <- function(indep.var){

  feature.name = deparse(substitute(indep.var))
  df1 <- data.frame(table(indep.var))
  colnames(df1) <- c(feature.name, "Frequency")
  df2 <- data.frame(prop.table(table(indep.var)))
  colnames(df2) <- c(feature.name, "Proportion")

  df <- merge(
    df1, df2, by = feature.name
  )
  ndf <- df[order(-df$Frequency),]
```

```
if (names(dev.cur()) != "null device"){
    dev.off()
  }
  grid.table(ndf)
}
```

The preceding function will summarize the categorical variable and talk about how many classes or categories are present in it and some other details such as frequency and proportion. If you remember, we had mentioned earlier that we will also be depicting the relationship of categorical variables with the class/dependent variable `credit.risk`. The following function will help us achieve the same in the form of contingency tables:

```
# generate contingency table
get.contingency.table <- function(dep.var, indep.var,
                                            stat.tests=F){
  if(stat.tests == F){
    CrossTable(dep.var, indep.var, digits=1,
               prop.r=F, prop.t=F, prop.chisq=F)
  }else{
    CrossTable(dep.var, indep.var, digits=1,
               prop.r=F, prop.t=F, prop.chisq=F,
               chisq=T, fisher=T)
  }
}
```

We will also build some functions for depicting visualizations. We will be visualizing `categorical variable` distribution using bar charts by using the following function:

```
# visualizations
# barcharts
visualize.barchart <- function(indep.var){
  qplot(indep.var, geom="bar",
        fill=I('gray'), col=I('black'),
        xlab = deparse(substitute(indep.var))) + theme_bw()
}
```

We will use mosaic plots to depict visualizations of the previously mentioned contingency tables using the following function:

```
# mosaic plots
visualize.contingency.table <- function(dep.var, indep.var){
  if (names(dev.cur()) != "null device"){
    dev.off()
  }
  mosaicplot(dep.var ~ indep.var, color=T,
             main = "Contingency table plot")
}
```

Now that we have built all the necessary utilities, we will begin analyzing our data in the following section.

Analyzing the dataset

We will be analyzing each feature of the dataset in this section and depicting our analysis in the form of summary statistics, relationships, statistical tests, and visualizations wherever necessary. We will denote necessary analysis which will be carried out for each variable in a table. An important point to remember is that the dependent feature denoted in code by dep.var will always be credit.rating since this is the variable which is dependent on the other features; these features are independent variables and will be denoted as indep.var in the tables and plots often.

We will carry out detailed analysis and transformations for some of the important features which have a lot of significance, especially data features having a large number of classes, so that we can clearly understand data distributions and how they change on transformation of the data. For the remaining features, we will not focus too much on the summary statistics but emphasize more on feature engineering through transformations and their relationships with the dependent credit.rating variable.

Now we will attach the data frame so that we can access the individual features easily. You can do that using the following code snippet:

```
> # access dataset features directly
> attach(credit.df)
```

Now we will be starting our analysis with the dependent variable credit.risk, also known as the class variable in our dataset, which we will be trying to predict in the next chapter.

The following code snippet helps us in getting the required summary statistics for this feature:

```
> # credit.rating stats
> get.categorical.variable.stats(credit.rating)
> # credit.rating visualizations
> visualize.barchart(credit.rating)
```

The following visualizations tell us that `credit.rating` has two classes, 1 and 0, and gives the necessary statistics. Basically, customers with a credit rating of 1 are credit worthy and those with a rating of 0 are not credit worthy. We also observe from the bar chart that the proportion of credit worthy customers in the bank is significantly high compared to the rest.

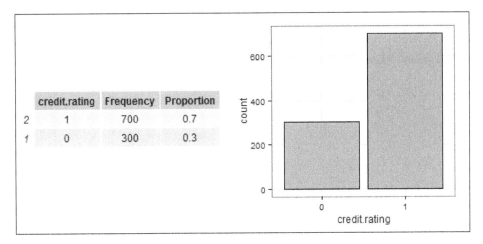

	credit.rating	Frequency	Proportion
2	1	700	0.7
1	0	300	0.3

Next, we will analyze the `account.balance` feature. Basically, this attribute indicates the current balance of the current account of the customer.

We will start with getting the summary statistics and plotting a bar-chart using the following code snippet. We will include both the outputs together for better understanding.

```
> # account.balance stats and bar chart
> get.categorical.variable.stats(account.balance)
> visualize.barchart(account.balance)
```

From the following visualizations, you can see that there are four distinct classes for `account.balance` and they each have some specific semantics which we will be talking about soon.

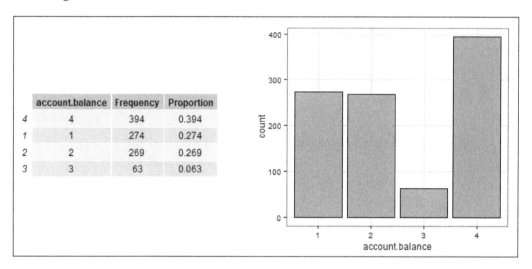

	account.balance	Frequency	Proportion
4	4	394	0.394
1	1	274	0.274
2	2	269	0.269
3	3	63	0.063

From the preceding output you can see that there are four distinct classes for `account.balance`, and they each have some semantics, as defined next. The currency DM indicates Deutsche Mark, the old currency name of Germany.

The four classes indicate the following as the main semantics or checking account held for at least a year:

- **1**: No running bank account
- **2**: No balance or debit
- **3**: Balance of < 200 DM
- **4**: Balance of >=200 DM

The currency DM indicates Deutsche Mark, the old currency name of Germany. We will be doing some feature engineering here and will combine classes 3 and 4 together to indicate customers who have a positive balance in their account. We will do this because the proportion of class 3 is quite small compared to the rest and we don't want to unnecessarily keep too many classes per feature unless they are critical. We will achieve this by using the following code snippets.

First, we will load the necessary package for doing this. Install it using the command `install.packages("car")` in case you do not have the package installed.

```
> #load dependencies
> library(car)
```

Now we will recode the necessary classes, as shown next:

```
> # recode classes and update data frame
> new.account.balance <- recode(account.balance,
+                     "1=1;2=2;3=3;4=3")
> credit.df$account.balance <- new.account.balance
```

We will now see the relationship between `new.account.balance` and `credit.rating` using a contingency table, as discussed earlier, and visualize it using a mosaic plot by using the following code snippet. We will also perform some statistical tests which I will explain in brief later.

```
> # contingency table and mosaic plot
> get.contingency.table(credit.rating, new.account.balance,
                                        stat.tests=T)
> visualize.contingency.table(credit.rating, new.account.balance)
```

In the following figure, you can now see how the various classes for `account.balance` are distributed with regards to `credit.rating` in both the table and the plot. An interesting thing to see is that 90% of people with funds in their account are not potential credit risks, which sounds reasonable.

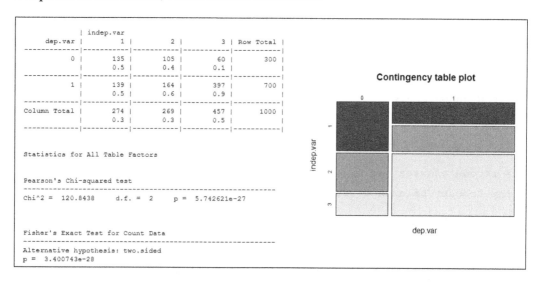

We also perform two statistical tests here: the Chi-squared test and Fisher's test, both relevant tests in contingency tables used extensively for hypothesis testing. Going into details of the statistical calculations involved in these tests is out of scope of this chapter. I will put it in a way which is easy to understand. Usually, we start with a null hypothesis that between the two variables as depicted previously, there exists no association or relationship, as well as an alternative hypothesis that there is a possibility of a relationship or association between the two variables. If the p-value obtained from the test is less than or equal to 0.05, only then can we reject the null hypothesis in favor of the alternative hypothesis. In this case, you can clearly see that both the tests give p-values < 0.05, which definitely favors the alternative hypothesis that there is some association between `credit.rating` and `account.balance`. These types of tests are extremely useful when we build statistical models. You can look up the preceding tests on the internet or any statistics book to get a deeper insight into what p-values signify and how they work.

Do note that going forward we will show only the most important analysis results for each feature. However, you can always try getting relevant information for the various analysis techniques using the functions we explained earlier. For contingency tables, use the `get.contingency.table()` function. Statistical tests can be performed by setting the `stat.tests` parameter as TRUE in the `get.contingency.table()` function. You can also use the `visualize.contingency.table()` function to view mosaic plots.

Now we will look at `credit.duration.months`, which signifies the duration of the credit in months. This is a numerical variable and the analysis will be a bit different from the other categorical variables.

```
> # credit.duration.months analysis
> get.numeric.variable.stats(credit.duration.months)
```

We can visualize the same from the following figure:

	Min.	1st Qu.	Median	Mean	3rd Qu.	Max.
credit.duration.months	4	12	18	20.9	24	72

The values we see are in months and we get the typical summary statistics for this feature, including the mean, median, and quartiles. We will now visualize the overall distribution of the values for this feature using both `histograms/density` plots and `boxplots`.

```
> # histogram\density plot
> visualize.distribution(credit.duration.months)
```

The preceding snippet produces the following plots. We can clearly observe that this is a multimodal distribution with several peaks.

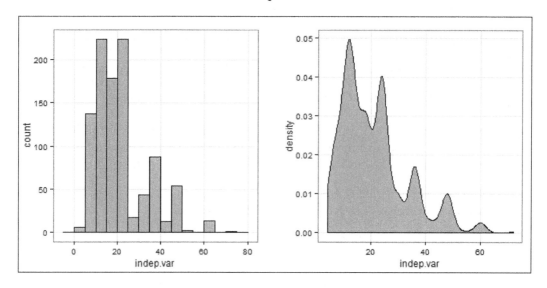

We now visualize the same in the form of box plots, including the one showing associations with `credit.rating` next.

```
> # box plot
> visualize.boxplot(credit.duration.months, credit.rating)
```

Interestingly, from the following plots we see that the median credit duration for people who have a bad credit rating is higher than those who have a good credit rating. This seems to be plausible if we assume that many customers with long credit durations defaulted on their payments.

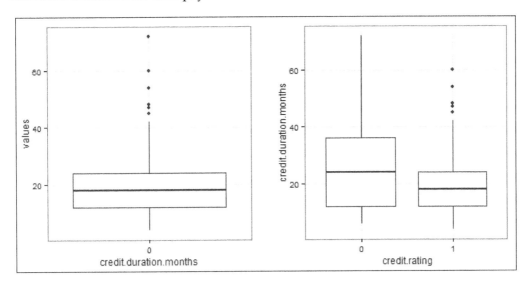

Moving on to the next variable, `previous.credit.payment.status` indicates what is the status of the customer with regards to paying his previous credits. This is a `categorical variable` and we get the statistics for it as shown next:

```
> # previous.credit.payment.status stats and bar chart
> get.categorical.variable.stats(previous.credit.payment.status)
> visualize.barchart(previous.credit.payment.status)
```

This gives us the following table and bar chart depicting the data distribution:

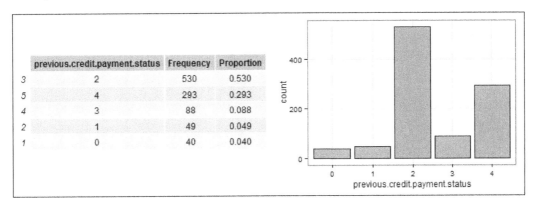

	previous.credit.payment.status	Frequency	Proportion
3	2	530	0.530
5	4	293	0.293
4	3	88	0.088
2	1	49	0.049
1	0	40	0.040

The classes indicate the following as the main semantics:

- **0**: Hesitant payment
- **1**: Problematic running account
- **2**: No previous credits left
- **3**: No problem with the current credits at this bank
- **4**: Paid back the previous credits at this bank

We will be applying the following transformations to this feature, so the new semantics will be:

- **1**: Some problems with payment
- **2**: All credits paid
- **3**: No problems and credits paid in this bank only

We will perform the transformations in the following code snippet:

```
> # recode classes and update data frame
> new.previous.credit.payment.status <-
                         recode(previous.credit.payment.status,
+                                       "0=1;1=1;2=2;3=3;4=3")
> credit.df$previous.credit.payment.status <-
                         new.previous.credit.payment.status
```

The contingency table for the transformed feature is obtained as follows:

```
> # contingency table
> get.contingency.table(credit.rating,
                        new.previous.credit.payment.status)
```

We observe from the following table that maximum people who have a good credit rating have paid their previous credits without any problem and those who do not have a good credit rating had some problem with their payments, which makes sense!

```
Total Observations in Table:  1000


             | indep.var
    dep.var  |        1 |         2 |         3 | Row Total |
-------------|----------|-----------|-----------|-----------|
          0  |       53 |      169 |        78 |       300 |
             |      0.6 |       0.3 |      0.2  |           |
-------------|----------|-----------|-----------|-----------|
          1  |       36 |      361 |       303 |       700 |
             |      0.4 |       0.7 |      0.8  |           |
-------------|----------|-----------|-----------|-----------|
Column Total |       89 |      530 |       381 |      1000 |
             |      0.1 |       0.5 |      0.4  |           |
-------------|----------|-----------|-----------|-----------|
```

The next feature we will look at is `credit.purpose`, which signifies the purpose of the credit amount. This is also a categorical variable and we get its summary statistics and plot the bar chart showing the frequency of its various classes as follows:

```
> # credit.purpose stats and bar chart
> get.categorical.variable.stats(credit.purpose)
> visualize.barchart(credit.purpose)
```

This gives us the following table and bar chart depicting the data distribution:

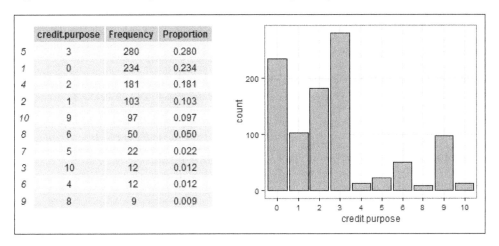

	credit.purpose	Frequency	Proportion
5	3	280	0.280
1	0	234	0.234
4	2	181	0.181
2	1	103	0.103
10	9	97	0.097
8	6	50	0.050
7	5	22	0.022
3	10	12	0.012
6	4	12	0.012
9	8	9	0.009

We observe that there are a staggering 11 classes just for this feature. Besides this, we also observe that several classes have extremely low proportions compared to the top 5 classes and class **label 7** doesn't even appear in the dataset! This is exactly why we need to do feature engineering by grouping some of these classes together, as we did previously.

The classes indicate the following as the main semantics:

- **0**: Others
- **1**: New car
- **2**: Used car
- **3**: Furniture items
- **4**: Radio or television
- **5**: Household appliances
- **6**: Repair
- **7**: Education
- **8**: Vacation
- **9**: Retraining
- **10**: Business

We will be transforming this feature by combining some of the existing classes and the new semantics after transformation will be the following:

- **1**: New car
- **2**: Used car
- **3**: Home related items
- **4**: Others

We will do this by using the following code snippet:

```
> # recode classes and update data frame
> new.credit.purpose <- recode(credit.purpose,"0=4;1=1;2=2;3=3;
+                                              4=3;5=3;6=3;7=4;
+                                              8=4;9=4;10=4")
> credit.df$credit.purpose <- new.credit.purpose
```

The contingency table for the transformed feature is then obtained by the following code snippet:

```
> # contingency table
> get.contingency.table(credit.rating, new.credit.purpose)
```

Based on the following table, we see that the customers who have credit purposes of home related items or other items seem to have the maximum proportion in the bad credit rating category:

```
             | indep.var
    dep.var  |       1 |       2 |       3 |       4 | Row Total |
-------------|---------|---------|---------|---------|-----------|
          0  |      17 |      58 |      96 |     129 |       300 |
             |     0.2 |     0.3 |     0.3 |     0.4 |           |
-------------|---------|---------|---------|---------|-----------|
          1  |      86 |     123 |     268 |     223 |       700 |
             |     0.8 |     0.7 |     0.7 |     0.6 |           |
-------------|---------|---------|---------|---------|-----------|
Column Total |     103 |     181 |     364 |     352 |      1000 |
             |     0.1 |     0.2 |     0.4 |     0.4 |           |
-------------|---------|---------|---------|---------|-----------|
```

The next feature we will analyze is `credit.amount`, which basically signifies the amount of credit in DM being asked from the bank by the customer. This is a numerical variable and we use the following code for getting the summary statistics:

```
> # credit.amount analysis
> get.numeric.variable.stats(credit.amount)
```

	Min.	1st Qu.	Median	Mean	3rd Qu.	Max.
credit.amount	250	1370	2320	3270	3970	18400

We see the normal statistics, such as the average credit amount as 3270 DM and the median as around 3270 DM. We will now visualize the distribution of the preceding data using a histogram and density plot as follows:

```
> # histogram\density plot
> visualize.distribution(credit.amount)
```

This will give us the histogram and density plot for `credit.amount`, and you can see that it is a right-skewed distribution in the following figure:

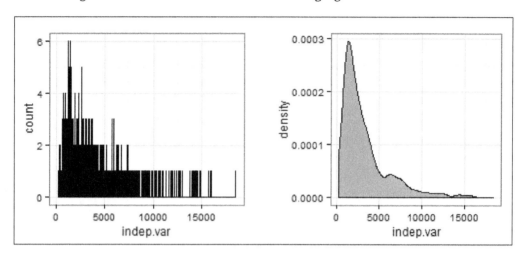

Next, we will visualize the data using boxplots to see the data distribution and its relationship with `credit.rating` using the following code snippet:

```
> # box plot
> visualize.boxplot(credit.amount, credit.rating)
```

This generates the following boxplots where you can clearly see the right skew in the distribution shown by the numerous dots in the boxplots. We also see an interesting insight that the median credit rating was bad for those customers who asked for a higher credit amount, which seems likely assuming many of them may have failed to make all the payments required to pay off the credit amount.

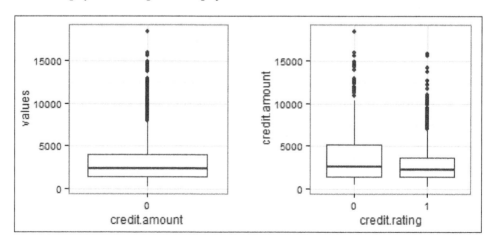

Now that you have a good idea about how to perform descriptive analysis for categorical and numerical variables, going forward we will not be showing outputs of all the different analysis techniques for each feature. Feel free to experiment with the functions we used earlier on the remaining variables to obtain the summary statistics and visualizations if you are interested in digging deeper into the data!

The next feature is savings, which is a categorical variable having the following semantics for the 5 class labels:

- **1**: No savings
- **2**: `< 100` DM
- **3**: Between `[100, 499]` DM
- **4**: Between `[500, 999]` DM
- **5**: `>= 1000` DM

The feature signifies the average amount of savings/stocks belonging to the customer. We will be transforming it to the following four class labels:

- **1**: No savings
- **2**: `< 100` DM
- **3**: Between `[100, 999]` DM
- **4**: `>= 1000` DM

We will be using the following code snippet:

```
> # feature: savings - recode classes and update data frame
> new.savings <- recode(savings,"1=1;2=2;3=3;
+                                 4=3;5=4")
> credit.df$savings <- new.savings
```

Now we analyze the relationship between savings and `credit.rating` using the following code for the contingency table:

```
> # contingency table
> get.contingency.table(credit.rating, new.savings)
```

This generates the following contingency table. On observing the table values, it is clear that people with no savings have the maximum proportion among customers who have a bad credit rating, which is not surprising! This number is also high for customers with a good credit rating since the total number of good credit rating records is also high compared to the total records in bad credit rating. However, we also see that the proportion of people having > 1000 DM and a good credit rating is quite high in comparison to the proportion of people having both a bad credit rating and > 1000 DM in their savings account.

```
              | indep.var
   dep.var |        1 |        2 |        3 |        4 | Row Total |
-----------|----------|----------|----------|----------|-----------|
         0 |      217 |       34 |       17 |       32 |       300 |
           |      0.4 |      0.3 |      0.2 |      0.2 |           |
-----------|----------|----------|----------|----------|-----------|
         1 |      386 |       69 |       94 |      151 |       700 |
           |      0.6 |      0.7 |      0.8 |      0.8 |           |
-----------|----------|----------|----------|----------|-----------|
Column Total |    603 |      103 |      111 |      183 |      1000 |
           |      0.6 |      0.1 |      0.1 |      0.2 |           |
-----------|----------|----------|----------|----------|-----------|
```

We will now look at the feature named `employment.duration`, which is a categorical variable signifying the duration for which the customer has been employed until present. The semantics for the five classes of the feature are:

- **1**: Unemployed
- **2**: < 1 year
- **3**: Between [1, 4] years
- **4**: Between [4, 7] years
- **5**: >= 7 years

We will be transforming it to the following four classes:

- **1**: Unemployed or < 1 year
- **2**: Between [1,4] years
- **3**: Between [4,7] years
- **4**: >= 7 years

We will be using the following code:

```
> # feature: employment.duration - recode classes and update data frame
> new.employment.duration <- recode(employment.duration,
+                                   "1=1;2=1;3=2;4=3;5=4")
> credit.df$employment.duration <- new.employment.duration
```

Now we analyze its relationship using the contingency table, as follows:

```
> # contingency table
> get.contingency.table(credit.rating, new.employment.duration)
```

What we observe from the following table is that the proportion of customers having none or a significantly low number of years in employment and a bad credit rating is much higher than similar customers having a good credit rating. In the case of `employment.duration` feature, the value 1 indicates the people who are unemployed or have < 1 year of employment. The proportion of these people having a bad credit rating in 93 out of 300 people. This gives 31% which is lot higher compared to the same metric for the customers having a good credit rating which is 141 out of 700 customers, or 20%.

```
              | indep.var
   dep.var    |     1 |      2 |      3 |      4 | Row Total |
--------------|-------|--------|--------|--------|-----------|
          0   |    93 |    104 |     39 |     64 |       300 |
              |   0.4 |    0.3 |    0.2 |    0.3 |           |
--------------|-------|--------|--------|--------|-----------|
          1   |   141 |    235 |    135 |    189 |       700 |
              |   0.6 |    0.7 |    0.8 |    0.7 |           |
--------------|-------|--------|--------|--------|-----------|
 Column Total |   234 |    339 |    174 |    253 |      1000 |
              |   0.2 |    0.3 |    0.2 |    0.3 |           |
--------------|-------|--------|--------|--------|-----------|
```

We now move on to the next feature named `installment.rate`, which is a categorical variable with the following semantics:

- **1**: `>=35%`
- **2**: Between `[25, 35]%`
- **3**: Between `[20, 25]%`
- **4**: `< 20%` for the four classes

There wasn't too much information in the original metadata for this attribute so there is some ambiguity, but what we assumed is that it indicates the percentage of the customer's salary which was used to pay the credit loan as monthly installments. We won't be doing any transformations here so we will directly go to the relationships.

```
> # feature: installment.rate - contingency table and statistical tests
> get.contingency.table(credit.rating, installment.rate,
+                       stat.tests=TRUE)
```

We performed the statistical tests for this variable in the code snippet because we weren't really sure if our assumption for its semantics was correct or whether it could be a significant variable. From the following results, we see that both statistical tests yield p-values of > 0.05, thus ruling the null hypothesis in favor of the alternative. This tells us that these two variables do not have a significant association between them and this feature might not be one to consider when we make feature sets for our predictive models. We will look at feature selection in more detail in the next chapter.

```
                | indep.var
     dep.var |       1 |       2 |       3 |       4 | Row Total |
-------------|---------|---------|---------|---------|-----------|
           0 |      34 |      62 |      45 |     159 |       300 |
             |     0.2 |     0.3 |     0.3 |     0.3 |           |
-------------|---------|---------|---------|---------|-----------|
           1 |     102 |     169 |     112 |     317 |       700 |
             |     0.8 |     0.7 |     0.7 |     0.7 |           |
-------------|---------|---------|---------|---------|-----------|
Column Total |     136 |     231 |     157 |     476 |      1000 |
             |     0.1 |     0.2 |     0.2 |     0.5 |           |
-------------|---------|---------|---------|---------|-----------|

Statistics for All Table Factors

Pearson's Chi-squared test
-----------------------------------------------------------------
Chi^2 =  5.5      d.f. =  3       p =   0.14

Fisher's Exact Test for Count Data
-----------------------------------------------------------------
Alternative hypothesis: two.sided
p =   0.15
```

The next variable we will analyze is `marital.status`, which indicates the marital status of the customer and is a categorical variable. It has four classes with the following semantics:

- **1**: Male divorced
- **2**: Male single
- **3**: Male married/widowed
- **4**: Female

We will be transforming them into three classes with the following semantics:

- **1**: Male divorced/single
- **2**: Male married/widowed
- **3**: Female

We will be using the following code:

```
> # feature: marital.status - recode classes and update data frame
> new.marital.status <- recode(marital.status, "1=1;2=1;3=2;4=3")
> credit.df$marital.status <- new.marital.status
```

We now observe the relationship between `marital.status` and `credit.rating` by building a contingency table using the following code snippet:

```
> # contingency table
> get.contingency.table(credit.rating, new.marital.status)
```

From the following table, we notice that the ratio of single men to married men for customers with a good credit rating is **1:2** compared to nearly **1:1** for customers with a bad credit rating. Does this mean that maybe more married men tend to pay their credit debts in time? That could be a possibility for this dataset, but do remember that correlation does not imply causation in general.

```
          | indep.var
  dep.var |       1 |         2 |       3 | Row Total |
 ---------|---------|-----------|---------|-----------|
        0 |   129 |     146 |     25 |      300 |
          |   0.4 |     0.3 |    0.3 |          |
 ---------|---------|-----------|---------|-----------|
        1 |   231 |     402 |     67 |      700 |
          |   0.6 |     0.7 |    0.7 |          |
 ---------|---------|-----------|---------|-----------|
Column Total |  360 |     548 |     92 |     1000 |
          |   0.4 |     0.5 |    0.1 |          |
 ---------|---------|-----------|---------|-----------|
```

The p-values from the statistical tests give us a value of `0.01`, indicating that there might be some association between the features.

The next feature is guarantor, which signifies if the customer has any further debtors or guarantors. This is a categorical variable with three classes having the following semantics:

- **1**: None
- **2**: Co-applicant
- **3**: Guarantor

We transform them into two variables with the following semantics:

- **1**: No
- **2**: Yes

For the transformation, we use the following code snippet:

```
> # feature: guarantor - recode classes and update data frame
> new.guarantor <- recode(guarantor, "1=1;2=2;3=2")
> credit.df$guarantor <- new.guarantor
```

Performing statistical tests on this yield a p-value of `1`, which is much greater than `0.05`, thus ruling the null hypothesis in favor and implying that there is probably no association between guarantor and `credit.rating`.

You can also run the statistical tests using direct functions instead of calling the get.contingency.table (...) function each time. For Fisher's exact test, call fisher.test(credit.rating, guarantor), and for Pearson's Chi-squared test, call chisq.test(credit,rating, guarantor). Feel free to substitute guarantor with any of the other independent variables to carry out these tests.

The next feature is residence.duration, which signifies how long the customer has been residing at his current address.

This is a categorical variable with the following semantics for the four classes:

- **1**: < 1 year
- **2**: Between [1,4] years
- **3**: Between [4,7] years
- **4**: >= 7 years

We will not be doing any transformations and will be directly doing statistical tests to see if this feature has any association with credit,rating. From in the previous tip, using the functions fisher.test and chisq.test both give us a p-value of 0.9, which is significantly > 0.05 and thus there is no significant relationship between them. We will show the outputs of both the statistical tests here, just so you can get an idea of what they depict.

```
> # perform statistical tests for residence.duration
> fisher.test(credit.rating, residence.duration)
> chisq.test(credit.rating, residence.duration)
```

You can see from the following outputs that we get the same p-value from both the tests we talked about earlier:

Fisher's Exact Test for Count Data	Pearson's Chi-squared test
data: credit.rating and residence.duration p-value = 0.9 alternative hypothesis: two.sided	data: credit.rating and residence.duration X-squared = 0.7, df = 3, p-value = 0.9

We now shift our focus to `current.assets`, which is a categorical variable having the following semantics for the four classes:

- **1**: No assets
- **2**: Car/other
- **3**: Life insurance/savings contract
- **4**: House/land ownership

We will not be doing any transformations on this data and will directly run the same statistical tests to check if it has any association with `credit.rating`. We get a p-value of 3×10^{-5}, which is definitely < 0.05, and thus we can conclude that the alternative hypothesis holds good that there is some association between the variables.

The next variable we will analyze is `age`. This is a numeric variable and we will get its summary statistics as follows:

```
> # age analysis
> get.numeric.variable.stats(age)
```

Output:

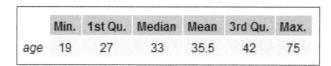

	Min.	1st Qu.	Median	Mean	3rd Qu.	Max.
age	19	27	33	35.5	42	75

We can observe that the average age of customers is 35.5 years and the median age is 33 years. To view the feature distributions, we will visualize it using a histogram and density plot using the following code snippet:

```
> # histogram\density plot
> visualize.distribution(age)
```

We can observe from the following plots that the distribution is a right-skewed distribution with the majority of customer ages ranging from 25 to 45 years:

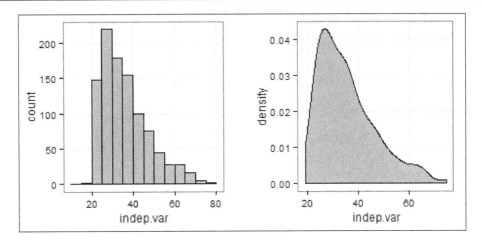

We will now observe the relationship between `age` and `credit.rating` by visualizing it through boxplots, as follows:

```
> # box plot
> visualize.boxplot(age, credit.rating)
```

The right-skew from the following plots is clearly distinguishable in the boxplots by the cluster of dots we see at the extreme end. The interesting observation we can make from the right plot is that people who have a bad credit rating have a lower median age than people who have a good credit rating.

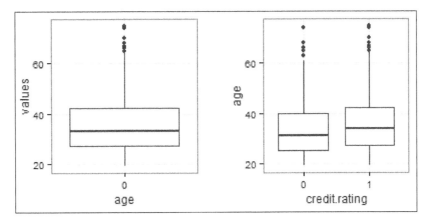

One reason for this association could be that younger people who are still not well settled and employed have failed to repay the credit loans which they had taken from the bank. But, once again, this is just an assumption which we cannot verify unless we look into the full background of each customer.

Next, we will look at the feature other.credits, which has the following semantics for the three classes:

- **1**: At other banks
- **2**: At stores
- **3**: No further credits

This feature indicates if the customer has any other pending credits elsewhere. We will transform this to two classes with the following semantics:

- **1**: Yes
- **2**: No

We will be using the following code snippet:

```
> # feature: other.credits - recode classes and update data frame
> new.other.credits <- recode(other.credits, "1=1;2=1;3=2")
> credit.df$other.credits <- new.other.credits
```

On performing statistical tests on the newly transformed feature, we get a p-value of 0.0005, which is < 0.05, and thus favors the alternative hypothesis over the null, indicating that there is some association between this feature and credit.rating, assuming there is no influence from anything else.

The next feature apartment.type is a categorical variable having the following semantics for the three classes:

- **1**: Free apartment
- **2**: Rents flat
- **3**: Owns occupied flat

This feature basically signifies the type of apartment in which the customer resides. We will not be doing any transformation to this variable and will be directly moving on to the statistical tests. Both the tests give us a p-value of < 0.05, which signifies that some association is present between apartment.type and credit.rating, assuming no other factors affect it.

Now we will look at the feature bank.credits, which is a categorical variable having the following semantics for the four classes:

- **1**: One
- **2**: Two/three
- **3**: Four/five
- **4**: Six or more

This feature signifies the total number of credit loans taken by the customer from this bank including the current one. We will transform this into a binary feature with the following semantics for the two classes:

- **1**: One
- **2**: More than one

We will be using the following code:

```
> # feature: bank.credits - recode classes and update data frame
> new.bank.credits <- recode(bank.credits, "1=1;2=2;3=2;4=2")
> credit.df$bank.credits <- new.bank.credits
```

Carrying out statistical tests on this transformed feature gives us a p-value of 0.2, which is much > 0.05, and hence we know that the null hypothesis still holds good that there is no significant association between bank.credits and credit.rating. Interestingly, if you perform statistical tests with the untransformed version of bank. credits, you will get an even higher p-value of 0.4, which indicates no significant association.

The next feature is occupation, which obviously signifies the present job of the customer. This is a categorical variable with the following semantics for its four classes:

- **1**: Unemployed with no permanent residence
- **2**: Unskilled with permanent residence
- **3**: Skilled worker/minor civil servant
- **4**: Executive/self-employed/higher civil servant

We won't be applying any transformations on this feature since each class is quite distinct in its characteristics. Hence, we will be moving on directly to analyzing the relationships with statistical tests. Both the tests yield a p-value of 0.6, which is definitely > 0.05, and the null hypothesis holds good that there is no significant relationship between the two features.

We will now look at the next feature dependents, which is a categorical variable having the following semantics for its two class labels:

- **1**: Zero to two
- **2**: Three or more

This feature signifies the total number of people who are dependents for the customer. We will not be applying any transformations since it is already a binary variable. Carrying out statistical tests on this feature yields a p-value of 1, which tells us that this feature does not have a significant relationship with credit.rating.

Next up is the feature telephone, which is a binary categorical variable which has two classes with the following semantics indicating whether the customer has a telephone:

- **1**: No
- **2**: Yes

We do not need any further transformations here since it is a binary variable. So, we move on to the statistical tests which give us a p-value of 0.3, which is > 0.05, ruling the null hypothesis in favor of the alternative, thus indicating that no significant association exists between telephone and `credit.rating`.

The final feature in the dataset is `foreign.worker`, which is a binary categorical variable having two classes with the following semantics indicating if the customer is a foreign worker:

- **1**: Yes
- **2**: No

We do not perform any transformations since it is already a binary variable with two distinct classes and move on to the statistical tests. Both the tests give us a p-value of < 0.05, which might indicate that this variable has a significant relationship with `credit.rating`.

With this, we come to an end of our data analysis phase for the dataset.

Saving the transformed dataset

We have performed a lot of feature engineering using data transformations for several categorical variables and since we will be building predictive models on the transformed feature sets, we need to store this dataset separately to disk. We use the following code snippet for the same:

```
> ## Save the transformed dataset
> write.csv(file='credit_dataset_final.csv', x = credit.df,
+           row.names = F)
```

We can load the above file into R directly the next time start building predictive models, which we will be covering in the next chapter.

Next steps

We have analyzed our dataset, performed necessary feature engineering and statistical tests, built visualizations, and gained substantial domain knowledge about credit risk analysis and what kind of features are considered by banks when they analyze customers. The reason why we analyzed each feature in the dataset in detail was to give you an idea about each feature that is considered by banks when analyzing credit rating for customers. This was to give you good domain knowledge understanding and also to help you get familiar with the techniques of performing an exploratory and descriptive analysis of any dataset in the future. So, what next? Now comes the really interesting part of using this dataset; building feature sets from this data and feeding them into predictive models to predict which customers can be potential credit risks and which of them are not. As mentioned previously, there are two steps to this: data and algorithms. In fact, we will go a step further and say that there are feature sets and algorithms which will help us in achieving our main objective.

Feature sets

A dataset is basically a file consisting of several records of observation where each tuple or record denotes one complete set of observations and the columns are specific attributes or features in that observation which talk about specific characteristics. In predictive analytics, usually there is one attribute or feature in the dataset whose class or category has to be predicted. This variable is `credit.rating` in our dataset, also known as the dependent variable. All the other features on which this depends are the independent variables. Taking a combination of these features forms a feature vector, which is also known popularly as a feature set. There are various ways of identifying what feature sets we should consider for predictive models, and you will see going ahead that for any dataset there is never a fixed feature set. It keeps changing based on feature engineering, the type of predictive model we are building, and the significance of the features based on statistical tests.

Each property in the feature set is termed as a feature or attribute and these are also known as independent or explanatory variables in statistics. Features can be of various types, as we saw in our dataset. We can have categorical features with several classes, binary features with two classes, ordinal features which are basically categorical features but have some order inherent in them (for example, low, medium, high), and numerical features which could be integer values or real values. Features are highly important in building predictive models and more often than not, the data scientists spend a lot of time in building the perfect feature sets to highly boost the accuracy of predictive models. This is why domain knowledge is highly essential, besides knowing about the machine learning algorithms.

Machine learning algorithms

Once we get the feature sets ready, we can start using predictive models to use them and start predicting the credit rating of customers based on their features. An important thing to remember is that this is an iterative process and we have to keep modifying our feature sets based on outputs and feedback obtained from our predictive models to further improve them. Several methods which are relevant in our scenario, which belong to the class of supervised machine learning algorithms, are explained briefly in this section.

- **Linear classification algorithms**: These algorithms perform classification in terms of a linear function which assigns scores to each class by performing a dot product of the feature set and some weights associated with them. The predicted class is the one which has the highest score. The optimal weights for the feature set are determined in various ways and differ based on the chosen algorithms. Some examples of algorithms include logistic regression, support vector machines, and perceptrons.

- **Decision trees**: Here we use decision trees as predictive models that map various observations from the data points to the observed class of the record we are to predict. A decision tree is just like a flowchart structure, where each internal nonleaf node denotes a check on a feature, each branch represents an outcome of that check, and each terminal leaf node contains a class label which we predict finally.

- **Ensemble learning methods**: These include using multiple machine learning algorithms to obtain better predictive models. An example is the Random Forest classification algorithm which uses an ensemble of decision trees during the model training phase, and at each stage it takes the majority output decision from the ensemble of decision trees as its output. This tends to reduce overfitting, which occurs frequently when using decision trees.

- **Boosting algorithms**: This is also an ensemble learning technique in the supervised learning family of algorithms. It consists of an iterative process of training several weak classification models and learning from them before adding them to a final classifier which is stronger than them. A weighted approach is followed when adding the classifiers, which is based on their accuracy. Future weak classifiers focus more on the records which were previously misclassified.

- **Neural networks**: These algorithms are inspired by the biological neural networks which consist of systems of interconnected neurons that exchange messages with each other. In predictive modeling, we deal with artificial neural networks which consist of interconnected groups of nodes. Each node consists of a function which is usually a mathematical function (that is, sigmoid function) and has an adaptive weight associated with it which keeps changing based on inputs fed to the nodes and constantly checking the error obtained from the outputs in several iterations also known as **epochs**.

We will be covering several of these algorithms when building predictive models in the next chapter.

Summary

Congratulations on staying until the end of this chapter! You have learnt several important things by now which we have covered in this chapter. You now have an idea about one of the most important areas in the financial domain, that is, Credit Risk analysis. Besides this, you also gained significant domain knowledge about how banks analyze customers for their credit ratings and what kind of attributes and features are considered by them. Descriptive and exploratory analysis of the dataset also gave you an insight into how to start working from scratch when you just have a problem to solve and a dataset given to you! You now know how to perform feature engineering, build beautiful publication quality visualizations using ggplot2, and perform statistical tests to check feature associations. Finally, we wrapped up our discussion by talking about feature sets and gave a brief introduction to several supervised machine learning algorithms which will help us in the next step of predicting credit risks. The most interesting part is yet to come, so stay tuned!

6
Credit Risk Detection and Prediction – Predictive Analytics

In the previous chapter, we covered a lot of ground in the financial domain where we took up the challenge of detecting and predicting bank customers who could be potential credit risks. We now have a good idea about our main objective regarding credit risk analysis. Besides this, the substantial knowledge gained from descriptive analytics of the dataset and its features will be useful for predictive analytics, as we had mentioned earlier.

In this chapter, we will be journeying through the world of predictive analytics, which sits at the core of machine learning and data science. Predictive analytics encompasses several things which include classification algorithms, regression algorithms, domain knowledge, and business logic which are combined to build predictive models and derive useful insights from data. We had discussed various machine learning algorithms at the end of the previous chapter which would be applicable for solving our objective, and we will be exploring several of them in this chapter when we build predictive models using the given dataset and these algorithms.

An interesting take on predictive analytics is that it holds a lot of promise for organizations who want to strengthen their business and profits in the future. With the advent of big data, most organizations now have more data than they can analyze! While this is a big challenge, a tougher challenge is to select the right data points from this data and build predictive models which would be capable of predicting outcomes correctly in the future. However, there are several caveats in this approach because each model is basically mathematical functions based on formulae, assumptions, and probability. Also, in the real world, conditions and scenarios keep changing and evolving and thus one must remember that a predictive model built today may be completely redundant tomorrow.

A lot of skeptics say that it is extremely difficult for computers to mimic humans to predict outcomes which even humans can't predict due of the ever changing nature of the environment with time, and hence all statistical methods are only valuable under ideal assumptions and conditions. While this is true to some extent, with the right data, a proper mindset, and by applying the right algorithms and techniques, we can build robust predictive models which can definitely try and tackle problems which would be otherwise impossible to tackle by conventional or brute-force methods.

Predictive modeling is a difficult task and while there might be a lot of challenges and results might be difficult to obtain always, one must take these challenges with a pinch of salt and remember the quotation from the famous statistician George E.P. Box, who claimed that *Essentially all models are wrong but some are useful!*, which is quite true based on what we discussed earlier. Always remember that a predictive model will never be 100% perfect but, if it is built with the right principles, it will be very useful!

In this chapter, we will focus on the following topics:

- Predictive analytics
- How to predict credit risk
- Important concepts in predictive modeling
- Getting the data
- Data preprocessing
- Feature selection
- Modeling using logistic regression
- Modeling using support vector machines
- Modeling using decision trees
- Modeling using random forests
- Modeling using neural networks
- Model comparison and selection

Predictive analytics

We had already discussed a fair bit about predictive analytics in the previous chapter to give you a general overview of what it means. We will be discussing it in more detail in this section. Predictive analytics can be defined as a subset of the machine learning universe, which encompasses a wide variety of supervised learning algorithms based on data science, statistics, and mathematical formulae which enable us to build predictive models using these algorithms and data which has already been collected. These models enable us to make predictions of what might happen in the future based on past observations. Combining this with domain knowledge, expertise, and business logic enables analysts to make data driven decisions using these predictions, which is the ultimate outcome of predictive analytics.

The data we are talking about here is data which has already been observed in the past and has been collected over a period of time for analysis. This data is often known as historical data or training data which is fed to the model. However, most of the time in the predictive modeling methodology, we do not feed the raw data directly but use features extracted from the data after suitable transformations. The data features along with a supervised learning algorithm form a predictive model. The data which is obtained in the present can then be fed to this model to predict outcomes which are under observation and also to test the performance of the model with regards to various accuracy metrics. This data is known as testing data in the machine learning world.

The analytics pipeline that we will be following for carrying out predictive analytics in this chapter is a standard process, which is explained briefly in the following steps:

1. **Getting the data**: Here we get the dataset on which we will be building the predictive model. We will perform some basic descriptive analysis of the dataset, which we have already covered in the previous chapter. Once we have the data we will move on to the next step.

2. **Data preprocessing**: In this step, we carry out data transformations, such as changing data types, feature scaling, and normalization, if necessary, to prepare the data for being trained by models. Usually this step is carried out after the dataset preparation step. However, in this case, the end results are the same, so we can perform these steps in any order.

3. **Dataset preparation**: In this step, we use some ratio like 70:30 or 60:40 to separate the instances from the data into training and testing datasets. We usually use the training dataset to train a model and then check its performance and predicting capability with the testing dataset. Often data is divided in proportions of 60:20:20 where we also have a validation dataset besides the other two datasets. However, we will just keep it to two datasets in this chapter.

4. **Feature selection**: This process is an iterative one which even occurs in a later stage if needed. The main objective in this step is to choose a set of attributes or features from the training dataset that enables the predictive model to give the best predictions possible, minimizing error rates and maximizing accuracy.

5. **Predictive modeling**: This is the main step where we select a machine learning algorithm best suited for solving the problem and build the predictive model using the algorithm by feeding it the features extracted from the data in the training dataset. The output of this stage is a predictive model which can be used for predictions on future data instances.

6. **Model evaluation**: In this phase, we use the testing dataset to get predictions from the predictive model and use a variety of techniques and metrics to measure the performance of the model.

7. **Model tuning**: We fine tune the various parameters of the model and perform feature selection again if necessary. We then rebuild the model and re-evaluate it until we are satisfied with the results.

8. **Model deployment**: Once the predictive model gives a satisfactory performance, we can deploy this model by using a web service in any application to provide predictions in real time or near real time. This step focuses more on software and application development around deploying the model, so we won't be covering this step since it is out of scope. However, there are a lot of tutorials out there regarding building web services around predictive models to enable *Prediction as a service*.

The last three steps are iterative and may be performed several times if needed.

Even though the preceding process might look pretty intensive at first glance, it is really a very simple and straight-forward process, which once understood would be useful in building any type of predictive modeling. An important thing to remember is that predictive modeling is an iterative process where we might need to analyze the data and build the model several times by getting feedback from the model predictions and evaluating them. It is therefore extremely important that you do not get discouraged even if your model doesn't perform well on the first go because a model can never be perfect, as we mentioned before, and building a good predictive model is an art as well as science!

In the next section, we will be focusing on how we would apply predictive analytics to solve our prediction problem and the kind of machine learning algorithms we will be exploring in this chapter.

How to predict credit risk

If you remember our main objective from the previous chapter, we were dealing with customer data from a German bank. We will quickly recap our main problem scenario to refresh your memory. These bank customers are potential candidates who ask for credit loans from the bank with the stipulation that they make monthly payments with some interest on the amount to repay the credit amount. In a perfect world there would be credit loans dished out freely and people would pay them back without issues. Unfortunately, we are not living in a utopian world, and so there will be customers who will default on their credit loans and be unable to repay the amount, causing huge losses to the bank. Therefore, credit risk analysis is one of the crucial areas which banks focus on where they analyze detailed information pertaining to customers and their credit history.

Now coming back to the main question, for predicting credit risk, we need to analyze the dataset pertaining to customers, build a predictive model around it using machine learning algorithms, and predict whether a customer is likely to default on paying the credit loan and could be labeled as a potential credit risk. The process which we will follow for achieving this is what we discussed in the previous section. You already have an idea about the data and features associated with it from the previous chapter. We will explore several predictive models, understand the concepts behind how the models work, and then build these models for predicting credit risk. Once we start predicting the outcomes, we will compare the performance of these different models and then talk about the business impact and how to derive insights from the model prediction outcomes. Do note that the predictions are not the output in the predictive analytics life cycle but the valuable insights that we derive from these predictions is the end goal. Businesses such as financial institutions get value only from using domain knowledge to translate prediction outcomes and raw numbers from machine learning algorithms to data driven decisions, which, when executed at the right time, help grow the business.

For this scenario, if you remember the dataset well, the feature `credit.rating` is the response or class variable, which indicates the credit rating of the customers. We will be predicting this value for the other customers based on other features which are independent variables. For modeling, we will be using machine learning algorithms which belong to the supervised learning family of algorithms. These algorithms are used for predictions and can be divided into two broad categories: classification and regression. However, they have some differences which we will talk about now. In the case of regression, the values for the variables to be predicted are continuous values, like predicting prices of houses based on different features such as the number of rooms, the area of the house, and so on. Regression mostly deals with estimating and predicting a response value based on input features. In the case of classification, the values for the variables to be predicted have discrete and distinct labels, such as predicting the credit rating for customers for our bank, where the credit rating can either be good, which is denoted by `1` or bad, which is denoted by `0`. Classification mostly deals with categorizing and identifying group memberships for each data tuple in the dataset. Algorithms such as logistic regression are special cases of regression models which are used for classification, where the algorithm estimates the odds that a variable is in one of the class labels as a function of the other features. We will be building predictive models using the following machine learning algorithms in this chapter:

- Logistic regression
- Support vector machines
- Decision trees
- Random forests
- Neural networks

We have chosen these algorithms to give a good flavor of the diverse set of supervised machine learning algorithms which are present, so that you gain knowledge not only about the concepts behind these models but also learn to implement building models using them, and compare model performances using various techniques. Before we begin our analysis, we will glance over some basic concepts in predictive modeling that are mentioned in this book and talk about some of them in detail so you get a good idea of what goes on behind the scenes.

Important concepts in predictive modeling

We already looked at several concepts when we talked about the machine learning pipeline. In this section, we will look at typical terms which are used in predictive modeling, and also discuss about model building and evaluation concepts in detail.

Preparing the data

The data preparation step, as discussed earlier, involves preparing the datasets necessary for feature selection and building the predictive models using the data. We frequently use the following terms in this context:

- **Datasets**: They are typically a collection of data points or observations. Most datasets usually correspond to some form of structured data which involves a two dimensional data structure, such as a data matrix or data table (in R this is usually represented using a data frame) containing various values. An example is our `german_credit_dataset.csv` file from *Chapter 5, Credit Risk Detection and Prediction – Descriptive Analytics.*

- **Data observations**: They are the rows in a dataset where each row consists of a set of observations against a set of attributes. These rows are also often called tuples. For our dataset, each row containing information about a customer is a good example.

- **Data features**: They are the columns in a dataset which describe each row in the dataset. These features are often called attributes or variables. Features such as `credit.rating`, `account.balance`, and so on form the features of our credit risk dataset.

- **Data transformation**: It refers to the act of transforming various data features as needed based on observations from descriptive analytics. Data type conversions, missing values imputation, and scaling and normalization are some of the most used techniques. Also, for categorical variables, if your algorithms are not able to detect the different levels in the variable, you need to convert it to several dummy variables; this process is known as one-hot encoding.

- **Training data**: It refers to the data which is solely used to train the predictive models. The machine learning algorithm picks up the tuples from this dataset and tries to find out patterns and learn from the various observation instances.

- **Testing data**: It refers to the data which is fed to the predictive model to get predictions and then we check the accuracy of the model using the class labels which are already present in the tuples for this dataset. We never train the model with the testing data because it would bias the model and give incorrect evaluations.

Building predictive models

We build the actual predictive models using machine learning algorithms and data features which finally start giving out predictions as we feed it new data tuples. Some concepts associated with building predictive models are as follows:

- **Model training**: It is analogous to building the predictive model where we use a supervised machine learning algorithm and feed the training data features to it and build the predictive model.

- **Predictive model**: It is based on some machine learning algorithm, which is essentially a mathematical model at heart, with some assumptions, formulae, and parameter values.

- **Model selection**: It is a process where the main objective is to select a predictive model from several iterations of predictive models. The criteria for selecting the best model can vary, depending on the metrics we want to choose, such as maximizing the accuracy, minimizing the error rate, or getting the maximum AUC, which is something we will discuss later. Cross-validation is a good way to run this iterative process.

- **Hyperparameter optimization**: It is basically trying to choose a set of the hyperparameters used by the algorithm in the model such that the performance of the model is optimal with regards to its prediction accuracy. This is usually done by a grid search algorithm.

- **Cross validation**: It is a model validation technique which is used to estimate how a model would perform in a generic fashion. It is mainly used in iterative processes where the end goal is to optimize the model and make sure it is not over fit to the data so that the model can generalize well with new data and make good predictions. Usually, several rounds of cross validation are run iteratively. Each round of cross validation involves splitting the data into train and test sets; using the training data to train the model and then evaluating its performance with the test set. At the end of this, we get a model which is the best of the lot.

Evaluating predictive models

The most important part in predictive modeling is testing whether the models created are actually useful. This is done by evaluating the models on the testing data and using various metrics to measure the performance of the model. We will discuss some popular model evaluation techniques here. To explain the concepts clearly, we will consider an example with our data. Let us assume we have 100 customers and 40 of them have a bad credit rating with class label 0 and the remaining 60 have a good credit rating with class label 1 in the test data. Let us now assume that our model predicts 22 instances out of the 40 bad instances as bad and the remaining 18 as good. The model also predicts 40 instances out of the 60 good customers as good and the remaining 20 as bad. We will now see how we evaluate the model performance with different techniques:

- **Prediction values**: They are usually discrete values which belong to a specific class or category and are often known as class labels. In our case, it is a binary classification problem where we deal with two classes where label 1 indicates customers with good credit rating and 0 indicates bad credit rating.

- **Confusion matrix**: It is a nice way to see how the model is predicting the different classes. It is a contingency table with usually two rows and two columns for a binary classification problem like ours. It reports the number of predicted instances in each class against the actual class values. For our preceding example, the confusion matrix would be a 2x2 matrix where two rows would indicate the predicted class labels and two columns would indicate the actual class labels. The total number of predictions with the bad (0) class label which are actually having the bad label is called **True Negative** (**TN**) and the remaining bad instances wrongly predicted as good are called **False Positive** (**FP**). Correspondingly, the total number of predictions with the good (1) class label that are actually labeled as good are called **True Positive** (**TP**) and the remaining good instances wrongly predicted as bad are called **False Negative** (**FN**).

We will depict this in the following figure and discuss some important metrics derived from the confusion matrix, also depicted in the same figure:

Predicted Labels		Actual Labels	
		0	1
	0	22	20
	1	18	40
Specificity (TNR):		22 / 40 = 0.55	
Sensitivity (TPR):		40 / 60 = 0.67	
Precision (PPV):		40 / 58 = 0.69	
NPV:		22 / 42 = 0.52	
FPR (1-Specificity):		18 / 40 = 0.45	
FNR (1- Sensitivity):		20 / 60 = 0.33	
Accuracy:		62 / 100 = 0.62	
F1 Score:		80 / 118 = 0.68	

In the preceding figure, the values which are highlighted in the 2x2 matrix are the ones which were correctly predicted by our model. The ones in white were incorrectly predicted by the model. We can therefore infer the following measures quite easily: TN is 22, **FP** is **18**, **TP** is **40**, and **FN** is **20**. Total **N** is **40** and total P is **60**, which add up to 100 customers in our example dataset.

Specificity is also known as **true negative rate**, and can be represented by the formula $\frac{TN}{FP+TN}$, which gives us the proportion of total true negatives correctly predicted by the total number of instances which are actually negative. In our case, we have a specificity of **55%**.

Sensitivity, also known as **true positive rate** and **recall**, has the formula $\frac{TP}{FN+TP}$, which indicates the proportion of total true positives correctly predicted by the total number of instances which are actually positive. Our example has a sensitivity of **67%**.

Precision, also known as **positive predictive value**, has the formula $\frac{TP}{FP+TP}$, which indicates the number of actual positive instances out of all the positive predictions. Our example has a precision of **69%**.

Negative predictive value has the formula $\frac{TN}{FN+TN}$, which indicates the number of actual negative instances out of all the negative predictions. Our example has an NPV of **52%**.

False positive rate, also known as **fall-out**, is basically the inverse of specificity; where the formula is $\frac{FP}{FP+TN}$, which indicates the number of false positive predictions out of all the negative instances. Our example has an FPR of **45%**.

False Negative Rate, also known as **miss rate**, is basically the inverse of sensitivity; where the formula is $\frac{FN}{TP+FN}$, which indicates the number of false negative predictions out of all the positive instances. Our example has an FNR of **33%**.

Accuracy is basically the metric which denotes how accurate the model is in making predictions, where the formula is $\frac{TP+TN}{P+N}$. Our prediction accuracy is **62%**.

F1 score is another metric of measuring a model's accuracy. It takes into account both the precision and recall values by computing the harmonic mean of the values, depicted by the formula $\frac{2TP}{2TP+FP+FN}$. Our model has an **f1** score of **68%**.

A **Receiver Operator Characteristic** (**ROC**) curve is basically a plot which is used to visualize the model performance as we vary its threshold. The ROC plot is defined by the FPR and TPR as the *x* and *y* axes respectively, and each prediction sample can be fit as a point in the ROC space. Perfect plot would involve a TPR of 1 and an FPR of 0 for all the data points. An average model or a baseline model would be a diagonal straight line from *(0, 0)* to *(1, 1)* indicating both values to be 0.5. If our model has an ROC curve above the base diagonal line, it indicates that it is performing better than the baseline. The following figure explains how a typical ROC curve looks like in general:

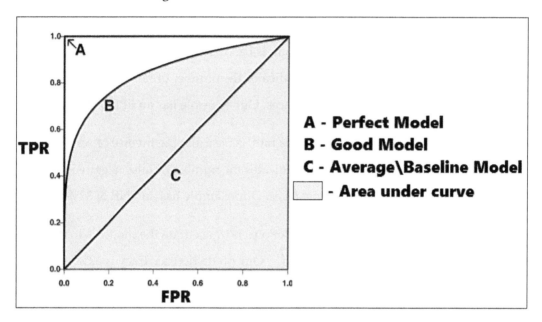

Area under curve (**AUC**) is basically the area under the ROC curve obtained from the model evaluation. The AUC is a value which indicates the probability that the model will rank a randomly chosen positive instance higher than a randomly chosen negative one. Therefore, the higher the AUC, the better it is. Do check out the file performance_plot_utils.R (shared with the code bundle of the chapter), which has some utility functions to plot and depict these values that we will be using later when we evaluate our model.

This should give you enough background on important terms and concepts related to predictive modeling, and now we will start with our predictive analysis on the data!

Getting the data

In *Chapter 5*, *Credit Risk Detection and Prediction – Descriptive Analytics*, we had analyzed the credit dataset from the German bank and performed several transformations already. We will be working on that transformed dataset in this chapter. We had saved the transformed dataset which you can check out by opening the `credit_dataset_final.csv` file. We will be doing all our analysis in R as usual. To load the data in memory, run the following code snippet:

```
> # load the dataset into data frame
> credit.df <- read.csv("credit_dataset_final.csv", header = TRUE, sep = ",")
```

This loads the dataset into a data frame which can now be readily accessed using the `credit.df` variable. Next, we will focus on data transformation and normalization.

Data preprocessing

In the data preprocessing step, we will be focusing on two things mainly: data type transformations and data normalization. Finally we will split the data into training and testing datasets for predictive modeling. You can access the code for this section in the `data_preparation.R` file. We will be using some utility functions, which are mentioned in the following code snippet. Remember to load them up in memory by running them in the R console:

```
## data type transformations - factoring
to.factors <- function(df, variables){
  for (variable in variables){
    df[[variable]] <- as.factor(df[[variable]])
  }
  return(df)
}


## normalizing - scaling
scale.features <- function(df, variables){
  for (variable in variables){
    df[[variable]] <- scale(df[[variable]], center=T, scale=T)
  }
  return(df)
}
```

The preceding functions operate on the data frame to transform the data. For data type transformations, we mainly perform factoring of the categorical variables, where we transform the data type of the categorical features from numeric to factor. There are several numeric variables, which include `credit.amount`, `age`, and `credit.duration.months`, which all have various values and if you remember the distributions in the previous chapter, they were all skewed distributions. This has multiple adverse effects, such as induced collinearity, gradients being affected, and models taking longer times to converge. Hence, we will be using z-score normalization, where each value represented by, let's say, e_i, for a feature named E, can be calculated using the formula $Znorm(e_i) = \dfrac{e_i - \bar{E}}{\sigma(E)}$ where $\bar{E}$ represents the overall mean and $\sigma(E)$ represents the standard deviation of the feature E. We use the following code snippet to perform these transformations on our data:

```
> # normalize variables
> numeric.vars <- c("credit.duration.months", "age",
                    "credit.amount")
> credit.df <- scale.features(credit.df, numeric.vars)
> # factor variables
> categorical.vars <- c('credit.rating', 'account.balance',
+                       'previous.credit.payment.status',
+                       'credit.purpose', 'savings',
+                       'employment.duration', 'installment.rate',
+                       'marital.status', 'guarantor',
+                       'residence.duration', 'current.assets',
+                       'other.credits', 'apartment.type',
+                       'bank.credits', 'occupation',
+                       'dependents', 'telephone',
+                       'foreign.worker')
> credit.df <- to.factors(df=credit.df,
                          variables=categorical.vars)
```

Once the preprocessing is complete, we will split our data into training and test datasets in the ratio of 60:40, where 600 tuples will be in the training dataset and 400 tuples will be in the testing dataset. They will be selected in a random fashion as follows:

```
> # split data into training and test datasets in 60:40 ratio
> indexes <- sample(1:nrow(credit.df), size=0.6*nrow(credit.df))
```

```
> train.data <- credit.df[indexes,]
> test.data <- credit.df[-indexes,]
```

Now that we have our datasets ready, we will explore feature importance and selection in the following section.

Feature selection

The process of feature selection involves ranking variables or features according to their importance by training a predictive model using them and then trying to find out which variables were the most relevant features for that model. While each model often has its own set of important features, for classification we will use a random forest model here to try and figure out which variables might be of importance in general for classification-based predictions.

We perform feature selection for several reasons, which include:

- Removing redundant or irrelevant features without too much information loss
- Preventing overfitting of models by using too many features
- Reducing variance of the model which is contributed from excess features
- Reducing training time and converging time of models
- Building simple and easy to interpret models

We will be using a recursive feature elimination algorithm for feature selection and an evaluation algorithm using a predictive model where we repeatedly construct several machine learning models with different features in different iterations. At each iteration, we keep eliminating irrelevant or redundant features and check the feature subset for which we get maximum accuracy and minimum error. Since this is an iterative process and follows the principle of the popular greedy hill climbing algorithm, an exhaustive search with a global optima outcome is generally not possible and depending on the starting point, we may end up at local optima with a subset of features which may be different from the subset of features we obtain in a different run. However, most of the features in the obtained subset will usually be constant if we run it several times using cross-validation. We will use the random forest algorithm, which we will explain in more detail later on. For now, just remember it is an ensemble learning algorithm that uses several decision trees at each stage in its training process. This tends to reduce variance and overfitting with a small increase towards bias of the model since we introduce some randomness into this process at each stage in the algorithm.

The code for this section is present in the `feature_selection.R` file. We will first load the necessary libraries. Install them in case you do not have them installed, as we did in the previous chapters:

```
> library(caret)   # feature selection algorithm
> library(randomForest) # random forest algorithm
```

Now we define the utility function for feature selection using recursive feature elimination and random forests for the model evaluation in the following code snippet. Remember to run it in the R console to load into memory for using it later:

```
run.feature.selection <- function(num.iters=20, feature.vars, class.var){
  set.seed(10)
  variable.sizes <- 1:10
  control <- rfeControl(functions = rfFuncs, method = "cv",
                        verbose = FALSE, returnResamp = "all",
                        number = num.iters)
  results.rfe <- rfe(x = feature.vars, y = class.var,
              sizes = variable.sizes,
              rfeControl = control)
  return(results.rfe)
}
```

By default, the preceding code uses cross-validation where the data is split into training and test sets. For each iteration, recursive feature elimination takes place and the model is trained and tested for accuracy and errors on the test set. The data partitions keep changing randomly for every iteration to prevent overfitting of the model and ultimately give a generalized estimate of how the model would perform in a generic fashion. If you observe, our function runs it for 20 iterations by default. Remember, in our case, we always train on the training data which is internally partitioned for cross-validation by the function. The variable `feature.vars` indicate all the independent feature variables that can be accessed in the training dataset using the `train.data[,-1]` subsetting, and to access the `class.var`,which indicates the class variable to be predicted, we subset using `train.data[,1]`.

We do not touch the test data at all because we will be using it only for predictions and model evaluations. Therefore, we would not want to influence the model by using that data since it would lead to incorrect evaluations.

We now run the algorithm using our defined function on the training data using the following code. It may take some time to run, so be patient if you see that R is taking some time to return the results:

```
rfe.results <- run.feature.selection(feature.vars=train.data[,-1],
                                     class.var=train.data[,1])
# view results
rfe.results
```

On viewing the results, we get the following output:

```
Recursive feature selection

Outer resampling method: Cross-Validated (20 fold)

Resampling performance over subset size:

 Variables Accuracy  Kappa AccuracySD KappaSD Selected
         1   0.7167 0.0000    0.01565  0.0000
         2   0.7584 0.2892    0.06599  0.2042
         3   0.7485 0.2467    0.06253  0.2006
         4   0.7551 0.3538    0.07602  0.1877
         5   0.7838 0.4382    0.07132  0.1712
         6   0.7869 0.4297    0.06066  0.1551
         7   0.7768 0.3915    0.04241  0.1220
         8   0.7868 0.4047    0.03559  0.1163
         9   0.7801 0.3997    0.05498  0.1517
        10   0.7869 0.4170    0.05725  0.1665        *
        20   0.7567 0.2858    0.05634  0.1856

The top 5 variables (out of 10):
   account.balance, credit.duration.months, savings, previous.credit.payment.status, credit.amount
```

From the output, you can see that it has found a total of 10 features that were the most important out of the 20 and it has returned the top five features by default. You can play around with this result variable even further and see all the variables with their importance by using the varImp(rfe.results) command in the R console. The values and importance values may differ for you because the training and test data partitions are done randomly, if you remember, so do not panic if you see different values from the screenshot. However, the top five features will usually remain consistent based on our observations. We will now start building predictive models using the different machine learning algorithms for the next stage of our analytics pipeline. However, do remember that since the training and test sets are randomly chosen, your sets might give slightly different results than what we depict here when we performed these experiments.

Modeling using logistic regression

Logistic regression is a type of regression model where the dependent or class variable is not continuous but categorical, just as in our case, credit rating is the dependent variable with two classes. In principle, logistic regression is usually perceived as a special case of the family of generalized linear models. This model functions by trying to find out the relationship between the class variable and the other independent feature variables by estimating probabilities. It uses the logistic or sigmoid function for estimating these probabilities. Logistic regression does not predict classes directly but the probability of the outcome. For our model, since we are dealing with a binary classification problem, we will be dealing with binomial logistic regression.

First we will load the library dependencies as follows and separate the testing feature and class variables:

```
library(caret) # model training and evaluation
library(ROCR) # model evaluation
source("performance_plot_utils.R") # plotting metric results
## separate feature and class variables
test.feature.vars <- test.data[,-1]
test.class.var <- test.data[,1]
```

Now we will train the initial model with all the independent variables as follows:

```
> formula.init <- "credit.rating ~ ."
> formula.init <- as.formula(formula.init)
> lr.model <- glm(formula=formula.init, data=train.data,
family="binomial")
```

We can view the model details using the `summary(lr.model)` command, which shows you the various variables and their importance based on their significance values. We show a part of these details in the following snapshot:

```
Call:
glm(formula = formula.init, family = "binomial", data = train.data)

Deviance Residuals:
    Min       1Q    Median        3Q       Max
-2.6551   -0.5141    0.3187    0.6335    2.1838

Coefficients:
                                    Estimate Std. Error z value Pr(>|z|)
(Intercept)                         0.156837   1.073803   0.146 0.883876
account.balance2                    0.246170   0.291234   0.845 0.397963
account.balance3                    1.678654   0.298253   5.628 1.82e-08 ***
credit.duration.months             -0.545377   0.153737  -3.547 0.000389 ***
previous.credit.payment.status2     0.588709   0.420863   1.399 0.161869
previous.credit.payment.status3     1.225405   0.431435   2.840 0.004507 **
```

You can see that the model automatically performs one-hot encoding of categorical variables, which is basically having a variable for each category in that variable. The variables with stars beside them have p-values < `0.05` (which we discussed in the previous chapter) and are therefore significant.

Next, we perform predictions on the test data and evaluate the results as follows:

```
> lr.predictions <- predict(lr.model, test.data, type="response")

> lr.predictions <- round(lr.predictions)

> confusionMatrix(data=lr.predictions, reference=test.class.var,
positive='1')
```

On running this, we get a confusion matrix with associated metrics, which we discussed earlier, which are shown in the following figure. It is quite interesting to see that we achieved an overall accuracy of **71.75%**, which is quite decent, considering this dataset has a majority of good credit rating customers. It is predicting bad credit ratings quite well, which is evident from the **specificity** of **48%**. **Sensitivity** is **83%**, which is quite good, **NPV** is **58%**, and **PPV** is **76%**.

```
Confusion Matrix and Statistics

          Reference
Prediction   0    1
         0  62   45
         1  68  225

              Accuracy : 0.7175
                95% CI : (0.6706, 0.7611)
   No Information Rate : 0.675
   P-Value [Acc > NIR] : 0.03788

                 Kappa : 0.3252
 Mcnemar's Test P-Value : 0.03849

           Sensitivity : 0.8333
           Specificity : 0.4769
        Pos Pred Value : 0.7679
        Neg Pred Value : 0.5794
            Prevalence : 0.6750
        Detection Rate : 0.5625
  Detection Prevalence : 0.7325
     Balanced Accuracy : 0.6551

      'Positive' Class : 1
```

We will now try to build another model with some selected features and see how it performs. If you remember, we had some generic features that are important for classification, which we obtained in the earlier section on feature selection. We will still run feature selection specifically for logistic regression to see feature importance using the following code snippet:

```
formula <- "credit.rating ~ ."
formula <- as.formula(formula)
control <- trainControl(method="repeatedcv", number=10, repeats=2)
model <- train(formula, data=train.data, method="glm",
               trControl=control)
```

```
importance <- varImp(model, scale=FALSE)

plot(importance)
```

We get the following plot from which we select the top five variables to build the next model. As you can see, reading the plot is pretty simple. The greater the importance, the more important the variable is. Feel free to add more variables and build different models using them!

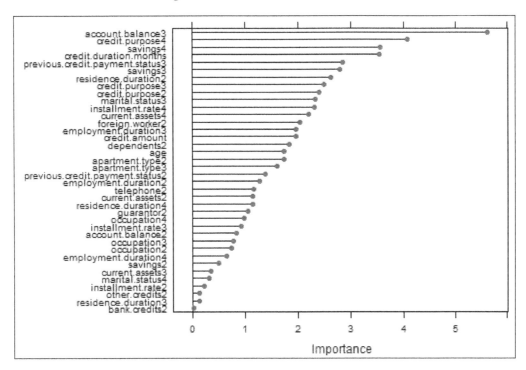

Next, we build the model using a similar approach to before and test the model performance on the test data using the following code snippet:

```
> formula.new <- "credit.rating ~ account.balance + credit.purpose
                    + previous.credit.payment.status + savings
                    + credit.duration.months"

> formula.new <- as.formula(formula.new)

> lr.model.new <- glm(formula=formula.new, data=train.data,
family="binomial")

> lr.predictions.new <- predict(lr.model.new, test.data, type="response")

> lr.predictions.new <- round(lr.predictions.new)

> confusionMatrix(data=lr.predictions.new, reference=test.class.var,
positive='1')
```

We get the following confusion matrix. However, if you look at the model evaluation results, as shown in following output, you will see that now accuracy has slightly increased and is **72.25%**. **Sensitivity** has shot up to **94%**, which is excellent, but sadly this has happened at the cost of specificity, which has gone down to **27%**, and you can clearly see that more bad credit ratings are being predicted as good, which is 95 out of the total 130 bad credit rating customers in the test data! **NPV** has gone up to **69%** because fewer positive credit ratings are being misclassified as false negatives because of higher sensitivity.

```
Confusion Matrix and Statistics

          Reference
Prediction   0   1
         0  35  16
         1  95 254

              Accuracy : 0.7225
                95% CI : (0.6758, 0.7658)
   No Information Rate : 0.675
   P-Value [Acc > NIR] : 0.02302

                 Kappa : 0.2492
 Mcnemar's Test P-Value : 1.327e-13

           Sensitivity : 0.9407
           Specificity : 0.2692
        Pos Pred Value : 0.7278
        Neg Pred Value : 0.6863
            Prevalence : 0.6750
        Detection Rate : 0.6350
  Detection Prevalence : 0.8725
     Balanced Accuracy : 0.6050

      'Positive' Class : 1
```

Now comes the question of which model we want to select for predictions. This does not solely depend on the accuracy but on the domain and business requirements of the problem. If we predict a customer with a **bad credit rating (0)** as **good (1)**, it means we are going to approve the credit loan for the customer who will end up not paying it, which will cause losses to the bank. However, if we predict a customer with **good credit rating (1)** as **bad (0)**, it means we will deny him the loan in which case the bank will neither profit nor will incur any losses. This is much better than incurring huge losses by wrongly predicting bad credit ratings as good.

Therefore, we choose our first model as the best one and now we will view some metric evaluation plots using the following code snippet:

```
> lr.model.best <- lr.model
> lr.prediction.values <- predict(lr.model.best, test.feature.vars,
type="response")
> predictions <- prediction(lr.prediction.values, test.class.var)
> par(mfrow=c(1,2))
> plot.roc.curve(predictions, title.text="LR ROC Curve")
> plot.pr.curve(predictions, title.text="LR Precision/Recall Curve")
```

We get the following plots from the preceding code:

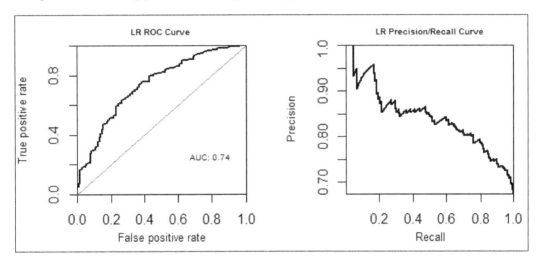

You can see from the preceding plot that the **AUC** is **0.74**, which is pretty good for a start. We will now build the next predictive model using support vector machines using a similar process and see how it fares.

Modeling using support vector machines

Support vector machines belong to the family of supervised machine learning algorithms used for both classification and regression. Considering our binary classification problem, unlike logistic regression, the SVM algorithm will build a model around the training data in such a way that the training data points belonging to different classes are separated by a clear gap, which is optimized such that the distance of separation is the maximum. The samples on the margins are typically called the support vectors. The middle of the margin which separates the two classes is called the optimal separating hyperplane.

Data points on the wrong side of the margin are weighed down to reduce their influence and this is called the soft margin compared to the hard margins of separation we discussed earlier. SVM classifiers can be simple linear classifiers where the data points can be linearly separated. However, if we are dealing with data consisting of several features such that a linear separation is not possible directly, then we make use of several kernels to achieve the same and these form the non-linear SVM classifiers. You will be able to visualize how an SVM classifier actually looks much better with the following figure from the official documentation for the svm library in R:

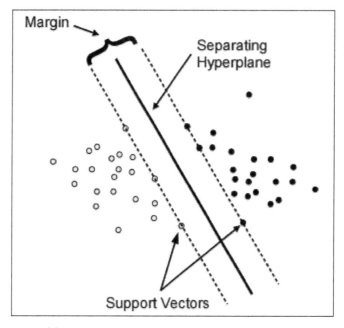

Image source: https://cran.r-project.org/web/packages/e1071/vignettes/svmdoc.pdf

From the figure, you can clearly see that we can place multiple hyperplanes separating the data points. However, the criterion for choosing the separating hyperplane is such that the distance of separation from the two classes is the maximum and the support vectors are the representative samples of the two classes as depicted on the margins. Revisiting the issue of non-linear classifiers, SVM has several kernels which can be used to achieve this besides the regular linear kernel used for linear classification. These include polynomial, **radial basis function (RBF)**, and several others. The main principle behind these non-linear kernel functions is that, even if linear separation is not possible in the original feature space, they enable the separation to happen in a higher dimensional transformed feature space where we can use a hyperplane to separate the classes. An important thing to remember is the curse of dimensionality that applies here; since we may end up working with higher dimensional feature spaces, the model generalization error increases and the predictive power of the model decreases. It we have enough data, it still performs reasonably. We will be using the RBF kernel, also known as the radial basis function, in our model and for that two important parameters are cost and gamma.

We will start by loading the necessary dependencies and preparing the testing data features:

```
library(e1071) # svm model
library(caret) # model training\optimizations
library(kernlab) # svm model for hyperparameters
library(ROCR) # model evaluation
source("performance_plot_utils.R") # plot model metrics
## separate feature and class variables
test.feature.vars <- test.data[,-1]
test.class.var <- test.data[,1]
```

Once this is done, we build the SVM model using the training data and the RBF kernel on all the training set features:

```
> formula.init <- "credit.rating ~ ."
> formula.init <- as.formula(formula.init)
> svm.model <- svm(formula=formula.init, data=train.data,
+                  kernel="radial", cost=100, gamma=1)
> summary(svm.model)
```

The properties of the model are generated as follows from the `summary` function:

```
Call:
svm(formula = formula.init, data = train.data, kernel = "radial", cost = 100, gamma = 1)

Parameters:
   SVM-Type:  C-classification
 SVM-Kernel:  radial
       cost:  100
      gamma:  1

Number of Support Vectors:   600

 ( 430 170 )

Number of Classes:   2

Levels:
 0 1
```

Now we use our testing data on this model to make predictions and evaluate the results as follows:

```
> svm.predictions <- predict(svm.model, test.feature.vars)
> confusionMatrix(data=svm.predictions, reference=test.class.var,
  positive="1")
```

This gives us the following confusion matrix like we saw in logistic regression and the details are depicted for the model performance. We observe that the **accuracy** is **67.5%**, **sensitivity** is **100%**, and **specificity** is **0%**, which means that it is a very aggressive model which just predicts every customer rating as good. This model clearly suffers from the major class classification problem and we need to improve this.

```
Confusion Matrix and Statistics


          Reference
Prediction   0   1
         0   0   0
         1 130 270


                Accuracy : 0.675
                  95% CI : (0.6267, 0.7207)
     No Information Rate : 0.675
     P-Value [Acc > NIR] : 0.5238

                   Kappa : 0
 Mcnemar's Test P-Value : <2e-16

             Sensitivity : 1.000
             Specificity : 0.000
          Pos Pred Value : 0.675
          Neg Pred Value :   NaN
              Prevalence : 0.675
          Detection Rate : 0.675
    Detection Prevalence : 1.000
       Balanced Accuracy : 0.500

        'Positive' Class : 1
```

To build a better model, we need some feature selection. We already have the top five best features which we had obtained in the *Feature selection* section. Nevertheless, we will still run a feature selection algorithm specifically for SVM to see feature importance, as follows:

```
> formula.init <- "credit.rating ~ ."
> formula.init <- as.formula(formula.init)
> control <- trainControl(method="repeatedcv", number=10, repeats=2)
> model <- train(formula.init, data=train.data, method="svmRadial",
+               trControl=control)
> importance <- varImp(model, scale=FALSE)
> plot(importance, cex.lab=0.5)
```

This gives us a plot and we see that the top five important variables are similar to our top five best features, except this algorithm ranks age as more important than `credit.amount`, so you can test this by building several models with different features and see which one gives the best results. For us, the features selected from random forests gave a better result. The variable importance plot is depicted as follows:

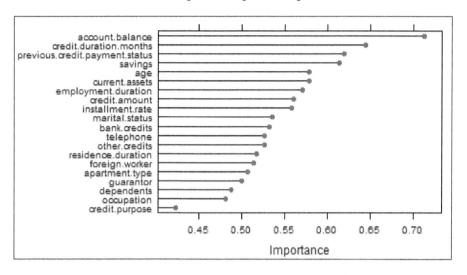

We now build a new SVM model based on the top five features that gave us the best results and evaluate its performance on the test data using the following code snippet:

```
> formula.new <- "credit.rating ~ account.balance +
                    credit.duration.months + savings +
                    previous.credit.payment.status + credit.amount"
> formula.new <- as.formula(formula.new)
> svm.model.new <- svm(formula=formula.new, data=train.data,
                    kernel="radial", cost=100, gamma=1)
> svm.predictions.new <- predict(svm.model.new, test.feature.vars)
> confusionMatrix(data=svm.predictions.new,
                    reference=test.class.var, positive="1")
```

The preceding snippet gives us a confusion matrix finally on the test data and we observe that the overall accuracy has in fact dropped by **1%** to **66.5%**. However, the most interesting part is that now our model is able to predict more bad ratings from bad, which can be seen from the confusion matrix. The **specificity** is now **38%** compared to **0%** earlier and, correspondingly, the **sensitivity** has gone down to **80%** from **100%**, which is still good because now this model is actually useful and profitable! You can see from this that feature selection can indeed be extremely powerful. The confusion matrix for the preceding observations is depicted in the following snapshot:

```
Confusion Matrix and Statistics

          Reference
Prediction   0    1
         0  49   53
         1  81  217

               Accuracy : 0.665
                 95% CI : (0.6164, 0.7111)
    No Information Rate : 0.675
    P-Value [Acc > NIR] : 0.68620

                  Kappa : 0.1913
 Mcnemar's Test P-Value : 0.01968

            Sensitivity : 0.8037
            Specificity : 0.3769
         Pos Pred Value : 0.7282
         Neg Pred Value : 0.4804
             Prevalence : 0.6750
         Detection Rate : 0.5425
   Detection Prevalence : 0.7450
      Balanced Accuracy : 0.5903

       'Positive' Class : 1
```

We will definitely select this model and move on to model optimization by hyperparameter tuning using a grid search algorithm as follows to optimize the cost and gamma parameters:

```
cost.weights <- c(0.1, 10, 100)
gamma.weights <- c(0.01, 0.25, 0.5, 1)
tuning.results <- tune(svm, formula.new,
                    data = train.data, kernel="Radial",
```

```
                    ranges=list(cost=cost.weights, gamma=gamma.
weights))
print(tuning.results)
```

Output:

```
Parameter tuning of 'svm':
- sampling method: 10-fold cross validation
- best parameters:
  cost gamma
    10  0.25
- best performance: 0.22
```

The grid search plot can be viewed as follows:

```
> plot(tuning.results, cex.main=0.6, cex.lab=0.8,xaxs="i", yaxs="i")
```

Output:

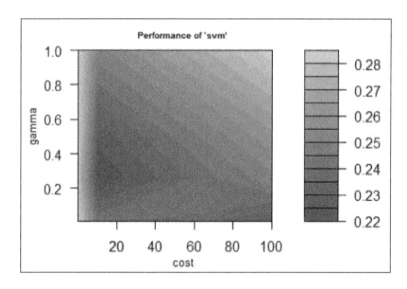

The darkest region shows the parameter values which gave the best performance. We now select the best model and evaluate it once again as follows:

```
> svm.model.best = tuning.results$best.model
> svm.predictions.best <- predict(svm.model.best,
                              test.feature.vars)
> confusionMatrix(data=svm.predictions.best,
                reference=test.class.var, positive="1")
```

On observing the confusion matrix results we obtained from the following output (we are henceforth depicting only the metrics which we are tracking), we see that the overall **accuracy** has increased to **71%**, **sensitivity** to **86%**, and **specificity** to **41%**, which is excellent compared to the previous model results:

```
          Reference
Prediction   0   1
         0  53  38
         1  77 232

                Accuracy : 0.7125
                  95% CI : (0.6654, 0.7564)
     No Information Rate : 0.675
     P-Value [Acc > NIR] : 0.0596891

                   Kappa : 0.2895
 Mcnemar's Test P-Value : 0.0003948

             Sensitivity : 0.8593
             Specificity : 0.4077
```

You see how powerful hyperparameter optimizations can be in predictive modeling! We also plot some evaluation curves as follows:

```
> svm.predictions.best <- predict(svm.model.best, test.feature.vars,
decision.values = T)

> svm.prediction.values <- attributes(svm.predictions.best)$decision.
values

> predictions <- prediction(svm.prediction.values, test.class.var)

> par(mfrow=c(1,2))

> plot.roc.curve(predictions, title.text="SVM ROC Curve")

> plot.pr.curve(predictions, title.text="SVM Precision/Recall Curve")
```

We can see how the predictions are plotted in the evaluation space, and we see that the AUC in this case is 0.69 from the following ROC plot:

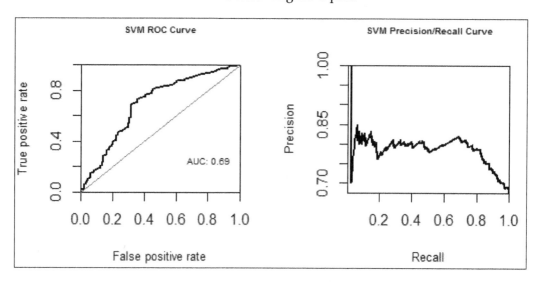

Now, let's say we want to optimize the model based on this ROC plot with the objective of maximizing the AUC. We will try that now, but first we need to encode the values of the categorical variables to include some letters because R causes some problems when representing column names of factor variables that have only numbers. So basically, if `credit.rating` has values 0, 1 then it gets transformed to **X0** and **X1**; ultimately our categories are still distinct and nothing changes. We transform our data first with the following code snippet:

```
> transformed.train <- train.data
> transformed.test <- test.data
> for (variable in categorical.vars){
+    new.train.var <- make.names(train.data[[variable]])
+    transformed.train[[variable]] <- new.train.var
+    new.test.var <- make.names(test.data[[variable]])
+    transformed.test[[variable]] <- new.test.var
+ }
> transformed.train <- to.factors(df=transformed.train,
variables=categorical.vars)
> transformed.test <- to.factors(df=transformed.test,
variables=categorical.vars)
> transformed.test.feature.vars <- transformed.test[,-1]
> transformed.test.class.var <- transformed.test[,1]
```

Now we build an AUC optimized model using grid search again, as follows:

```
> grid <- expand.grid(C=c(1,10,100), sigma=c(0.01, 0.05, 0.1, 0.5,
                                              1))
> ctr <- trainControl(method='cv', number=10, classProbs=TRUE,
                    summaryFunction=twoClassSummary)
> svm.roc.model <- train(formula.init, transformed.train,
+                        method='svmRadial', trControl=ctr,
+                        tuneGrid=grid, metric="ROC")
```

Our next step is to perform predictions on the test data and evaluate the confusion matrix:

```
> predictions <- predict(svm.roc.model,
                        transformed.test.feature.vars)
> confusionMatrix(predictions, transformed.test.class.var,
                positive = "X1")
```

This gives us the following results:

```
          Reference
Prediction  X0   X1
       X0   52   33
       X1   78  237

              Accuracy : 0.7225
                95% CI : (0.6758, 0.7658)
   No Information Rate : 0.675
   P-Value [Acc > NIR] : 0.02302

                 Kappa : 0.3052
 Mcnemar's Test P-Value : 2.963e-05

           Sensitivity : 0.8778
           Specificity : 0.4000
```

We see now that **accuracy** has increased further to **72**% and **specificity** has decreased slightly to **40**%, but **sensitivity** has increased to **87**%, which is good. We plot the curves once again, as follows:

```
> svm.predictions <- predict(svm.roc.model, transformed.test.feature.
vars, type="prob")
> svm.prediction.values <- svm.predictions[,2]
```

```
> predictions <- prediction(svm.prediction.values, test.class.var)
> par(mfrow=c(1,2))
> plot.roc.curve(predictions, title.text="SVM ROC Curve")
> plot.pr.curve(predictions, title.text="SVM Precision/Recall Curve")
```

This gives us the following plots, the same as we did in our earlier iterations:

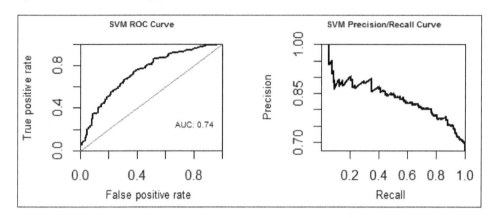

It is quite pleasing to see that the AUC has indeed increased from 0.69 earlier to 0.74 now, which means the AUC based optimization algorithm indeed worked, since it has given better performance than the previous model in all the aspects we have been tracking. Up next, we will look at how to build predictive models using decision trees.

Modeling using decision trees

Decision trees are algorithms which again belong to the supervised machine learning algorithms family. They are also used for both classification and regression, often called **CART**, which stands for **classification and regression trees**. These are used a lot in decision support systems, business intelligence, and operations research.

Decision trees are mainly used for making decisions that would be most useful in reaching some objective and designing a strategy based on these decisions. At the core, a decision tree is just a flowchart with several nodes and conditional edges. Each non-leaf node represents a conditional test on one of the features and each edge represents an outcome of the test. Each leaf node represents a class label where predictions are made for the final outcome. Paths from the root to all the leaf nodes give us all the classification rules. Decision trees are easy to represent, construct, and understand. However, the drawback is that they are very prone to overfitting and often these models do not generalize well. We will follow a similar analytics pipeline as before, to build some models based on decision trees.

We start with loading the necessary dependencies and test data features:

```
> library(rpart)# tree models
> library(caret) # feature selection
> library(rpart.plot) # plot dtree
> library(ROCR) # model evaluation
> library(e1071) # tuning model
> source("performance_plot_utils.R") # plotting curves
> ## separate feature and class variables
> test.feature.vars <- test.data[,-1]
> test.class.var <- test.data[,1]
```

Now we will build an initial model with all the features as follows:

```
> formula.init <- "credit.rating ~ ."
> formula.init <- as.formula(formula.init)
> dt.model <- rpart(formula=formula.init,
                 method="class",data=train.data,control =
                      rpart.control(minsplit=20, cp=0.05))
```

We predict and evaluate the model on the test data with the following code:

```
> dt.predictions <- predict(dt.model, test.feature.vars,
                        type="class")
> confusionMatrix(data=dt.predictions, reference=test.class.var,
                 positive="1")
```

From the following output, we see that the model **accuracy** is around **68%**, **sensitivity** is **92%**, which is excellent, but **specificity** is only **18%**, which we should try and improve:

```
          Reference
Prediction   0   1
         0  23  22
         1 107 248

                Accuracy : 0.6775
                  95% CI : (0.6293, 0.7231)
     No Information Rate : 0.675
     P-Value [Acc > NIR] : 0.4812
                   Kappa : 0.1149
 Mcnemar's Test P-Value : 1.406e-13
             Sensitivity : 0.9185
             Specificity : 0.1769
```

We will now try feature selection to improve the model. We use the following code to train the model and rank the features by their importance:

```
> formula.init <- "credit.rating ~ ."
> formula.init <- as.formula(formula.init)
> control <- trainControl(method="repeatedcv", number=10, repeats=2)
> model <- train(formula.init, data=train.data, method="rpart",
+                trControl=control)
> importance <- varImp(model, scale=FALSE)
> plot(importance)
```

This gives us the following plot showing the importance of different features:

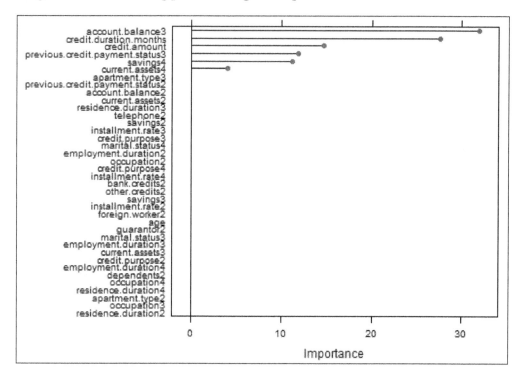

If you observe closely, the decision tree does not use all the features in the model construction and the top five features are the same as those we obtained earlier when we talked about feature selection. We will now build a model using these features as follows:

```
> formula.new <- "credit.rating ~ account.balance + savings +
                  credit.amount +
```

```
                    credit.duration.months +

                    previous.credit.payment.status"
> formula.new <- as.formula(formula.new)
> dt.model.new <- rpart(formula=formula.new, method="class",data=train.
data,
+                       control = rpart.control(minsplit=20, cp=0.05),
+                       parms = list(prior = c(0.7, 0.3)))
```

We now make predictions on the test data and evaluate it, as follows:

```
> dt.predictions.new <- predict(dt.model.new, test.feature.vars,
                        type="class")
> confusionMatrix(data=dt.predictions.new,
            reference=test.class.var, positive="1")
```

This gives us the following confusion matrix with other metrics:

```
            Reference
Prediction   0   1
         0 100 121
         1  30 149

                   Accuracy : 0.6225
                     95% CI : (0.573, 0.6702)
        No Information Rate : 0.675
        P-Value [Acc > NIR] : 0.9884
                      Kappa : 0.2718
     Mcnemar's Test P-Value : 2.405e-13
                Sensitivity : 0.5519
                Specificity : 0.7692
```

You can see now that the overall model **accuracy** has decreased a bit to **62%**. However, we have increased our bad credit rating prediction where we predict a 100 bad credit rating customers out of 130, which is excellent! Consequently, **specificity** has jumped up to **77%** and **sensitivity** is down to **55%**, but we still classify a substantial number of good credit rating customers as good. Though this model is a bit aggressive, it is a reasonable model because though we deny credit loans to more customers who could default on the payment, we also make sure a reasonable number of good customers get their credit loans approved.

The reason we obtained these results is because we have built the model with a parameter called prior, if you check the modeling section earlier. This prior basically empowers us to apply weightages to the different classes in the class variable. If you remember, we had **700** people with a **good credit rating** and **300** people with a **bad credit rating** in our dataset, which was highly skewed, so while training the model, we can use prior to specify the importance of each of the classes in this variable and thus adjust the importance of misclassification of each class. In our model, we give more importance to the bad credit rating customers.

You can reverse the priors and give more importance to the good rating customers by using the parameter as prior = c(0.7, 0.3), which would give the following confusion matrix:

```
          Reference
Prediction   0   1
         0  23  22
         1 107 248

                  Accuracy : 0.6775
                    95% CI : (0.6293, 0.7231)
       No Information Rate : 0.675
       P-Value [Acc > NIR] : 0.4812
                     Kappa : 0.1149
    Mcnemar's Test P-Value : 1.406e-13
               Sensitivity : 0.9185
               Specificity : 0.1769
```

You can clearly see now that, since we gave more importance to good credit ratings, the **sensitivity** has jumped up to **92%** and **specificity** has gone down to **18%**. You can see that this gives you a lot of flexibility over your modeling depending on what you want to achieve.

To view the model, we can use the following code snippet:

```
> dt.model.best <- dt.model.new
> print(dt.model.best)
```

Output:

```
n= 600

node), split, n, loss, yval, (yprob)
      * denotes terminal node

1) root 600 180.00000 0 (0.7000000 0.3000000)
   2) account.balance=1,2 322   76.18605 0 (0.8194936 0.1805064) *
   3) account.balance=3 278   74.11765 1 (0.4165513 0.5834487) *
```

To visualize the preceding tree, you can use the following:

```
> par(mfrow=c(1,1))
> prp(dt.model.best, type=1, extra=3, varlen=0, faclen=0)
```

This gives us the following tree, and we can see that, using the priors, the only feature that is being used now out of the five features is account.balance and it has ignored all the other features. You can try and optimize the model further by using hyperparameter tuning by exploring the tune.rpart function from the e1071 package:

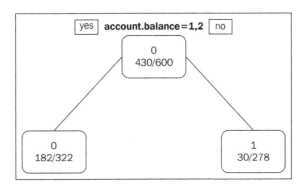

We finish our analysis by plotting some metric evaluation curves as follows:

```
> dt.predictions.best <- predict(dt.model.best, test.feature.vars,
                                 type="prob")
> dt.prediction.values <- dt.predictions.best[,2]
> predictions <- prediction(dt.prediction.values, test.class.var)
> par(mfrow=c(1,2))
> plot.roc.curve(predictions, title.text="DT ROC Curve")
> plot.pr.curve(predictions, title.text="DT Precision/Recall
            Curve")
```

The **AUC** is around **0.66**, which is not the best but definitely better than the baseline denoted by the red line in the following plot:

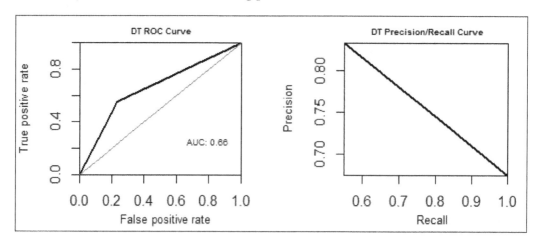

Based on our business requirements, this model is quite fair. We will discuss model comparison later on in this chapter. We will now use random forests to build our next set of predictive models.

Modeling using random forests

Random forests, also known as random decision forests, are a machine learning algorithm that comes from the family of ensemble learning algorithms. It is used for both regression and classification tasks. Random forests are nothing but a collection or ensemble of decision trees, hence the name.

The working of the algorithm can be described briefly as follows. At any point in time, each tree in the ensemble of decision trees is built from a bootstrap sample, which is basically sampling with replacement. This sampling is done on the training dataset. During the construction of the decision tree, the split which was earlier being chosen as the best split among all the features is not done anymore. Now the best split is always chosen from a random subset of the features each time. This introduction of randomness into the model increases the bias of the model slightly but decreases the variance of the model greatly which prevents the overfitting of models, which is a serious concern in the case of decision trees. Overall, this yields much better performing generalized models. We will now start our analytics pipeline by loading the necessary dependencies:

```
> library(randomForest) #rf model
> library(caret) # feature selection
```

```
> library(e1071) # model tuning
> library(ROCR) # model evaluation
> source("performance_plot_utils.R") # plot curves
> ## separate feature and class variables
> test.feature.vars <- test.data[,-1]
> test.class.var <- test.data[,1]
```

Next, we will build the initial training model with all the features as follows:

```
> formula.init <- "credit.rating ~ ."
> formula.init <- as.formula(formula.init)
> rf.model <- randomForest(formula.init, data = train.data,
                           importance=T, proximity=T)
```

You can view the model details by using the following code:

```
> print(rf.model)
```

Output:

```
No. of variables tried at each split: 4
        OOB estimate of  error rate: 23.67%
Confusion matrix:
    0   1 class.error
0 61 109  0.64117647
1 33 397  0.07674419
```

This gives us information about the **out of bag error (OOBE)**, which is around **23%**, and the confusion matrix which is calculated on the training data, and also how many variables it is using at each split.

Next, we will perform predictions using this model on the test data and evaluate them:

```
> rf.predictions <- predict(rf.model, test.feature.vars,
                            type="class")
> confusionMatrix(data=rf.predictions, reference=test.class.var,
                 positive="1")
```

The following output depicts that we get an overall **accuracy** of **73%**, **sensitivity** of **91%**, and **specificity** of **36%**:

```
              Reference
Prediction    0    1
         0   47   24
         1   83  246

                  Accuracy : 0.7325
                    95% CI : (0.6863, 0.7753)
       No Information Rate : 0.675
       P-Value [Acc > NIR] : 0.007434
                     Kappa : 0.309
    Mcnemar's Test P-Value : 2.058e-08
               Sensitivity : 0.9111
               Specificity : 0.3615
```

The initial model yields quite decent results. We see that a fair amount of bad credit rating customers are classified as bad and most of the good rating based customers are rated as good.

We will now build a new model with the top five features from the feature selection section, where we had used the random forest algorithm itself for getting the best features. The following code snippet builds the new model:

```
formula.new <- "credit.rating ~ account.balance + savings +
                        credit.amount +
                        credit.duration.months +
                        previous.credit.payment.status"
formula.new <- as.formula(formula.new)
rf.model.new <- randomForest(formula.new, data = train.data,
                    importance=T, proximity=T)
```

We now make predictions with this model on the test data and evaluate its performance as follows:

```
> rf.predictions.new <- predict(rf.model.new, test.feature.vars,
                        type="class")
> confusionMatrix(data=rf.predictions.new,   reference=test.class.var,
positive="1")
```

This gives us the following confusion matrix as the output with the other essential performance metrics:

```
              Reference
Prediction    0    1
        0    55   42
        1    75  228
                Accuracy : 0.7075
                  95% CI : (0.6602, 0.7517)
     No Information Rate : 0.675
     P-Value [Acc > NIR] : 0.090176
                   Kappa : 0.2864
 Mcnemar's Test P-Value : 0.003092
             Sensitivity : 0.8444
             Specificity : 0.4231
```

We get a slightly decreased **accuracy** of **71%**, which is obvious because we have eliminated many features, but now the **specificity** has increased to **42%**, which indicates it is able to classify more bad instances correctly as bad. **Sensitivity** has decreased slightly to **84%**. We will now use grid search to perform hyperparameter tuning on this model as follows, to see if we can improve the performance further. The parameters of interest here include ntree, indicating the number of trees, nodesize, indicating the minimum size of terminal nodes, and mtry, indicating the number of variables sampled randomly at each split.

```
nodesize.vals <- c(2, 3, 4, 5)
ntree.vals <- c(200, 500, 1000, 2000)
tuning.results <- tune.randomForest(formula.new,
                        data = train.data,
                        mtry=3,
                        nodesize=nodesize.vals,
                        ntree=ntree.vals)

print(tuning.results)
```

Output:

```
Parameter tuning of 'randomForest':
- sampling method: 10-fold cross validation
- best parameters:
 nodesize mtry ntree
        5    3   500
- best performance: 0.215
```

We now get the best model from the preceding grid search, perform predictions on the test data, and evaluate its performance with the following code snippet:

```
> rf.model.best <- tuning.results$best.model
> rf.predictions.best <- predict(rf.model.best, test.feature.vars,
                        type="class")
> confusionMatrix(data=rf.predictions.best,
                reference=test.class.var, positive="1")
```

We can make several observations from the following output. Performance has improved very negligibly as the overall **accuracy** remains the same at **71%** and **specificity** at **42%**. **Sensitivity** has increased slightly to **85%** from **84%**:

```
            Reference
Prediction   0   1
         0  55  41
         1  75 229

                Accuracy : 0.71
                  95% CI : (0.6628, 0.754)
    No Information Rate : 0.675
    P-Value [Acc > NIR] : 0.073747
                   Kappa : 0.291
 Mcnemar's Test P-Value : 0.002184
             Sensitivity : 0.8481
             Specificity : 0.4231
```

We now plot some performance curves for this model, as follows:

```
> rf.predictions.best <- predict(rf.model.best, test.feature.vars,
type="prob")
> rf.prediction.values <- rf.predictions.best[,2]
> predictions <- prediction(rf.prediction.values, test.class.var)
> par(mfrow=c(1,2))
> plot.roc.curve(predictions, title.text="RF ROC Curve")
> plot.pr.curve(predictions, title.text="RF Precision/Recall Curve")
```

We observe that the total **AUC** is about **0.7** and is much better than the red baseline **AUC** of **0.5** in the following plot:

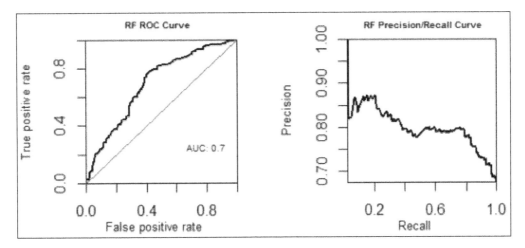

The last algorithm we will explore is neural networks and we will build our models using them in the following section.

Modeling using neural networks

Neural networks, or to be more specific in this case, artificial neural networks, is a family of machine learning models whose concepts are based on the working of biological neural networks, just like our nervous system. Neural networks have been there for a long time, but recently there has been an upsurge of interest in building highly intelligent systems using deep learning and artificial intelligence. Deep learning makes use of deep neural networks, which are essentially neural networks with a huge number of hidden layers between the input and output layers. A typical neural network can be visualized with the following figure:

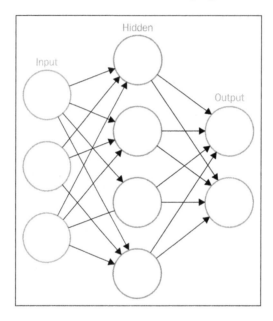

From the figure, you can deduce that this neural network is an interconnected network of various nodes, also called neurons. Each node represents a neuron which is nothing but a mathematical function. It is impossible to go into every detail of how to represent a node mathematically but we will give the gist here. These mathematical functions receive one or more inputs with weights, which are represented in the preceding figure as edges, and then it performs some computation on these inputs to give an output. Various popular functions used in these nodes include step function and the sigmoid function, which you have already seen in use in the logistic regression algorithm. Once the inputs are weighed and transformed by the function, the activation of these functions is sent to further nodes until it reaches the output layer. A collection of nodes form a layer, just like in the earlier figure, we have three layers.

So, a neural network depends on several neurons or nodes and the pattern of interconnection between them, the learning process that is used to update the weights of the connections at each iteration (popularly called as epoch), and the activation functions of the nodes that convert the node's inputs with weights to its output activation, which is passed layer by layer till we get the output prediction. We will start with loading the necessary dependencies as follows:

```
> library(caret) # nn models
> library(ROCR) # evaluate models
> source("performance_plot_utils.R") # plot curves
> # data transformation
> test.feature.vars <- test.data[,-1]
> test.class.var <- test.data[,1]
```

We will now have to do some feature value encoding, similar to what we did when we did AUC optimization for SVM. To refresh your memory, you can run the following code snippet:

```
> transformed.train <- train.data
> transformed.test <- test.data
> for (variable in categorical.vars){
+    new.train.var <- make.names(train.data[[variable]])
+    transformed.train[[variable]] <- new.train.var
+    new.test.var <- make.names(test.data[[variable]])
+    transformed.test[[variable]] <- new.test.var
+ }
> transformed.train <- to.factors(df=transformed.train,
variables=categorical.vars)
> transformed.test <- to.factors(df=transformed.test,
variables=categorical.vars)
> transformed.test.feature.vars <- transformed.test[,-1]
> transformed.test.class.var <- transformed.test[,1]
```

Once we have our data ready, we will build our initial neural network model using all the features as follows:

```
> formula.init <- "credit.rating ~ ."
> formula.init <- as.formula(formula.init)
> nn.model <- train(formula.init, data = transformed.train,
method="nnet")
```

The preceding code snippet might ask you to install the `nnet` package if you do not have it installed, so just select the option when it asks you and it will install it automatically and build the model. If it fails, you can install it separately and run the code again. Remember, it is an iterative process so the model building might take some time. Once the model converges, you can view the model details using the `print(nn.model)` command which will show several iteration results with different size and decay options, and you will see that it does hyperparameter tuning internally itself to try and get the best model!

We now perform predictions on the test data and evaluate the model performance as follows:

```
> nn.predictions <- predict(nn.model,
                     transformed.test.feature.vars, type="raw")
> confusionMatrix(data=nn.predictions,
                  reference=transformed.test.class.var,
                  positive="X1")
```

You can observe from the following output that our model has an **accuracy** of **72%**, which is quite good. It is predicting bad ratings as bad quite well, which is evident from the **specificity** which is **48%**, and as usual **sensitivity** is good at **84%**.

```
            Reference
Prediction   X0   X1
        X0   62   43
        X1   68  227

               Accuracy : 0.7225
                 95% CI : (0.6758, 0.7658)
    No Information Rate : 0.675
    P-Value [Acc > NIR] : 0.02302
                  Kappa : 0.3343
 Mcnemar's Test P-Value : 0.02273
            Sensitivity : 0.8407
            Specificity : 0.4769
```

We will now use the following code snippet to plot the features of importance for neural network based models:

```
> formula.init <- "credit.rating ~ ."
> formula.init <- as.formula(formula.init)
> control <- trainControl(method="repeatedcv", number=10, repeats=2)
> model <- train(formula.init, data=transformed.train, method="nnet",
                 trControl=control)
```

```
> importance <- varImp(model, scale=FALSE)
> plot(importance)
```

This gives us the following plot ranking variables according to their importance:

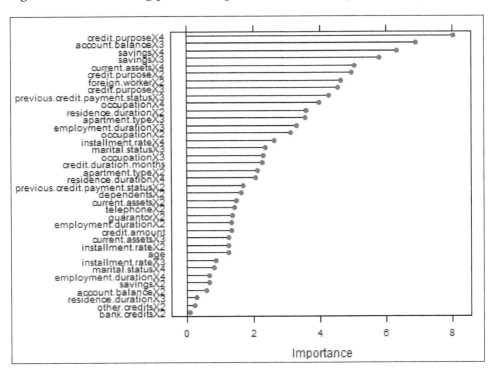

We select some of the most important features from the preceding plot and build our next model as follows:

```
> formula.new <- "credit.rating ~ account.balance + credit.purpose +
savings + current.assets +
foreign.worker + previous.credit.payment.status"
> formula.new <- as.formula(formula.new)
> nn.model.new <- train(formula.new, data=transformed.train,
method="nnet")
```

We now perform predictions on the test data and evaluate the model performance:

```
> nn.predictions.new <- predict(nn.model.new,
                    transformed.test.feature.vars,
                    type="raw")
```

```
> confusionMatrix(data=nn.predictions.new,
                  reference=transformed.test.class.var,
                  positive="X1")
```

This gives us the following confusion matrix with various metrics of our interest. We observe from the following output that the **accuracy** has increased slightly to **73%** and **sensitivity** has now increased to **87%** at the cost of **specificity**, which has dropped to **43%**:

```
              Reference
Prediction  X0   X1
        X0   56   34
        X1   74  236

                 Accuracy : 0.73
                   95% CI : (0.6836, 0.7729)
      No Information Rate : 0.675
      P-Value [Acc > NIR] : 0.0100321
                    Kappa : 0.3313
   Mcnemar's Test P-Value : 0.0001749
              Sensitivity : 0.8741
              Specificity : 0.4308
```

You can check the hyperparameter tuning which it has done internally, as follows:

```
> plot(nn.model.new, cex.lab=0.5)
```

The following plot shows the accuracy of the various models with different numbers of nodes in the hidden layer and the weight decay:

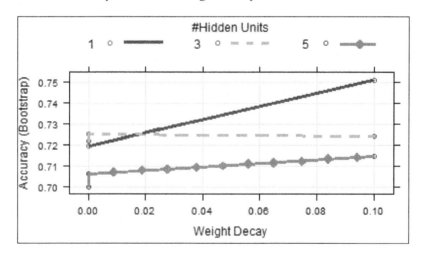

Based on our requirement that the bank makes minimum losses, we select the best model as the initial neural network model that was built, since it has an accuracy similar to the new model and its specificity is much higher which is extremely important. We now plot some performance curves for the best model as follows:

```
> nn.model.best <- nn.model
> nn.predictions.best <- predict(nn.model.best, transformed.test.feature.
vars, type="prob")
> nn.prediction.values <- nn.predictions.best[,2]
> predictions <- prediction(nn.prediction.values, test.class.var)
> par(mfrow=c(1,2))
> plot.roc.curve(predictions, title.text="NN ROC Curve")
> plot.pr.curve(predictions, title.text="NN Precision/Recall Curve")
```

We observe from the following plot that the **AUC** is **0.74**, which is quite good and performs a lot better than the baseline denoted in red:

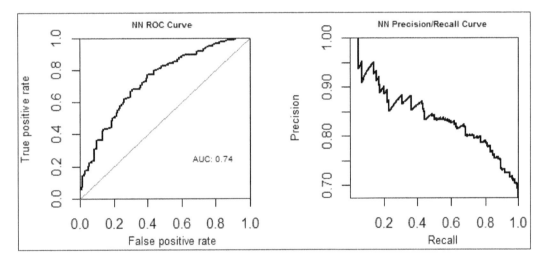

This concludes our predictive modeling session and we will wrap it up with model selection and comparisons.

Model comparison and selection

We have explored various machine learning techniques and built several models to predict the credit ratings of customers, so now comes the question of which model we should select and how the models compare against each other. Our test data has 130 instances of customers with a **bad credit rating** (0) and 270 customers with a **good credit rating** (1).

If you remember, earlier we had talked about using domain knowledge and business requirements after doing modeling to interpret results and make decisions. Right now, our decision is to choose the best model to maximize profits and minimize losses for the German bank. Let us consider the following conditions:

- If we incorrectly predict a customer with bad credit rating as good, the bank will end up losing the whole credit amount lent to him since he will default on the payment and so loss is 100%, which can be denoted as -1 for our ease of calculation.

- If we correctly predict a customer with bad credit rating as bad, we correctly deny him a credit loan and so there is neither any loss nor any profit.

- If we correctly predict a customer with good credit rating as good, we correctly give him the credit loan. Assuming the bank has an interest rate on the sum of money lent, let us assume the profit is 30% from the interest money that is paid back monthly by the customer. Therefore, profit is denoted as 30% or +0.3 for our ease of calculation.

- If we incorrectly predict a customer with good credit rating as bad, we incorrectly deny him the credit loan but there is neither any profit nor any loss involved in this case.

Keeping these conditions in mind, we will make a comparison table for the various models, including some of the metrics we had calculated earlier for the best model for each machine learning algorithm. Remember that considering all the model performance metrics and business requirements, there is no one model that is the best among them all. Each model has its own set of good performance points, which is evident in the following analysis:

	Logistic Regression	Support Vector Machines	Decision Trees	Random Forests	Neural Networks
Accuracy	71.75%	72.25%	62.25%	71%	72.25%
Sensitivity	83.30%	87.80%	55.20%	85%	84.10%
Specificity	47.70%	40%	77%	42.30%	47.70%
AUC	0.74	0.74	0.66	0.7	0.74
Profit	225 x 0.3 = 67.5	237 x 0.3 = 71.1	149 x 0.3 = 44.7	229 x 0.3 = 68.7	227 x 0.3 = 68.1
Loss	68 x (-1) = -68	78 x (-1) = -78	30 x (-1) = -30	75 x (-1) = -75	68 x (-1) = -68
Total gain	-0.5	-6.9	14.7	-6.3	0.1

Best Accuracy:	SVM, NN
Best Sensitivity:	SVM
Best Specificity:	DT
Best AUC:	LR, SVM, NN
Most Profit:	SVM
Least loss:	DT
Best Overall Gain:	DT

The cells highlighted in the preceding table show the best performance for that particular metric. As we mentioned earlier, there is no best model and we have listed down the models that have performed best against each metric. Considering the total overall gain, decision tree seems to be the model of choice. However, this is assuming that the credit loan amount requested is constant per customer. Remember that if each customer requests loans of different amounts then this notion of total gain cannot be compared because then the profit from one loan might be different to another and the loss incurred might be different on different loans. This analysis is a bit complex and out of the scope of this chapter, but we will mention briefly how this can be computed. If you remember, there is a `credit.amount` feature, which specifies the credit amount requested by the customer. Since we already have the customer numbers in the training data, we can aggregate the rated customers with their requested amount and sum up the ones for which losses and profits are incurred, and then we will get the total gain of the bank for each method!

Summary

We explored several important areas in the world of supervised learning in this chapter. If you have followed this chapter from the beginning of our journey and braved your way till the end, give yourself a pat on the back! You now know what constitutes predictive analytics and some of the important concepts associated with it. Also, we have seen how predictive modeling works and the full predictive analytics pipeline in actual practice. This will enable you to build your own predictive models in the future and start deriving valuable insights from model predictions. We also saw how to actually use models to make predictions and evaluate these predictions to test model performance so that we can optimize the models further and then select the best model based on metrics as well and business requirements. Before we conclude and you start your own journey into predictive analytics, I will like to mention that you should always remember Occam's razor, which states that *Among competing hypotheses, the one with the fewest assumptions should be selected,* which can be also interpreted as *Sometimes, the simplest solution is the best one.* Do not blindly jump into building predictive models with the latest packages and techniques, because first you need to understand the problem you are solving and then start from the simplest implementation, which will often lead to better results than most complex solutions.

7
Social Media Analysis – Analyzing Twitter Data

Connected is the word that describes life in the 21st century. Though various factors contribute to the term connected, there's one aspect which has played a pivotal role. It's called the Web. The Web, which has made distance an irrelevant metric and blurred socio-economic boundaries, is a world in itself and we all are a part of it. The Web or Internet in particular has been a central entity in this data-driven revolution. As we have seen in our previous chapters, for most modern day problems, it is the Web/Internet (henceforth used interchangeably) that acts as a source of data. Be it e-commerce platforms or financial domain, the Internet provides us with huge amounts of data every second. There's another ocean of data within this virtual world which touches our lives at a very personal level. Social networks, or social media, is a behemoth of information and the topic for this chapter.

In the previous chapter, we covered the financial domain, where we analyzed and predicted credit risk for customers of a certain bank. We now shift gears and move into the realm of social media and see how machine learning and R empower us to uncover insights from this ocean of data.

In this chapter, we will cover the following topics:

- Data mining specifics for social networks
- The importance and use of different data visualizations
- An overview of how to connect and collect Twitter data
- Utilizing Twitter data to uncover amazing insights
- Seeing how social networks pose new challenges to the data mining process

Social networks (Twitter)

We all use social networks day in and day out. There are numerous social networks catering to all sorts of ideologies and philosophies, but Facebook and Twitter (barring a couple more) have become synonymous with the term social network itself. These two social networks enjoy popularity not only because of their uniqueness and the quality of service but because of the way they enable us to interact in a very intuitive way. As we saw with recommendation engines used in e-commerce websites (see *Chapter 4, Building a Product Recommendation System*), social networks have existed long before Facebook, Twitter, or even the Internet.

Social networks have interested scientists and mathematicians alike. It is an interdisciplinary topic which spans but is not limited to sociology, psychology, biology, economics, communication studies, and information science. Various theories have been developed to analyze social networks and their impact on human lives in the form of factors influencing economics, demographics, health, language, literacy, crime, and more.

Studies done as early as the late 1800s form the basis of what we today refer to as social networks. A social network, as the word itself says, is a sort of connection/network between nodes or entities represented by humans and elements affecting social life. More formally, it is a network depicting relationships and interactions. Hence, it is not surprising to see various graph theories and algorithms being employed to understand social networks. Where the 19th and 20th centuries were limited to theoretical models and painstaking social experiments, the 21st century's technology has opened the doors for these theories to be tested, fine tuned, and modeled to help understand the dynamics of social interactions. Though testing these theories by some social networks (called social experiments) have been caught in controversies, such topics are beyond the scope of this book. We shall limit ourselves to the algorithmic/data science space and leave the controversies for the experts to discuss.

The Milgram Experiment, or the small world experiment, was conducted in the late 1960s to examine the average path length for people in United States. As part of this experiment, random people were selected as starting points of a mail chain. These random people were tasked to send the mail to the next person so that the mail gets one step closer to its destination (somewhere in Boston) and so on. An average of six hops to the destination is the documented result of this famous experiment. Urban folklore suggests the phrase *6 degrees of separation* originated from this experiment, even though Dr. Milgram never used the term himself! He conducted many more experiments; search and be amazed.

Source:

http://www.simplypsychology.org/milgram.html

Before we jump into the specifics, let us try and understand the reason behind choosing Twitter as our point of analysis for this and the upcoming chapter. Let us begin with understanding what Twitter is and why is it so popular with both end users and data scientists alike.

Twitter, as we all know, is a social network/micro-blogging service that enables its users to send and receive tweets of a maximum of 140 characters. But what makes Twitter so popular is the way it caters to the basic human instincts. We, humans, are curious creatures with an incessant need to be heard. It is important for us to have someone or some place to voice our opinions. We love to share our experiences, feats, failures, and ideas. At some level or other, we also want to know what our peers are up to, what's keeping celebrities busy, or simply what's on the news. Twitter addresses just that.

With multiple social networks existing long before Twitter came into existence, it wasn't some other service which Twitter replaced. In our view, it was the way Twitter organized the information and its users that clicked. Its unique *Follow* model of relationship caters to our hunger for curiosity, while its short, free, and high-speed communication platform enables the users to speak out and be heard globally. By allowing users to follow a person or an entity of interest, it enables us to keep up with their latest happenings without the other user following us back. The *Follow* model tips Twitter's relationships towards more of an interest graph rather than the friendship model usually found in social networks such as Facebook.

Twitter is known and used across the globe for the super-fast spread of information (and rumors). It has been innovatively used in certain circumstances unimaginable before, such as finding people in times of natural calamities such as earthquakes or typhoons. It has been used to spread information so far and deep that it takes viral proportions. The asymmetric relationships and high speed information exchange aid in making Twitter such a dynamic entity. If we closely analyze and study the data and dynamics of this social network we can uncover many insights. Hence, it is the topic for this chapter.

Interesting links:

https://www.technologyreview.com/s/419368/how-twitter-helps-in-a-disaster/

http://www.citylab.com/tech/2015/04/how-twitter-maps-can-be-useful-during-disasters/391436/

https://www.researchgate.net/publication/282150020_A_Systematic_Literature_Review_of_Twitter_Research_from_a_Socio-Political_Revolution_Perspective?channel=doi&linkId=56050b3f0 8ae5e8e3f3125cb&showFulltext=true

http://www.tandfonline.com/doi/abs/10.1080/136911 8X.2012.696123

http://www.psmag.com/nature-and-technology/how-to-use-social-media-usefully

Let's apply some data science to tweets using #RMachineLearningByExample!

Data mining @social networks

We have traveled quite a distance so far through the chapters of this book, understanding various concepts and learning some amazing algorithms. We have even worked on projects that have applications in our daily lives. In short, we have done data mining without using the term explicitly. Let us now take this opportunity to formally define data mining.

Mining, in the classical sense of the word, refers to the extraction of useful minerals from the Earth (such as coal mining). Put in the context of the information age, mining refers to the extraction of useful information from large pools of data. Thus, if we look carefully, **Knowledge Mining** or **Knowledge Discovery from Data (KDD)** seems to be a better representation than the term data mining. As is the case with many keywords, short and sweet catches the attention. Thus, you may find in many places the terms Knowledge Discovery from Data and data mining being used interchangeably, which is rightly so. The process of data mining, analogous to the mining of minerals, involves the following steps:

1. Data cleansing to remove noise and unwanted data

2. Data transformation to transform the data into relevant form for analysis

3. Data/pattern evaluation to uncover interesting insights

4. Data presentation to visualize knowledge in a useful form

Data mining isn't about using a search engine to get information, say regarding snakes. Rather it is about uncovering hidden insights like snakes are the only creatures found on every continent except Antarctica!

If we take a minute to understand the preceding steps, we can see that we used exactly the same process across our projects. Please keep in mind that we have simply formalized and presented the process we have been following across chapters and not missed or modified any step done in previous chapters.

Mining social network data

Now that we have formally defined data mining and seen the steps involved in transforming data to knowledge, let us focus on data from social networks. While data mining methodology is independent of the source of data, there are certain things to be kept in mind which could lead to better processing and improved results.

Like the mining of any other type of data, domain knowledge is definitely a plus for mining social network data. Even though social network analysis is an interdisciplinary subject (as discussed in the previous section), it primarily involves the analysis of data pertaining to users or entities and their interactions.

In previous chapters, we have seen all sorts of data from e-commerce platforms to banks to data related to the characteristics of flowers. The data we have seen has had different attributes and characteristics. But if we look carefully, the data was a result of some sort of measurement or event capture.

Coming onto the social network's domain, the playground is a little, if not completely different. Unlike what we have seen so far, data from social media platforms is extremely dynamic. When we say dynamic, we refer to the actual content on a data point and not its structure. The data point itself may (or may not) be structured, but the content itself is not.

Let us be specific and talk about data contained in a tweet. A sample tweet looks something like this:

President Obama @POTUS · 26 Dec 2015

From the Obama family to yours, Merry Christmas! And a special thank you to all our men and women in uniform this holiday season.

 8.2K   30K   ● ● ●

Image source: `https://twitter.com/POTUS/status/680464195993911296`

A tweet, as we all know, is a 140 character message. Since the message is generated by a user (usually), the actual message may be of a different length, language, and or it may contain images, links, videos, and more. Thus, a tweet is a structured data point which contains the handle of the user (`@POTUS`), the name of the user (`President Obama`), the message (`From the Obama family...`), along with information related to when was it tweeted (`26 Dec 2015`), the number of likes, and the number of retweets. A tweet may also contain hashtags, hyperlinks, images, and videos embedded within the message. As we will see in the coming sections, a tweet contains tons of metadata (data about the data) apart from the attributes discussed preceding. Similarly, data from other social networks also contains a lot more information than what usually meets the eye.

This much information from a single tweet coupled with millions of users tweeting frantically every second across the globe presents a huge amount of data with interesting patterns waiting to be discovered.

In its true sense, Twitter's data (and of social networks in general) represents the 3 Vs (Volume, Variety, and Velocity) of big data very well.

143,199 tweets per second is a record achieved during the airing of the film Castle in the Sky in Japan on August 3, 2013. The average tweets per second is usually around 5700; the record multiplied it 25 times! Read more about it on the Twitter blog: `https://blog.twitter.com/2013/new-tweets-per-second-record-and-how`

Thus, the mining of data from a social network involves understanding the structure of the data point, the underlying philosophy or use of the social network (Twitter is used for quick exchange of information, while LinkedIn is used for professional networking), the velocity and volume of the data being generated, along with the thinking cap of a data scientist.

Towards the end of the chapter, we will also touch upon the challenges presented by social networks to the usual mining methodology.

Data and visualization

When the amount of data is growing exponentially every passing minute, the outcome of data mining activity must empower decision-makers to quickly identify action points. The outcome should be free of noise/excess information, yet be crisp and complete enough to be useable.

This unique challenge of presenting information in its most convenient and useable form for easy consumption by its intended audience (which may be nontechnical) is an important aspect of the data mining process. So far in this book, we have analyzed data and made use of line graphs, bar graphs, histograms, and scatter plots to uncover and present insights. Before we make use of these and a few more visualizations/graphs in this chapter as well, let us try and understand their importance and use them wisely.

While working on a data mining assignment, we usually get so engrossed in the data, its complexities, algorithms, and whatnot, that we tend to overlook the part where we have to make the outcome consumable rather than a difficult to read sheet of numbers and jargon. Apart from making sure that the final report/document contains the correct and verified figures, we also need to make sure that the figures are presented in such a manner that it is easy for the end user to make use of it. To enable easy consumption of this information/knowledge, we take the help of different visualizations.

Since this isn't a book on visualizations, we've taken the liberty of skipping the usual line graphs, bar graphs, pie charts, histograms, and other details. Let us understand some unconventional yet widely known/used visualizations before we use them in the coming sections.

Word clouds

Social networks generate data in different forms and formats. The data on such platforms may be created, shared, modified, quoted, or used in various different ways. To represent complex relationships, one of the most widely used visualizations for social network data are **tag clouds** or **word clouds**. For example, objects such as text, images, videos, and blogs on these platforms are frequently tagged. Thus, a tag cloud/word cloud represents statistics of user-generated tags. These tags may represent the relative frequency of the use of words or their presence in multiple objects. The words/tags are differentiated using different font sizes and colors to represent the statistic of choice (mostly frequency).

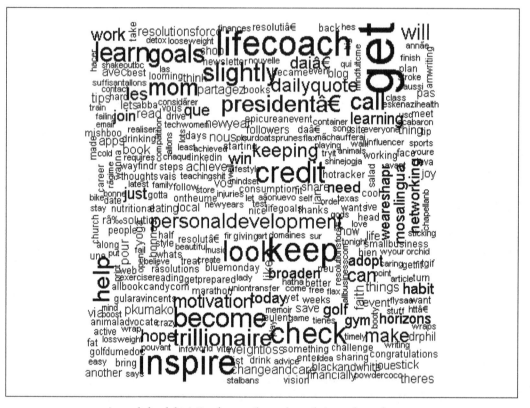

A word cloud depicting frequently used words in a subset of tweets

Treemaps

To represent data of high dimensionality, it is usually not possible to visualize all dimensions at the same time. Treemaps are one such type of visualization that partition all dimensions into subsets and present them in a hierarchical manner. Specifically, treemaps partition dimensions into a set of nested rectangles. One of the mostly widely cited examples of a treemap is the newsmap, which visualizes news aggregated by Google news and displays it in different categories shown by different colors; color gradients denote the appearance of the article (on a time scale), while the size of the rectangle denotes the popularity of the news item.

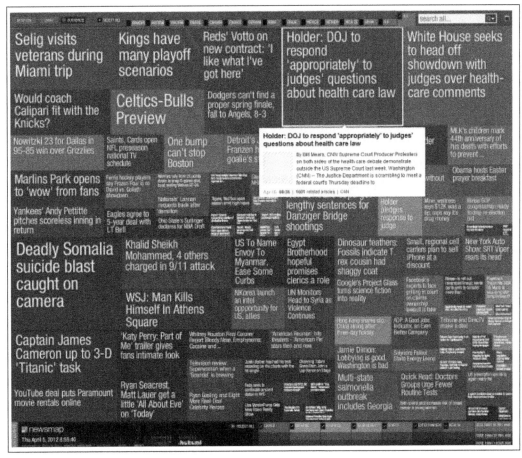

Treemap showing news aggregated by Google News

Image source: http://newsmap.jp/

Pixel-oriented maps

Visualizations not only make outcomes easier to understand, they are very utilitarian as well. Most of the time, the outcome of an analysis process is multidimensional. To represent this data graphically on a two dimensional screen/piece of paper is a challenge. This is where pixel-oriented visualizations come into the picture. For an *n-dimensional* data set, pixel-oriented visualizations map each *n-dimensional* data point to a single pixel in *n* different sub-windows. Thus, each data point is split across *n* windows, one for each dimension. These help us map a large amount of data in single visualization. Pixel-oriented visualization look like this:

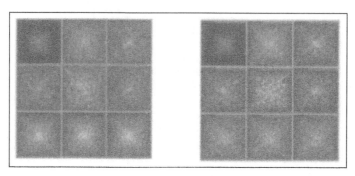

Sample pixel-oriented maps
Image source: http://bib.dbvis.de/uploadedFiles/163.pdf

Other visualizations

Apart from the already mentioned visualizations, there are many other interesting visualizations, which come in handy for different use cases. For example, visualizations such as box plots come in handy for understanding data distribution and outlier detection. Similarly, there are visualizations such as Chernoff faces, scatter plots, network graphs, and so on which have their own merits and use cases.

Please do note that visualization is in itself a field of study and this section is merely trying to touch the tip of the iceberg. We urge readers to go through books/online content as shared in the *References* section of the chapter to read more on this.

Getting started with Twitter APIs

Twitter is as much a delight for tweeple (people using Twitter to tweet) as it is for data scientists. The APIs and the documentation are well updated and easy to use. Let us get started with the APIs.

Overview

Twitter has one of easiest yet most powerful set of APIs available of any social network out there. These APIs have been used by Twitter itself and data scientists to understand the dynamics of the Twitter world. Twitter APIs make use of four different objects, namely:

- **Tweets**: A tweet is the central entity that defines Twitter itself. As discussed in the previous section, a tweet contains far more information (metadata) than just the content/message of the tweet.

- **Users**: Anybody or anything that can tweet, follow, or perform any of Twitter's actions is a user. Twitter is unique in its definition of user, which need not necessarily be a human. @MarsCuriosity is one such nonhuman popular Twitter handle with over 2 million followers!

- **Entities**: These are structured pieces of information extracted from the tweet object itself. These may include information on URLs, hashtags, user mentions, and so on. These objects enable quicker processing without parsing the tweet text.

- **Places**: A tweet may also have location attached to it. This information may be used for various purposes, such as displaying *Trending Topics Near You* or targeted marketing.

The preceding objects from the Twitter APIs have been explained at length on the website https://dev.twitter.com/. We urge readers to go through it to understand the objects and APIs even better.

Twitter has libraries available in all major programming languages/platforms. We will be making use of TwitteR, that is, Twitter's library for R.

Twitter Best Practices

Twitter has a set of *best practices* and a list of dos and don'ts specified clearly on its developer site, https://dev.twitter.com/, which talks about security/authentication, privacy, and more. Since Twitter supports a huge customer base with high availability, it tracks the usage of its APIs as well to keep its systems healthy. There is a defined rate limit on the number of times their APIs are queried. Kindly go through the best practices and be a #gooddeveloper!

Registering the application

Now that we have enough background about Twitter and its API objects, let us get our hands dirty. The first step when starting to use the APIs is to inform Twitter about your application. Twitter uses the standard **Open Authentication (OAuth)** protocol for authorizing a third party app. OAuth uses an application's consumer key, consumer secret, access token, and access token secret to allow it to use APIs and data of the connected service.

The following quick steps will set us up for the game:

1. Go to Twitter's Application Management Console at `https://apps.twitter.com/` and log in with your credentials or create an account if you don't have one.

2. Click on **Create New App** and fill in the details for the app's name, website, and so on. For our purposes, we will name our app `TwitterAnalysis_rmre`. For callback URL use `http://127.0.0.1:1410` to point back to your local system. You may choose any other port number as well.

3. Click on **Create your Twitter Application** to complete the process. Your Application Management Console would look like the following screenshot:

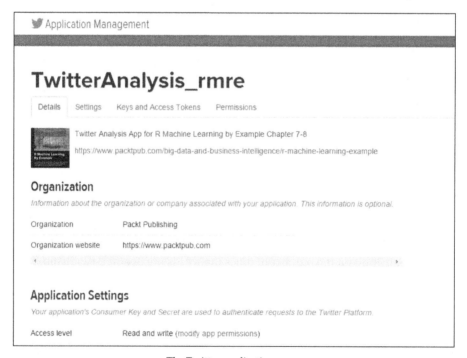

The Twitter application page

Congratulations, your app is created and registered with Twitter. But before we can use it, there's one more piece to it. We need to create access tokens, and to do that we perform the following steps.

1. Go to the link **Keys and Access Tokens** on the Twitter app's details page.

2. Scroll down and click on **Create My Access Token** to generate an access token for your profile.

3. The **Keys and Access Tokens** page looks like the following screenshot after completing the preceding steps:

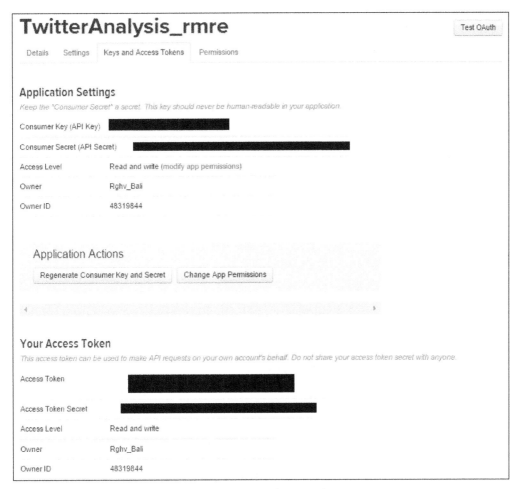

Application keys and access tokens

We will be using the same application for this as well as in the coming chapter. Make a note of the consumer key, consumer secret, access token and access secret; we will need these in our application.

 The keys and secrets generated for OAuth are sensitive pieces of information. They enable access for your app to Twitter's data. Please keep them as safe as you would keep your passwords (even safer than that). #SafetyFirst.

Connect/authenticate

Now that we have everything ready at Twitter's end, let us set things up at R's end as well. Before we start playing with the data from Twitter, the first step would be to connect and authenticate ourselves through the app we just created using R.

We will make use of R's TwitteR library by Jeff Gentry. This library or client allows us to use Twitter's web APIs through R. We will use the method setup_twitter_oauth() to connect to Twitter using our app's credentials (keys and access tokens). Kindly replace xxxx in the following code with your access keys/tokens generated in the previous step:

```
> # load library
> library(twitteR)
> # set credentials
> consumerSecret = "XXXXXXXXXXXXX"
> consumerKey = "XXXXXXXXXXXXXXXXXXXXXXXXXXx"
```

Upon executing the preceding snippet of code, it will prompt you to use a local file to cache credentials or not. For now, we will say No to it:

```
[1] "Using browser based authentication"
Use a local file to cache OAuth access credentials between R sessions?
1: Yes
2: No

Selection:
```

This will open up your browser and ask you to log in using your Twitter credentials and authorize this app, as shown in the following screenshot:

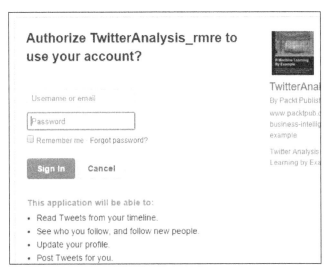

Authorize app to fetch data

Once authorized, the browser will be redirected to the callback URL we mentioned when we created the app on Twitter. You may use a more informative URL for the user as well.

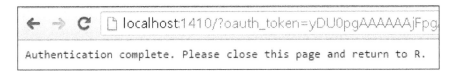

Congratulations, you are now connected to the ocean of tweets.

Extracting sample tweets

Now that we are connected to Twitter using R, it's time to extract some latest tweets and analyze what we get. To extract tweets, we will use the handle for Twitter's account 001 (Twitter's founder and first user), Jack Dorsey, @jack. The following snippet of code extracts the latest 300 tweets from him:

```
> twitterUser <- getUser("jack")
> # extract jack's tweets
> tweets <- userTimeline(twitterUser, n = 300)
> tweets
```

The output contains text combined with unprintable characters and URLs due to Twitter's content-rich data. We will look at the metadata of a tweet in a bit, but before that, the extracted information looks like this:

```
[[1]]
[1] "jack: \xed��\xed�\u0099@KillerMike Represents @BernieSanders in Post-Debate Spin Room /@p
itchfork  https://t.co/60sdEhZ18f"

[[2]]
[1] "jack: The @NBA goes all-in for MLK Day tribute with impact /@USATODAY  https://t.co/SF068gs
fUk"

[[3]]
[1] "jack: \"The time is always right to do what's right.\" https://t.co/V0fIveLpY8"
```

Sample tweets

To see the attributes and functions available to analyze and manipulate each tweet, use the getClass method as follows:

```
> # get tweet attributes
> tweets[[1]]$getClass()
>
> # get retweets count
> tweets[[1]]$retweetCount
>
> # get favourite count
> tweets[[1]]$favoriteCount
```

The following output will be generated:

```
> # get tweet attributes
> tweets[[1]]$getClass()
Reference Class "status":

Class fields:

Name:        text      favorited favoriteCount    replyToSN     created    truncated    replyToSID            id
Class:  character        logical       numeric    character      POSIXct      logical    character     character

Name: replyToUID statusSource    screenName  retweetCount   isRetweet    retweeted    longitude      latitude
Class:  character   character     character       numeric     logical      logical    character     character

Name:        urls
Class: data.frame

Class Methods:
    "setUrls", "getRetweets", "getRefClass", "getUrls", "setTruncated", "setText", "getReplyToSID", "getText", "export",
    "setCreated", "setFavoriteCount", "getCreated", "initialize", "callSuper", "getRetweeters", "initFields", "getClass",
    "setReplyToUID", "import", "setLatitude", "setIsRetweet", "getFavoriteCount", "getRetweetCount", "getIsRetweet", "setId",
    "setScreenName", "getLatitude", "getScreenName", "toDataFrame#twitterobj", "setRetweetCount", "setReplyToSID", "getId",
    "getReplyToUID", "setFavorited", "getRetweeted", "getFavorited", "toDataFrame", "setStatusSource", "setReplyToSN", "copy",
    "usingMethods", "setRetweeted", "field", ".objectParent", "getTruncated", "untrace", "trace", "setLongitude",
    "getStatusSource", "getStatusSource", ".objectPackage", "getReplyToSN", "show"

Reference Superclasses:
    "twitterobj", "envRefClass"

> # get retweets count
> tweets[[1]]$retweetCount
[1] 21
> # get favourite count
> tweets[[1]]$favoriteCount
[1] 47
```

Twitter data mining

Now that we have tested our tools, libraries, and connections to Twitter APIs, the time has come to begin our search for the hidden treasures in Twitter land. Let's wear our data miner's cap and start digging!

In this section, we will be working on Twitter data gathered from searching keywords (or hashtags in Twitter vocabulary) and user timelines. Using this data, we will be uncovering some interesting insights while using different functions and utilities from TwitteR and other R packages.

Please note that our process will implicitly follow the steps outlined for data mining. In the spirit of brevity, we might take the liberty to not mention each of the steps explicitly. We are mining for some *gold-plated* insights; rest assured nothing is skipped!

Every year, we begin with a new zeal to achieve great feats and improve upon our shortcomings. Most of us make promises to ourselves in the form of New Year's resolutions. Let us explore what tweeple are doing with their resolutions in 2016!

Note: Twitter data changes very rapidly and your results/plots may vary from the ones depicted in this chapter.

We will use the same app and its credentials to connect and tap into Twitter for data. The following code works in exactly the same way that we extracted sample tweets in the previous section:

```
library(twitteR)
library(ggplot2)
library(stringr)
library(tm)
library(wordcloud)


consumerSecret = "XXXXXXXXX"
consumerKey = "XXXXXXXXXXXXXXXXXXXXXXXXXXXXXXX"


setup_twitter_oauth(consumer_key = consumerKey,consumer_secret =
consumerSecret)
```

Apart from connecting to Twitter, we have also loaded required packages, such as `ggplot`, `stringr`, `tm`, and `wordcloud`. We will see where and how these packages are useful as we proceed.

Once connected to our data source, we can proceed towards collecting the required data. Since we are planning to learn about tweeple and their New Year's resolutions, we will extract data for the hashtag `#ResolutionsFor2016`. We can also use any hashtag, such as `#NewYearResolutions`, `#2016Resolutions`, or a combination of hashtags to get relevant tweets. The following piece of code not only extracts tweets, but also converts the list of tweet/status objects into an R data frame. We also convert each of the tweets to UTF-8 to handle text from different languages.

> **Amazing fact**: Twitter is available in 48 different languages and counting!

```
# trending tweets

trendingTweets = searchTwitter("#ResolutionsFor2016",n=1000)

trendingTweets.df = twListToDF(trendingTweets)

trendingTweets.df$text <- sapply(trendingTweets.df$text,function(x)
iconv(x,to='UTF-8'))
```

As we saw in the previous section, a tweet contains far more information than mere text. One of the various attributes is the status source. The status source denotes the device from where the tweet was made. It may be a mobile phone, tablet, and so on. Before we apply major transformations and clean up tweet objects, we apply a quick transformation to transform status source to meaningful form:

```
trendingTweets.df$tweetSource = sapply(trendingTweets.df$statusSource,fun
ction(sourceSystem) enodeSource(sourceSystem))
```

The preceding code transforms `statusSource` from values such as `<a href=\"http://twitter.com/download/android\" rel=\"nofollow\">Twitter for Android</a>` to simply Android and assigns it to a new attribute named `tweetSource`.

Once we have the data, the next set of steps in the data mining process is to clean up the data. We use the text mining package `tm` to perform transformation and cleanup. The `Corpus` function in particular helps us handle tweet/status objects as a collection of documents. We then use the `tm_map` utility from the same package to apply/map transformations such as converting all text to lower case, removing punctuation, numbers, and stop words. Stop words is a list of the most commonly used words, such as a, an, the, and so on, which can safely be removed while analyzing text without loss of meaning.

```
# transformations
tweetCorpus <- Corpus(VectorSource(trendingTweets.df$text))
tweetCorpus <- tm_map(tweetCorpus, tolower)
tweetCorpus <- tm_map(tweetCorpus, removePunctuation)
tweetCorpus <- tm_map(tweetCorpus, removeNumbers)


# remove URLs
removeURL <- function(x) gsub("http[[:alnum:]]*", "", x)
tweetCorpus <- tm_map(tweetCorpus, removeURL)


# remove stop words
twtrStopWords <- c(stopwords("english"),'resolution','resolutions',
'resolutionsfor','resolutionsfor2016','2016','new','year','years',
'newyearresolution')
tweetCorpus <- tm_map(tweetCorpus, removeWords, twtrStopWords)


tweetCorpus <- tm_map(tweetCorpus, PlainTextDocument)
```

The final transformation before we proceed to the next step of analyzing our data for hidden patterns/insights is a term-document matrix. As the name itself says, a term-document matrix is a matrix representation in which terms act as rows while columns are represented by documents. Each entry in this matrix represents the number of occurrences of a term in a given document. More formally, a term-document matrix is a matrix representation that describes the frequency of terms in a collection of documents. This representation is extremely useful in natural language processing applications. It is an optimized data structure that enables quick searches, topical modeling, and more. The data structure can be explained using the following simple example where we have two text documents, **TD1** and **TD2**:

TD1:	I tweet all the time!	
TD2:	I rarely tweet.	
	TD1	TD2
tweet	1	1
all	1	0
time	1	0
rarely	0	1

Sample term-document matrix

The tm package provides us another easy-to-use utility called term-document matrix (TermDocumentMatrix is also available), which we use to convert our Corpus object into the required form:

```
# Term Document Matrix

> twtrTermDocMatrix <- TermDocumentMatrix(tweetCorpus, control =
list(minWordLength = 1))
```

Frequent words and associations

The term-document matrix thus prepared contains words from each of the tweets (post the cleanup and transformations) as rows, while columns represent the tweet themselves.

As a quick check, let us see which of the words are most frequently used in our dataset. Let the threshold be set to 30 occurrences or more. We use the apply utility to iterate each term in our term-document matrix and sum its occurrences. The function helps us filter out the terms that have appeared 30 times or more.

```
# Terms occuring in more than 30 times
> which(apply(twtrTermDocMatrix,1,sum)>=30)
```

The result will be as shown in the following screenshot:

```
> which(apply(twtrTermDocMatrix,1,sum)>=30)
                    amp              check             credit
                     66                297                406
              dailymojo                get            healthy
                    425                710                806
                inspire               keep               less
                    901                962               1005
              lifecoach               look   motivationquotes
                   1014               1042               1182
newyearsresolutioninwords   notebkblogairy                one
                   1229               1246               1281
             positivity            swagger
                   1417               1807
```

Terms with 30 or more occurrences across tweets

As the preceding screenshot shows, words such as healthy, inspire, and positivity feature in the list of words with 30 or more occurrences. We all have a lot in common when it comes to yearly goals, no?

The preceding manipulation was a quick check to see if we really have tweets that help us find out something interesting about New Year's resolutions. Let us now take a formal approach and identify frequent terms in our data set. We will also try and present the information in a creative yet easy-to-understand representation. To get the most frequent terms in our data set, we use the function findFreqTerms from the tm package again. This function provides us an abstraction over quick hacks, such as the one we previously used. findFreqTerms also lets us set a minimum and maximum threshold for term frequencies. For our case, we will only mention the lower bound and see the results:

```
# print the frequent terms from termdocmatrix
> (frequentTerms<-findFreqTerms(twtrTermDocMatrix,lowfreq = 10))
```

The results look something like the following screenshot:

```
> (frequentTerms<-findFreqTerms(twtrTermDocMatrix,lowfreq = 10))
  [1] "adopt"                       "already"              "amp"
  [4] "avec"                        "become"               "book"
  [7] "broaden"                     "business"             "call"
 [10] "can"                         "cest"                 "change"
 [13] "check"                       "credit"               "crochet"
 [16] "daiâ€"                       "dailymojo"            "dailyquote"
 [19] "danisnotonfire"             "day"                  "decided"
 [22] "des"                         "diet"                 "digitalwomen"
 [25] "dont"                        "elected"              "end"
 [28] "faith"                       "femticdev"            "find"
 [31] "first"                       "fitness"              "forward"
 [34] "get"                         "give"                 "goal"
 [37] "goals"                       "going"                "golf"
 [40] "gym"                         "habit"                "happy"
 [43] "health"                      "healthy"              "healthyliving"
 [46] "help"                        "hope"                 "horizons"
 [49] "include"                     "infographic"          "inspire"
 [52] "interesting"                 "january"              "join"
 [55] "just"                        "keep"                 "keeping"
 [58] "language"                    "learn"                "learning"
 [61] "les"                         "less"                 "lifecoach"
 [64] "like"                        "look"                 "make"
 [67] "mishacollins"               "mom"                  "mosalingua"
 [70] "motivation"                  "motivationquotes"     "narechh"
 [73] "need"                        "networking"           "newyear"
 [76] "newyearsresolutioninwords"  "noellbernard"         "notebkblogairy"
 [79] "nous"                        "one"                  "personaldevelopment"
 [82] "positivity"                  "post"                 "presidentâ€"
 [85] "que"                         "slightly"             "start"
 [88] "started"                     "still"                "success"
 [91] "swagger"                     "things"               "time"
 [94] "tips"                        "today"                "trillionaire"
 [97] "try"                         "tweet"                "via"
[100] "vos"                         "way"                  "weareshapr"
[103] "week"                        "wellcrafted"          "will"
[106] "win"                         "work"
```

We get about 107 terms with a minimum occurrence of 10. If you look carefully, the terms we saw with frequencies of at least 30 also appear in this list, and rightly so.

Now that we are certain that there are terms/words with occurrences of more than 10, let us create a data frame and plot the terms versus their frequencies as we decided previously. We use the rowSums function to calculate the total occurrence of each term/word. We then pick a subset of terms which have more than 10 occurrences and plot them using ggplot:

```
# calculate frequency of each term
term.freq <- rowSums(as.matrix(twtrTermDocMatrix))


# picking only a subset
subsetterm.freq <- subset(term.freq, term.freq >= 10)



# create data frame from subset of terms
frequentTermsSubsetDF <- data.frame(term = names(subsetterm.freq), freq =
subsetterm.freq)


# create data frame with all terms
frequentTermsDF <- data.frame(term = names(term.freq), freq = term.freq)


# sort by subset DataFrame frequency
frequentTermsSubsetDF <- frequentTermsSubsetDF[with(frequentTermsSubset
DF, order(-frequentTermsSubsetDF$freq)), ]


# sort by complete DataFrame frequency
frequentTermsDF <- frequentTermsDF[with(frequentTermsDF, order(-
frequentTermsDF$freq)), ]


# words by frequency from subset data frame
ggplot(frequentTermsSubsetDF, aes(x = reorder(term,freq), y = freq)) +
geom_bar(stat = "identity") +xlab("Terms") + ylab("Frequency") + coord_
flip()
```

The preceding piece of code generates the following frequency graph:

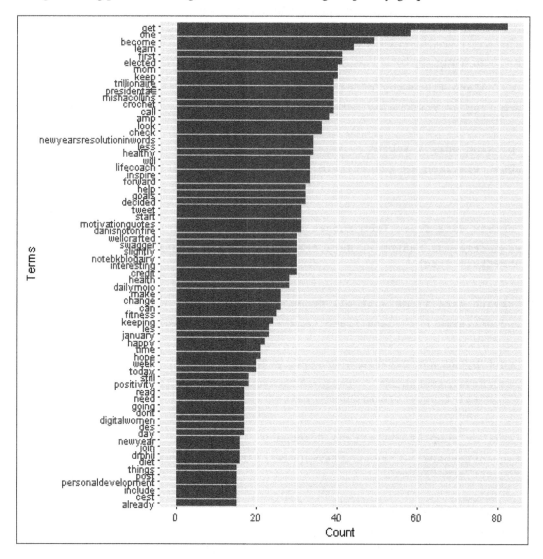

Upon analyzing the preceding graph, we can quickly get some interesting points:

- The words **mom**, **elected**, **president**, and **trillionaire** feature in the top 10. Strange set, yet interesting. More on this in a bit.

- Health features high in the list, but doesn't make it to the top 10. So, it seems like health is on the cards but not very high. This is the same for **fitness** and **diet**.

- Most of the words in this list are positive in essence. Words such as **happy**, **hope**, **positivity**, **change**, and so on all point to the upbeat mood while taking up New Year's resolutions!

Though the preceding graph gives us quite a lot of information regarding the words and their frequencies in a nice layout, it still doesn't show us the full picture. Remember that we crafted a subset of items from our data set before generating this graph? We did that on purpose, otherwise the graph would have become too long and words with lesser frequencies would clutter the whole thing. Another point which this graph misses out is the relative difference in the frequencies.

If our aim is to see the relative difference between the frequencies, we need a different visualization altogether. Here comes word cloud to the rescue. Using the `wordcloud` library, we can easily generate word clouds from a dataframe using a one liner:

```
# wordcloud
> wordcloud(words=frequentTermsDF$term, freq=frequentTermsDF$freq,random.
order=FALSE)
```

The wordcloud using the complete data frame looks something like this:

The preceding word cloud renders words in decreasing order of frequency. The size of each word emphasizes its frequency. You can play around with the `wordcloud` function to generate some interesting visualizations or even art!

A lot of words appear in the preceding graphs, but isn't it rather interesting to see the word trillionaire pop up in the top 10? What could be the reason for it? Was it a spam post by a bot, or a tweet by some celebrity that went viral, or something completely different altogether? Let's check out the top tweet in this list and see if it contains the word trillionaire:

```
# top retweets
> head(subset(trendingTweets.df$text, grepl("trillionaire",trendingTwee
ts.df$text) ),n=1)
```

The following screenshot is what you get:

```
> head(subset(trendingTweets.df$text, grepl("trillionaire",trendingTweets.df$text) ),n=1)
[1] "RT @mishacollins: my #ResolutionsFor2016: 1-call my mom more. 2-learn to crochet. 3-Become the first
trillionaire. 4-Get elected President.â€¦"
```

It turns out that our hunch was right. It was a New Year resolution tweet by a celebrity that went viral. A quick search on Twitter reveals the tweet:

Image source: `https://twitter.com/mishacollins?lang=en`

A bit further searching reveals Misha Collins is a famous actor from the television series Supernatural. We can also see that the above resolution was retweeted a staggering 5k times! It's interesting to note that the number of likes is 14k, outnumbering the retweets. Can we infer that tweeple prefer likes/hearts to retweets? It can also be seen that words such as mom, learn, trillionaire, elected, and President all occur as most frequent words without a doubt. Indirectly, we can also infer that Supernatural has a huge fan following on Twitter and that Castiel (Misha's role in the TV series) is a popular character from the show. A bit of a surprise is his resolution to learn to crochet, no?

Moving on from supernatural stuff, let us go back to the fitness debate. Fitness is important to most of us. Activities such as exercising or hitting the gym see a surge during the initial months/weeks of the year. Let's see how health-conscious our friends on Twitter are!

Since a lot of words such as health, diet, fitness, gym, and so on point towards a healthy lifestyle, let us try and find words associated with the word *fitness* itself. `findAssocs` is a handy function which helps us find words from a term-document matrix that have at least a specified level of correlation to a given word. We will use the output from this function to prepare a term-association (correlation) graph using `ggplot`. The process is similar to how we prepared the preceding frequency graph:

```
# Associatons
(fitness.associations <- findAssocs(twtrTermDocMatrix,"fitness",0.25))


fitnessTerm.freq <- rowSums(as.matrix(fitness.associations$fitness))


fitnessDF <- data.frame(term=names(fitnessTerm.freq),freq=fitnessTerm.freq)

fitnessDF <- fitnessDF[with(fitnessDF, order(-fitnessDF$freq)), ]
ggplot(fitnessDF,aes(x=reorder(term,freq),y=freq))
+geom_bar(stat = "identity") +xlab("Terms")
+ ylab("Associations")
+ coord_flip()
```

The words most closely correlated to the word fitness are as follows:

```
$fitness
   lossweight          getfit       workout   blogsretweet fredericksburg  fridayfeeling
         0.39            0.34          0.34           0.32           0.32           0.32
         fxbg       lbloggers solluswellness      yogavideos     meditation
         0.32            0.32          0.32           0.32           0.26
```

The same data is more readable in graphical form, as follows:

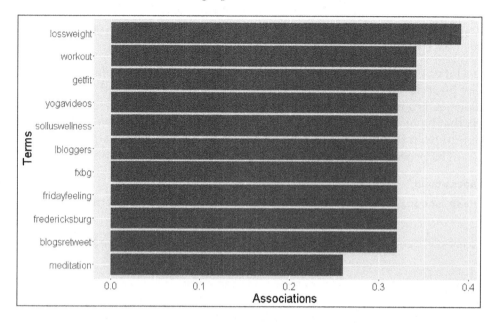

As evident from the preceding graph, terms such as **lossweight**, **workout**, **getfit**, and so on. prove our point that tweeple are as concerned about health as we are. It is interesting to note the occurrence of the term *yogavideos* in this list. It looks like yoga is catching up with other techniques of staying fit in 2016. There's **meditation** on the list too.

Popular devices

So far, we have dealt with the visible components of a tweet, such as the text, retweet counts, and so on, and we were able to extract many interesting insights. Let us take out our precision tools and dig deeper into our data.

As mentioned a couple times in the above sections, a tweet has far more information than what meets the eye. One such piece of information is about the source of the tweet. Twitter was born of the SMS era, and many of its characteristics, such as the 140 character word limit, are reminiscent of that era. It would be interesting to see how tweeple use Twitter, that is, what devices are used to access and post on Twitter frequently. Though the world has moved a long way from the SMS era, mobile phones are ubiquitous. To get this information, we will make use of the attribute `tweetSource` from our dataframe `trendingTweets.df`. We created this additional attribute from the `statusSource` attribute already existing in the `tweet` object (see the beginning of this section for a quick recap).

We shall use a subset of the data frame `trendingTweets.df` based upon retweet counts for the sake of clarity. We will use `ggplot` again to visualize our results.

```
# Source by retweet count
trendingTweetsSubset.df <- subset(trendingTweets.df, trendingTweets.
df$retweetCount >= 5000 )


ggplot(trendingTweetsSubset.df, aes(x =tweetSource, y =retweetCount/100))
+ geom_bar(stat = "identity") +xlab("Source") + ylab("Retweet Count")
```

The following plot is your result:

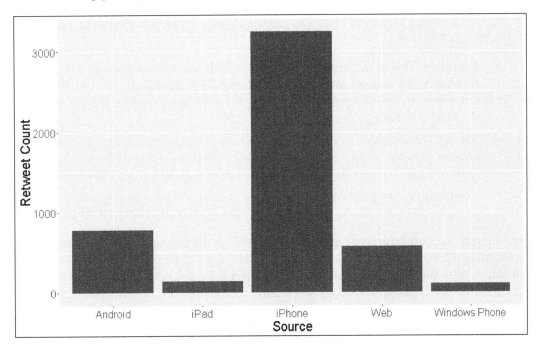

Without a doubt, the iPhone is the most preferred device, followed by Android and the Web. It is interesting to see that people use the Web/website to retweet more than the iPad! Windows Phone clearly has some serious issues to tackle here. Can we also infer that the iPhone is the preferred device amongst tweeples? Or does the iPhone provide a better experience than any other device for Twitter? Or we could even go deeper and say that Twitter on iPhone has an easier-to-access "retweets" button than any other device. Inferences such as these and many more, require a bit more digging than this, but all of this has a lot of knowledge/potential that could be used by managements, UX teams, and so on to improve and change things around.

Hierarchical clustering

We have seen clustering and classification in previous chapters (see *Chapter 2, Let's Help Machines Learn*) and uncovered some interesting facts about the data at hand. For our current use case, even though our tweets are all related to 2016 resolutions, we can never be sure of the kinds of resolutions tweeple make. This makes it a very apt use case for hierarchical clustering. Unlike k-means or other clustering algorithms that require a preset number of clusters before computation, hierarchical clustering algorithms work independently of it.

Let us take this opportunity to understand hierarchical clustering before we apply it to our data. Hierarchical clustering, like any other clustering algorithm, helps us group similar items together. The exact details for this algorithm in general can be explained as follows:

- **Initialize**: This is the first step, where each element is assigned to a cluster of its own. For a dataset containing *n* elements, the algorithm creates *n* different clusters with one element in each of them. A distance/similarity measure is decided at this step.

- **Merge**: During this step, depending upon the distance/similarity measure chosen, the closest pair of clusters are identified and merged into a single cluster. This step results in one fewer clusters than the total clusters so far.

- **Compute/recompute**: We compute/recompute distances/similarities between the new cluster formed in the Merge step and the existing clusters.

The **merge** and **compute** steps are repeated until we are left with a single cluster containing all *n* items. As the name suggests, this algorithm generates a hierarchical structure with the leaves denoting individual elements as clusters combined based upon similarity/distance as we go toward the root of the tree. The output tree is generally referred to as a **dendrogram**.

The merge step is where variations of this algorithm exist. There are several ways in which the closest clusters could be identified. From simple methods, such as single-link, which consider the shortest distance between any two elements of the two clusters in consideration as the distance measure, to complex ones such as Ward's method which uses variance to find the most compact clusters, there are several methods that could be employed depending upon the use case.

Coming back to the Twitter world, let us use hierarchical clustering to see which terms/tweets are the closest. For our current use case, we will use the single method for our merge criteria. You may try out different algorithms and observe the differences.

To perform hierarchical clustering, we first treat our dataset to remove sparse terms for the sake of clarity. For this, the `removeSparseTerms` function helps us remove rows of data that have sparsity below a specified limit. We then use the `hclust` utility to form clusters. The output of this utility is directly plottable. Let us write some code for this:

```
# remove sparse terms
twtrTermDocMatrix2 <- removeSparseTerms(twtrTermDocMatrix, sparse = 0.98)


tweet_matrix <- as.matrix(twtrTermDocMatrix2)


# cluster terms
distMatrix <- dist(scale(tweet_matrix))


fit <- hclust(distMatrix,method="single")
plot(fit)
```

The output *dendrogram* is amazingly simple to understand:

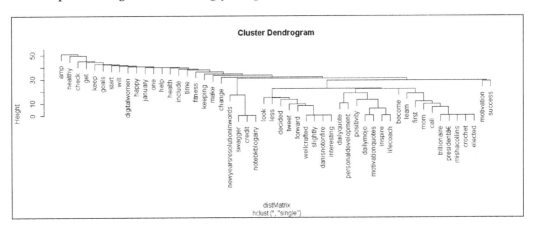

If you observe the second cluster from right, it contains terms **trillionaire**, **elected**, **mom**, **call**, and so on. Mapping back to the top retweeted tweet from Mischa Collins, all these terms are mentioned in that single tweet and our algorithm has rightly clustered them together. Smart, isn't it? As a small exercise, observe other clusters and see how the terms occur in the tweets that contain them. One important observation to make here is that the *dendrogram* correctly maps all frequent terms under a single root, which reaffirms that all these terms point to our central theme of 2016 resolutions!

Topic modeling

So far, our analysis has been about tweets related to New Year's resolutions from users across the world. We have analyzed tweets related to a topic of our choice. Ignoring spam and other noisy tweets, more or less, our data conformed to a single topic. The topic itself constituted a group of words (such as health, trillionaire, fitness, diet, mom, and so on) which broadly describe different resolutions. To broaden our scope of analysis and to discover even more insights, let us touch upon the concept of topic modeling.

Topic modeling is a process of discovering patterns in a corpus of unlabeled text that represents the gist of the corpus. A topic itself may be described as a group of words that occur together to describe a large body of text.

Another definition tweeted during one of the conferences on topic modeling:

Image source: `https://twitter.com/footnotesrising/`
`status/264823621799780353`

The aim of topic modeling is to automatically identify the underlying theme of a corpus and thus be useful in applications that require information retrieval based on a theme but in absence of known keywords (the exact opposite of our current usage of search engines). For example, wouldn't it be amazing to learn about relations between two countries from a newspaper's archive by using the theme *relations between country one and country two* rather than searching for a keyword and then following link after link. Please note that following links to discover information is equally powerful, but it leaves a lot to be desired.

One of the ways to perform topic modeling is through **Latent Dirichlet Allocation (LDA)**; it is one of the most powerful and widely used models.

LDA was presented by David M Blie in his paper *Introduction to Probabilistic Topic Models* in 2003. LDA, as his paper says, can be defined as a generative model that allows sets of observations to be explained by unobserved groups that explain why some parts of the data is similar. LDA works upon the assumption that documents exhibit multiple topics.

LDA is a probabilistic model and the mathematics of it are fairly involved and beyond the scope of this book. In a nonmathematical way, LDA can be explained as a model/process that helps identify the topics that have resulted in the generation of a collection of documents.

 For further reading, refer to Blei's paper.

`https://www.cs.princeton.edu/~blei/papers/Blei2011.pdf`

A blog which explains everything in simple words:

`http://tedunderwood.com/2012/04/07/topic-modeling-made-just-simple-enough/`

For our purpose/use case, we can assume LDA as a model/process which helps us to identify the underlying (hidden/latent) topics from a corpus of unlabeled text. Luckily, R abstracts most of the mathematical details in the form of a library called `topicmodels`.

For the purpose of topic modeling, we shall use a new set of tweets. The **International Space Station (ISS)** has multiple Twitter handles, and one of them is `@ISS_Research`, which particularly caters to research related tweets from the ISS. Let us explore what `@ISS_Research` is up to these days by analyzing the tweets from its timeline. We will analyze these tweets to identify the underlying topics of research at the ISS. For this purpose, we will use the same process to extract tweets and perform transformations/cleanup as we have done before. The following snippet of code does this:

```
# set user handle
atISS <- getUser("ISS_Research")


# extract iss_research tweets
tweets <- userTimeline(atISS, n = 1000)


tweets.df=twListToDF(tweets)


tweets.df$text <- sapply(tweets.df$text,function(x) iconv(x,to='UTF-8'))


#Document Term Matrix
twtrDTM <- DocumentTermMatrix(twtrCorpus, control = list(minWordLength =
1))
```

Please note that the preceding snippet prepares a *document-term matrix,* unlike last time where we prepared a *term-document matrix.*

Once we have tweets in the required format, the LDA utility from the `topicmodels` package helps us uncover the hidden topics/patterns. The LDA utility requires the number of topics as input along with the document-term matrix. We will try eight topics for now. The following code uses LDA to extract six terms for each of the eight topics:

```
#topic modeling


# find 8 topics
ldaTopics <- LDA(twtrDTM, k = 8)


#first 6 terms of every topic
ldaTerms <- terms(ldaTopics, 6)


# concatenate terms
(ldaTerms <- apply(ldaTerms, MARGIN = 2, paste, collapse = ", "))
```

The list of topics generated using LDA is as follows:

```
                                                          Topic 1
                    "like, lettuce, experiment, force, microgravity, now"
                                                          Topic 2
                       "flowers, earth, get, helping, mars, astrotimpeakes"
                                                          Topic 3
         "questions, get, asknasa, astrotimpeake, countermeasures, effects"
                                                          Topic 4
                  "aboard, conducting, earth, even, httpstcoxptaxswv, leds"
                                                          Topic 5
                       "earth, good, read, youre, astrokimiya, astrokjell"
                                                          Topic 6
                  "astrokjell, cygnus, ready, capture, csaasc, astrotimpeake"
                                                          Topic 7
    "stationcdrkelly, heres, sciearthnet, astronauts, aboard, astronicole"
                                                          Topic 8
                          "read, learn, many, astrotim, want, gardening"
```

A visual representation would be easier to understand. We can make use of `qplot` to quickly plot the topics across time on an area chart, as follows:

```
# first topic identified for every tweet
firstTopic <- topics(ldaTopics, 1)


topics <- data.frame(date=as.Date(tweets.df$created), firstTopic)


qplot(date, ..count.., data=topics, geom="density",fill=ldaTerms[firstTop
ic], position="stack")+scale_fill_grey()
```

The generated chart looks like the following screenshot:

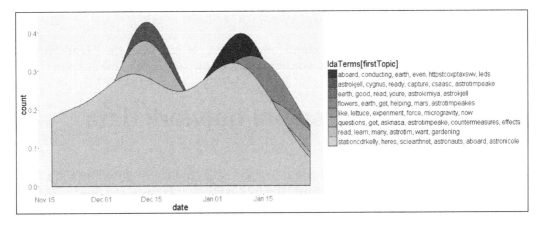

Let us now analyze the outputs. The list of terms per topic generated by LDA seems to give us a nice insight into the kind of work/research going on at the ISS. Terms such as mars, microgravity, flower, Cygnus, and so on tell us about the main areas of research or at least the topics about which scientists/astronauts on the ISS are talking. Terms such as stationcdrkelly and astrotimpeake look more like Twitter handles.

A quick exercise would be to use the current `@ISS_Research` timeline data and mine for the handles, such as `stationcdrkelly`, to discover more information. Who knows, it may turn out be a nice list of astronauts to follow!

The `qplot` output adds the time dimension to our plain list of topics. Analyzing topics across the time dimension helps us understand when a particular research topic was discussed or when something amazing was announced. Topic two in the list, or the fourth one from the top in the graph legend comprises the word flower. Since scientists were successful in blooming some orange flowers in space recently, the above graph helps us get an idea that the news first broke on Twitter on/around 15th January. A quick look on Twitter/news websites confirms that the news broke by tweet on 18th January 2016…close enough!

Colorful area charts

Try removing the option `scale_fill_grey()` from `qplot` to get some beautiful charts that are far easier to read than plain gray scale.

So, finally we learnt about topic modeling using LDA on data from the ISS and found what amazing things scientists and astronauts are doing up there in outer space.

Challenges with social network data mining

Before we close the chapter, let us look at the different challenges posed by social networks to the process of data mining. The following points present a few arguments, questions, and challenges:

- No doubt the data generated by social networks classifies as big data in every aspect. It has all the volume, velocity, and variety in it to overwhelm any system. Yet, interestingly, the challenge with such a huge source of data is the availability of enough granular data. If we zoom into our data sets and try to use data on a per user basis, we find that there isn't enough data to do some of the most common tasks, such as making recommendations!

- Social networks such as Twitter handle millions of users creating and sharing tons of data every second. To keep their systems up and running at all times, they put limits upon the amount of data that can be tapped using their APIs (security is also a major reason behind these limits, though). These limits put data science efforts in a quandary as it is difficult to obtain sufficient samples of data that represent the population correctly/completely. Insufficient samples may result in incorrect patterns or missing out on patterns altogether.

- Preprocessing and evaluation of results is also a challenge with social network analysis. While preprocessing data, we remove noisy content. With data coming in all shapes and sizes, determining noisy content is far more of a challenge than simply removing stopwords. Evaluation of results is another challenge, as there is no ground truth available in most cases, and due to the limitations presented here and otherwise, it is difficult to ascertain the validity of results with confidence.

The arguments/challenges presented above call for innovative and creative ways to be devised by data scientists, and that is what makes their job interesting and highly rewarding.

References

Some of the well-known books on visualization are as follows :

- http://www.amazon.in/Information-Dashboard-Design-At-Glance/dp/1938377001
- http://www.amazon.com/Visual-Display-Quantitative-Information/dp/096139210X
- http://www.amazon.com/Information-Visualization-Second-Interactive-Technologies/dp/1558608192

Some well known blogs on this are as follows:

- **Tableau specific**: http://www.jewelloree.com/
- http://flowingdata.com/
- http://www.informationisbeautiful.net/
- http://infosthetics.com/
- http://www.visualisingdata.com/
- https://eagereyes.org/
- http://thedailyviz.com/
- **D3**: https://d3js.org/

Summary

Social network analysis is one the trending topics in the world of data science. As we have seen throughout the chapter, these platforms not only provide us with ways to connect but they also present a unique opportunity to study human dynamics at a global scale. Through this chapter, we have learned some interesting techniques. We started off by understanding data mining in the social network context followed by the importance of visualizations. We focused on Twitter and understood different objects and APIs to manipulate them. We used various packages from R, such as TwitteR and TM, to connect, collect, and manipulate data for our analysis. We used data from Twitter to learn about frequency throughout. Finally, we presented some of the challenges posed by social networks words and associations, popular devices used by tweeple, hierarchical clustering and even touched upon topic modeling. We used ggplot2 and wordcloud to visualize our results to the data mining process in general. While concluding this chapter, we are sure that by now you can appreciate the amazing dynamics behind these platforms and R's ability to analyze it all. We aren't done with @Twitter yet, hold on to your #sentiments!

8
Sentiment Analysis of Twitter Data

"He who molds the public sentiment... makes statutes and decisions possible or impossible to make."

– Abraham Lincoln.

What people think matters not only to politicians and celebrities but also to most of us social beings. This need to know opinions about ourselves has affected people for a long time and is aptly summarized by the preceding famous quote. The opinion bug not only affects our own outlook, it affects the way we use products and services as well. As discussed while learning about market basket analysis and recommender engines (see *Chapter 3, Predicting Customer Shopping Trends with Market Basket Analysis* and *Chapter 4, Building a Product Recommendation System* respectively), our behavior can be approximated or predicted by observing the behavior of a group of people with similar characteristics such as price sensitivity, color preferences, brand loyalty, and so on. We also discussed in the earlier chapters that, for a long time, we have asked our friends and relatives for their opinions before making that next big purchase. While those opinions are important to us at an individual level, there are far more valuable insights we can derive from such information.

To say that the advent of the World Wide Web has simply accelerated and widened our circle would be an understatement. Without being repetitive, it is worth mentioning that the web has opened new doors for analyzing human behavior.

In the previous chapter, social networks were the object of discussion. We not only used social networks as tools to derive insights but we also discussed the fact that these platforms satisfy our inherent curiosity about what others are thinking or doing. Social networks provide us all with a platform where we can voice our opinions and be heard. The *be heard* aspect of it is a little tricky to define and handle. For instance, our opinions and feedback (assuming they are genuine) about someone or something on these platforms will certainly be heard by the people in our circles (directly or indirectly), but they may or may not be heard by the people or organizations they are intended for. Nevertheless, such opinions or feedback do impact the people connected to them and their behavior from then on. This impact of opinions and our general curiosity about what people think, coupled with more such use cases, is the motivation for this chapter.

In this chapter, we will:

- Learn about sentiment Analysis and its key concepts
- Look into the applications and challenges presented by sentiment analysis
- Understand the different approaches to perform opinion mining
- Apply the concepts of sentiment analysis on Twitter data

Understanding Sentiment Analysis

The fact that Internet-based companies and their CEOs feature as some of the most profitable entities in the global economy says a lot about how the world is being driven by technology and shaped by the Internet. Unlike any other medium, the Internet has become ubiquitous and has penetrated every aspect of our lives. It is no surprise that we are using and relying on the Internet and Internet-based solutions for advice and recommendations, apart from using it for many other purposes.

As we saw in the previous chapters, the relationship between the Internet and domains such as e-commerce and financial institutions goes way too deep. But our use of and trust in the online world doesn't stop there. Be it about booking a table at the new restaurant in your neighborhood or deciding which movie to see tonight, we take help from the Internet to know what opinions others have, or what others have to share, before we make the final call. As we will see later, such decision aids are not just limited to the commerce platforms but also apply to many other domains.

Opinion mining or sentiment analysis (as it is widely and interchangeably known) is the process of automatically identifying the subjectivity in text using natural language processing, text analytics, and computational linguistics. Sentiment analysis aims to identify the positive, negative, or neutral opinion, sentiment, or attitude of the speaker using said techniques. Sentiment analysis (henceforth used interchangeably with opinion mining) finds its application in areas from commerce to service domains across the world.

Key concepts of sentiment analysis

We will now examine the key terms and concepts related to sentiment analysis. These terms and concepts will help us formalize our discussions in the coming sections.

Subjectivity

Opinions or sentiments are one's own expression of views and beliefs. Furthermore, subjectivity (or subjective text) expresses our sentiments about entities such as products, people, governments, and so on. For instance, a subjective sentence could be *I love to use Twitter*, which shows a person's love towards a particular social network, while an objective sentence would be *Twitter is a social network*. The second example simply states a fact. Sentiment analysis revolves around subjective texts or subjectivity classification. It is also important to understand that not all subjective texts express sentiment. For example, *I just created my Twitter account*.

Sentiment polarity

Once we have a piece of text which is subjective in nature (and expresses some sentiment), the next task is to classify it into one of the sentiment classes of positive or negative (sometimes neutral is also considered). The task may also involve placing the text's sentiment on a continuous (or discrete) scale of polarities, thus defining the degree of positivity (or sentiment polarity). The sentiment polarity classification may deal with a different set of classes depending upon the context. For example, in a rating system for movies, sentiment polarities may be defined as liked versus disliked, or in a debate the views may be classified as for versus against.

Opinion summarization

Opinion classification or sentiment extraction from a piece of text is an important task in the process of sentiment analysis. This is often followed by a summarization of sentiments. To draw insights or conclusions from different texts related to the same topic (say, reviews of a given movie), it is important to aggregate (or summarize) the sentiments into a consumable form to draw conclusions (whether the movie is a blockbuster or a dud). This may involve the use of visualizations to infer the overall sentiment.

Feature extraction

As we have seen across the chapters, feature identification and extraction is what makes or breaks a machine learning algorithm. It is the most important factor after the data itself. Let us look at some of the feature sets utilized in solving the problem of sentiment analysis:

- **TF-IDF**: Information Retrieval makes heavy use of **Term Frequency-Inverse Document Frequency (tf-idf)** to enable quick information retrieval and analysis. In the context of tf-idf, a piece of text is represented as a feature vector containing words as its constituents. Recent research has also shown that, in the context of sentiment analysis, the presence of a word improves the performance and accuracy as compared to the frequency of the word.

Source:

Bo Pang, Lillian Lee, and Shivakumar Vaithyanathan. Thumbs up? Sentiment classification using machine learning techniques. In Proceedings of the Conference on **Empirical Methods in Natural Language Processing (EMNLP)**, pages 79–86, 2002.

TF-IDF is given as: $tfidf(t,d,D) = tf(t,d).idf(t,D)$

Where,

$tf(t,d)$ is the term frequency of term t in document d.

$idf(t,D)$ is the inverse document frequency for term t in document set D.

For example, we have the following screenshots of two documents with their terms and their corresponding frequencies:

Document A		Document B	
Term	**Frequency**	**Term**	**Frequency**
Twitter	3	I	3
internet	2	is	1
text	1	social	1
is	1	network	2

In its simplest form, TF-IDF for the term Twitter can be given as:

$$tfifd\left(Twitter\right) = tf\left(Twitter, Document\ A\right).idf\left(Twitter, Document\ Set\ D\right)$$
$$= 3 X 0.3010 = 0.9030$$

Different weight schemes can be used for calculating tfidf; the preceding example uses log with base 10 to calculate idf.

- n-Grams: Computational linguistics and probability consider a text corpus as a contiguous sequence of terms, which may be phonemes, letters, words, and so on. The n-gram-based modeling techniques find their roots in information theory, where the likelihood of the next character or word is based upon the *n* previous terms. Depending upon the value of n, the feature vector or model is termed as unigram (for n=1), bigram (for n=2), trigram (for n=3), and so on. n-grams are particularly useful with out-of-vocabulary words and approximate matches. For example, considering a sequence of words, a sentence such as *A chapter on sentiment analysis* would have bigrams such as *a chapter, chapter on, on sentiment, sentiment analysis*, and so on.

 Interesting work by Google on using n-grams: http://googleresearch.blogspot.in/2006/08/all-our-n-gram-are-belong-to-you.html.

- **Parts of Speech (POS)**: Understanding and making use of the underlying structure of the language for analysis has obvious advantages. POS are rules of language which are used to create sentences, paragraphs and documents. In its simplest form, adjectives are usually pretty good indicators of subjectivity (not always, though). A number of approaches make use of the polarity of adjectives while classifying subjective texts. Using phrases containing adjectives has been shown to improve performance even further. Research into using other parts of speech, such as verbs and nouns, along with adjectives has also shown positive results.

Reference:

Peter Turney. Thumbs up or thumbs down? Semantic orientation applied to unsupervised classification of reviews. In Proceedings of the **Association for Computational Linguistics (ACL)**, pages 417–424, 2002.

The following example shows the parts of speech (adjectives, nouns, and so on) tagged in a sample sentence, for example, *We saw the yellow dog*:

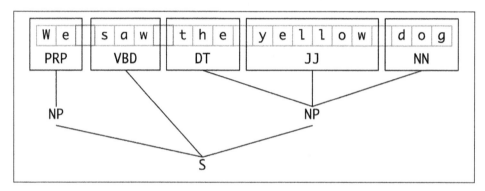

Source: `http://www.nltk.org/`

- **Negation**: In the case of sentiment analysis, negation plays an important role. For example, sentences such as *I like oranges* and *I don't like oranges* differ only in the word *don't*, but the negation term flips the polarity of sentences to opposite classes (positive and negative respectively). Negation may be used as a secondary feature set where the original feature vector is generated as is, but is flipped in polarity later on based on the negation term. There are other variants to this approach as well, and they show an improvement in the results as compared to approaches which do not take into account the effects of negation.

- **Topic specific features**: Topic plays an important role in setting the context. Since sentiment analysis is about the speaker's opinion, the subjectivity is influenced by the topic being discussed. Extensive research has gone into analyzing the effects of and relationship between the topic and sentiment of the text corpus.

Reference:

Tony Mullen and Nigel Collier. Sentiment analysis using support vector machines with diverse information sources. In Proceedings of the Conference on **Empirical Methods in Natural Language Processing (EMNLP)**, pages 412–418, July 2004. Poster paper.

Approaches

Now that we have a basic understanding of the key concepts from the world of sentiment analysis, let us look at different approaches for tackling this problem.

Sentiment analysis is mostly performed at the following two levels of abstraction:

- **Document level**: At this level of abstraction, the task is to analyze a given document to determine whether its overall sentiment is positive or negative (or neutral in certain cases). The basic assumption is that the whole document expresses opinions related to a single entity. For example, given a product review, the system analyzes it to determine whether the review is positive or negative.

- **Sentence level**: Sentence level analysis is a more granular form of sentiment analysis. This level of granularity counters the fact that not all sentences in a document are subjective and thus makes better use of subjectivity classification to determine the sentiment on a per sentence basis.

Pretty much like other machine learning techniques, sentiment analysis can also be tackled using supervised and unsupervised methods:

- **Supervised Approach**: Research on sentiment analysis has been going on for quite some time. While the earlier research was constrained by the availability of labeled datasets and performed rather shallow analysis, modern day supervised learning approaches for sentiment analysis have seen a boost, both in terms of systems utilizing these techniques as well as the overall performance of such systems due to the availability of labeled datasets. Datasets such as WordNet, SentiWordNet, SenticNet, newswire, Epinions, and so on enormously assist researchers in improving supervised algorithms by providing datasets with polar words, documents classified into categories, user opinions, and so on. Algorithms such as **Naïve Bayes**, **Support Vector Machines (SVM)**, as discussed in *Chapter 6, Credit Risk Detection and Prediction – Predictive Analytics*, and **Maximum-Entropy-based** classification algorithms are classic examples of supervised learning approaches.

- **Unsupervised Approach**: Unsupervised algorithms for sentiment analysis usually begin with building or learning a sentiment lexicon and then determining the polarity of the text input. Lexicon generation has been done through techniques such as linguistic heuristics, bootstrapping, and so on. One famous approach was detailed by Turney in his 2002 paper where he describes unsupervised sentiment analysis using some fixed syntactic patterns which were based on POS.

Reference:

Linguistic heuristics: Vasileios Hatzivassiloglou and Kathleen McKeown. Predicting the semantic orientation of adjectives. In Proceedings of the Joint ACL/EACL Conference, pages 174–181, 1997.

Bootstrapping: Ellen Riloff and Janyce Wiebe. Learning extraction patterns for subjective expressions. In Proceedings of the Conference on **Empirical Methods in Natural Language Processing (EMNLP)**, 2003.

Turney: Peter Turney. Thumbs up or thumbs down? Semantic orientation applied to unsupervised classification of reviews. In Proceedings of the **Association for Computational Linguistics (ACL)**, pages 417–424, 2002.

Applications

As we have been discussing throughout, our reliance upon online opinions is something of a surprise. We knowingly or unknowingly check these opinions or are influenced by them before buying products, downloading software, selecting apps, or choosing a restaurant. Sentiment analysis or opinion mining finds its application in many areas; they can be summarized into the following broad categories:

- **Online and Offline Commerce**: Customer preferences can make or break brands in an instant. For a product to be a hot seller, everything including pricing, packaging, and marketing has to be perfect. Customers form opinions about all aspects related to products, and thus affect their sales. It is not just the case with online commerce where customers check product reviews on multiple websites or blogs before making the actual purchase, but word of mouth and other such factors affect customer opinions in the world of offline commerce as well. Sentiment analysis thus forms an important factor which brands or companies track and analyze to be on top of the game. Analysis of social media content such as tweets, Facebook posts, blogs, and so on provide brands with an insight into how customers perceive their product. In certain cases, brands roll out specific marketing campaigns to set the general sentiment or hype about a product.

- **Governance**: In a world where most activities have online counterparts, governments are no exceptions. There have been projects by various governments across the globe which have made use of sentiment analysis in matters of policy making and security (by analyzing and monitoring any increase in hostile or negative communications). Sentiment Analysis has also been used by analysts to determine or predict outcomes of elections as well. Tools such as *eRuleMaking* have sentiment analysis as a key component.

Apart from the aforementioned two categories, opinion mining acts as an augmenting technology in fields such as recommendation engines and general prediction systems. For example, opinion mining may be used in conjunction with recommender engines to exclude products from recommendation lists which have opinions or sentiments below certain thresholds. Sentiment analysis may also find innovative use in predicting whether an upcoming movie will be a blockbuster or not based on sentiments related to the star cast, production house, topic of the movie, and so on.

Challenges

To understand the opinions and/or sentiments of others is an inherently difficult task. To be able to handle such a problem algorithmically is equally hard. The following are some of the challenges faced while performing Sentiment Analysis:

- **Understanding and Modeling Natural Language Constructs**: Sentiment analysis is inherently a **natural language processing (NLP)** problem, albeit a restricted one. Even though sentiment analysis is a restricted form of NLP, involving classification into positive, negative or neutral, it still faces issues like coreference resolution, word sense disambiguation, and negation handling to name a few. Advancements in NLP, as well as Sentiment Analysis, in recent years have helped in overcoming these issues to a certain extent, yet there is a long way to travel before we will be able to model the rules of a natural language perfectly.

- **Sarcasm**: Sentiments can be expressed in pretty subtle ways. It is not just negative sentiments; positive sentiments can also be nicely disguised within sarcastic sentences. Since understanding sarcasm is a trick only a few can master, it is not easy to model sarcasm and identify sentiment correctly. For example, the comment *Such a simple to use product, you just need to read 300 pages from the manual*, contains only positive words yet has a negative flavor to it which is not easy to model.

- **Review and reviewer quality**: Opinions vary from person to person. Some of us may present our opinions very strongly while others may not. Another issue is that everyone has an opinion, whether they know about a subject or not. This creates a problem of review and reviewer quality, which may affect overall analysis. For example, a person who is a casual reader may not be the most apt person to ask for a review of a new book. Similarly, it may not be advisable to get a new author's book reviewed by a critic. Both extremes may result in biased outcomes or incorrect insights.

- **Opinion data size and skew**: The web has loads and loads of blogs and sites which provide users with a platform to voice and share opinions on everything possible on and beyond the planet. Still, the opinion data at a granular level is an issue. As we discussed in the previous chapter, the amount of data related to a particular context (say a brand or a person) is so limited that it affects the overall analysis. Moreover, the data available is sometimes skewed in favor of (or against) entities due to prejudices, incorrect facts, or rumors.

Sentiment analysis upon Tweets

Now that we are equipped with the key terms and concepts from the world of Sentiment Analysis, let us put our theory to the test. We have seen some major application areas for Sentiment Analysis and the challenges faced, in general, to perform such analytics. In this section we will perform Sentiment Analysis categorized into:

- **Polarity analysis**: This will involve the scoring and aggregation of sentiment polarity using a labeled list of positive and negative words.
- **Classification-based analysis**: In this approach we will make use of R's rich libraries to perform classification based on labeled tweets available for public usage. We will also discuss their performance and accuracy.

R has a very robust library for the extraction and manipulation of information from Twitter called TwitteR. As we saw in the previous chapter, we first need to create an application using Twitter's application management console before we can use TwitteR or any other library for sentiment analysis. For this chapter, we will be reusing the application from the previous chapter (keep your application keys and secrets handy). Also, in the coming sections, we will be utilizing our code from previous chapters in a more structured format to enable reuse and to follow #bestCodingPractices.

Before we begin our analysis, let us first restructure our existing code and write some helper functions, which will come in handy later on. As we know, data from Twitter can be extracted using search terms or from a user's timeline. The following two helper functions help us to do exactly the same tasks in a reusable fashion:

```
#extract search tweets
extractTweets <- function(searchTerm,tweetCount){
  # search term tweets
  tweets = searchTwitter(searchTerm,n=tweetCount)
  tweets.df = twListToDF(tweets)
  tweets.df$text <- sapply(tweets.df$text,function(x)
iconv(x,to='UTF-8'))

  return(tweets.df)
}


#extract timeline tweets
extractTimelineTweets <- function(username,tweetCount){
```

```
# timeline tweets
twitterUser <- getUser(username)
tweets = userTimeline(twitterUser,n=tweetCount)
tweets.df = twListToDF(tweets)
tweets.df$text <- sapply(tweets.df$text,function(x)
iconv(x,to='UTF-8'))


return(tweets.df)
}
```

The function `extractTweets` takes the `search` term and number of tweets to
be extracted as inputs and returns the data in a data frame which contains text
converted to UTF8 encoding. Similarly, the function `extractTimelineTweets` takes
the username and number of tweets as inputs and returns data in a data frame with
the text converted to UTF8 encoding. Therefore, the preceding two functions will
help us to extract tweets multiple times (based on different `search` terms or users)
without rewriting the same lines of code again and again.

Continuing with the same theme, we will write another helper function to clean and
transform our data set. As we saw in the previous chapter, R's `tm` library provides
us with various utility functions to quickly clean and transform text corpus. In this
function, we will make use of `tm_map` to transform our tweets:

```
# clean and transform tweets
transformTweets <- function(tweetDF){
  tweetCorpus <- Corpus(VectorSource(tweetDF$text))
  tweetCorpus <- tm_map(tweetCorpus, tolower)
  tweetCorpus <- tm_map(tweetCorpus, removePunctuation)
  tweetCorpus <- tm_map(tweetCorpus, removeNumbers)


  # remove URLs
  removeURL <- function(x) gsub("http://[[:alnum:]]*", "", x)
  tweetCorpus <- tm_map(tweetCorpus, removeURL)


  # remove stop words
  twtrStopWords <- c(stopwords("english"),'rt','http','https')
```

```
tweetCorpus <- tm_map(tweetCorpus, removeWords, twtrStopWords)


tweetCorpus <- tm_map(tweetCorpus, PlainTextDocument)


#convert back to dataframe
tweetDataframe <- data.frame(text=unlist(sapply(tweetCorpus,
                    `[`, "content")), stringsAsFactors=F)


#split each doc into words
splitText <- function(x) {
  word.list = str_split(x, '\\s+')
  words = unlist(word.list)
}


# attach list of words to the data frame
tweetDataframe$wordList = sapply(
                  tweetDataframe$text,
                  function(text) splitText(text))


  return (tweetDataframe)
}
```

In addition to the usual transformations, such as stop word removal, change to lower case, punctuation removal, and so on, the function `transformTweets` tokenizes each tweet at word level and attaches the list of words in each tweet to the object. Also, the function returns the transformed tweets in a data frame for further manipulation.

Polarity analysis

Polarity, as discussed in the section *Key Concepts*, is the positive, negative or neutral classification of the piece of text in consideration. The class labels may change depending upon the context (liked versus disliked or favorable versus unfavorable). Polarity may also have a degree attached to it which places the analyzed text on a continuous (or discrete) scale of polarities (say from -5 to 5). This degree of polarity helps us analyze the extent (or degree) of positivity (or negativity) in the text. This is particularly useful in comparative studies as we have the opportunity to view analyzed text with reference to certain benchmarks.

In this section, we will analyze tweets and score each of them based on the polar words identified in each of the tweets. The simple and easy-to-code algorithm is outlined in the following steps:

1. Extract tweets based on selected search terms or Twitter handles.

2. Clean and transform tweets into a suitable format for ease of analysis. Tokenize tweets into a constituent list of words.

3. Load the list of positive and negative words to be used for polar word identification.

4. For each tweet, count the number of positive and negative words that match the list of positive and negative words obtained in the preceding step 3.

5. Assign a polarity score to each tweet based on the difference between positive and negative matches in the preceding step.

The preceding steps are represented diagrammatically as follows:

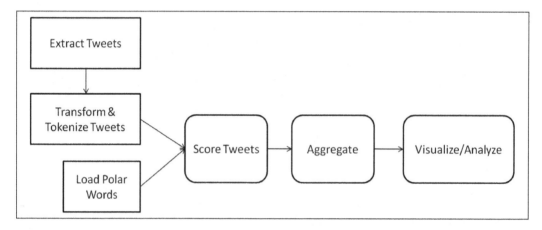

Once each tweet in the dataset has been scored, we may aggregate the scores to understand the overall sentiment distribution related to the search terms or Twitter handle. Positive values define a positive sentiment; larger numbers denote a greater degree of positivity, and similarly for negative sentiments. A neutral stance is represented by a score of 0. For example, *This car is amazingly fast and beautiful* has a greater degree of positivity than *This is a nice car*, though both are positive sentences.

Let us use this algorithm to analyze sentiments using search terms and Twitter handles. As discussed previously, opinion mining has become essential, not just for brands but for governments as well. Every entity out there wants to gauge how its target audience feels about it and its initiatives, and governments are no exception. Of late, the Indian Government has been utilizing Twitter and other social media platforms effectively to reach its audience and make them aware about its initiatives and policies. One such initiative is the recently launched Make in India initiative. Consider a scenario where one is tasked with analyzing the effectiveness of and public opinion related to such an initiative. To analyze public opinion, which changes dynamically over time, Twitter would be a good choice. So, to analyze sentiments for the Make in India initiative, let us analyze some tweets.

As previously outlined, we start by connecting to Twitter and extracting tweets related to the search term *Make In India*. This is followed by the preprocessing step, where we remove stop words, URLs, and so on to transform the tweets into a usable format. We also tokenize each tweet into a list of constituent words for use in the coming steps. Once our dataset is ready and in a consumable format, we load the precompiled list of positive and negative words. The list is available from `https://www.cs.uic.edu/~liub/FBS/sentiment-analysis.html`.

We first write a reusable `analyzeTrendSentiments` function which takes the search term and number of tweets to be extracted as inputs. It makes use of the functions `extractTweets` and `transformTweets` to get the job done:

```
analyzeTrendSentiments <- function(search,tweetCount){


  #extract tweets
  tweetsDF <- extractTweets(search,tweetCount)


  # transformations
  transformedTweetsDF <- transformTweets(tweetsDF)


  #score the words
  transformedTweetsDF$sentiScore = sapply(transformedTweetsDF$wordList,function(wordList) scoreTweet(wordList))


  transformedTweetsDF$search <- search


  return(transformedTweetsDF)
}
```

We then use the function `analyzeTrendSentiments` to get a data frame consisting of tweets scored using a precompiled list of polar words. We use `twitteR`, `ggplot2`, `stringr` and `tm` libraries as well:

```
library(twitteR)
library(stringr)
library(tm)
library(ggplot2)


consumerSecret = "XXXXXXXXXX"
consumerKey = "XXXXXXXXXXXXXXXXXXXXXXXXXXX"


setup_twitter_oauth(consumer_key = consumerKey,consumer_secret =
consumerSecret)


# list of positive/negative words from opinion lexicon
pos.words = scan(file= 'positive-words.txt', what='character', comment.
char=';')


neg.words = scan(file= 'negative-words.txt', what='character', comment.
char=';')


#extract 1500 tweets on the given topic
makeInIndiaSentiments <- analyzeTrendSentiments("makeinindia",1500)


#plot the aggregated scores on a histogram
qplot(makeInIndiaSentiments $sentiScore)
```

In the last chapter, we learned and used different visualizations to grasp the insights hidden in our analysis. Continuing with the same thought process, we generate a histogram of aggregated scores. The visualization looks like this:

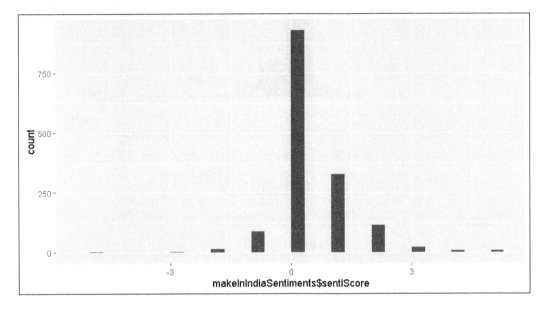

The histogram is easy to interpret. It shows the tweets distributed across a polarity scale on the *x*-axis and frequency of tweets on the *y*-axis. The results show a normal distribution with a general tilt towards the positive side. It seems the initiative is getting a positive response from its audience.

Going a bit deeper into the analysis itself, let us analyze the sentiments for the same search term and see how the opinions change over time.

The tweets for this analysis were extracted on the day the initiative was launched as well as a day later. Your results may vary due to the dynamic nature of Twitter. You may observe a difference in outcomes across other examples in this chapter as well. We urge you to be creative and try out other trending topics while working through examples from this chapter.

The output looks like this:

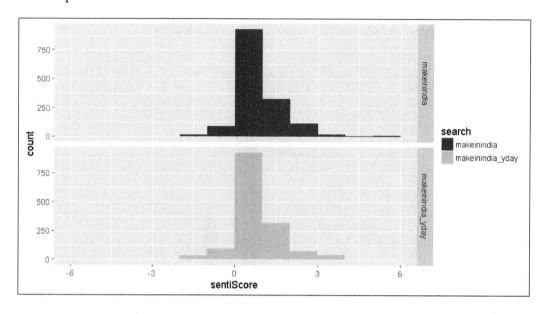

The preceding two histograms show a shift in opinions over the course of two days. If you were following the news at the time, in one of the events for this initiative a sudden fire broke out and burnt the whole stage. The graph on top is based upon tweets after the fire broke out while the graph labeled **makeinindia_yday** refers to the tweets from the day before. Though the shift in sentiments isn't drastic, it is clearly visible that the shift has been more towards the positive side (some tweets are even hitting a score of 6+). Could this be because tweeple started praising the emergency teams and police for their quick action in preventing casualties? Well, it looks like Twitter isn't just about people ranting on random stuff!

World leaders

Twitter has caught the frenzy of celebrities and politicians alike. As a quick exercise, try analyzing tweets from the twitter handles of world leaders such as @potus, @pmoindia, and @number10gov to see what kind of opinions our leaders project through Twitter. Don't be surprised if their timelines are neutral...oops, diplomatic!

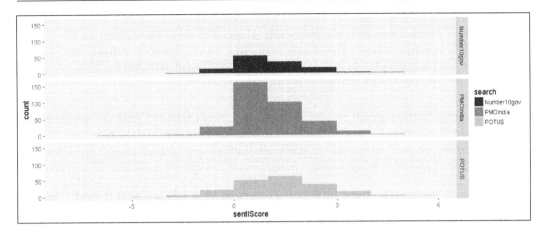

Classification-based algorithms

A classification problem requires the labeling of input data into required classes based on some defined characteristics of each class (see *Chapter 2, Let's Help Machines Learn*, for details). In the case of sentiment analysis, the classes are positive and negative (or neutral in certain cases). We have learned about different classification algorithms and seen how they are used across domains to solve categorization and classification problems in the previous chapters, and sentiment analysis is yet another domain where these algorithms are highly useful.

In this section, we will perform opinion mining using classification algorithms such as SVM and boosting. We will also touch upon ensemble methods and see how they help to improve performance. Note that, for this section, we will concentrate only on the positive and negative polarities, but the approach is generic enough to be easily extended to include the neutral polarity as well.

Labeled dataset

Since this is a supervised learning approach, we require labeled data for training and testing the performance of our algorithms. For the purpose of this chapter, we will utilize a labeled dataset from `http://www.sentiment140.com/`. It contains tweets labeled as 0, 2, and 4 for negative, neutral and positive sentiments, respectively. There are various attributes such as `tweet ID`, `date`, `search query`, `username`, and the `tweet text`, apart from the sentiment label. For our case we will be considering only the tweet text and its corresponding label.

polarity	id	tweet_date	search qui	username	tweet text
4	12	Mon May 11 03:29:20 UTC 2009	obama	mandanicole	how can you not love Obama? he makes jokes about himself.
2	13	Mon May 11 03:32:42 UTC 2009	obama	jpeb	Check this video out -- President Obama at the White House Correspondents' Dinner http://bit.ly/IMXUM
0	14	Mon May 11 03:32:48 UTC 2009	obama	kylesellers	@Karoli I firmly believe that Obama/Pelosi have ZERO desire to be civil. It's a charade and a slogan, but they want to destroy

Another source of labeled tweets is available at `https://github.com/guyz/twitter-sentiment-dataset`. This source makes use of a python script to download around 5000 labeled tweets keeping Twitter API guidelines in mind.

Before we get into the algorithm-specific details, let us look into the labeled dataset and perform the initial steps of collecting and transforming our data into the required forms. We will make use of libraries such as `caret` and `RTextTools` for these steps.

As mentioned previously, the dataset contains polarities labeled as 0, 2, and 4 for negative, neutral, and positive. We will load the `csv` file in R and apply a quick transformation to change the labels to positive and negative. Once the polarities have been transformed into intelligible names, we will filter out the rows of data containing neutral sentiments. Also, we will keep only the columns for polarity and tweet text, and remove the rest.

```
# load labeled dataset
labeledDSFilePath = "labeled_tweets.csv"
labeledDataset = read.csv(labeledDSFilePath, header = FALSE)

# transform polarity labels
labeledDataset$V1 = sapply(labeledDataset$V1,
    function(x)
      if(x==4)
        x <- "positive"
      else if(x==0)
        x<-"negative"
      else x<- "none")

#select required columns only
requiredColumns <- c("V1","V6")

# extract only positive/negative labeled tweets
tweets<-as.matrix(labeledDataset[labeledDataset$V1
      %in% c("positive","negative")
      ,requiredColumns])
```

The tweets object is now available as a matrix with each row representing a tweet, and with columns referring to polarity and tweet text. Before we transform this matrix into the formats required by the classification algorithms, we need to split our data into training and testing datasets (see *Chapter 2, Let's Help Machines Learn*, for more on this). Since both the training and testing datasets should contain a good enough distribution of samples of all classes for the purposes of training and testing, we use the createDataPartition function available from the caret package. For our use case, we split our data into 70/30 training and testing datasets:

```
indexes <- createDataPartition(tweets[,1], p=0.7, list = FALSE)


train.data <- tweets[indexes,]
test.data <- tweets[-indexes,]
```

We perform a quick check to see how our data is split across the positive and negative classes in our original dataset, and the training and testing datasets. You will see the result in the following screenshot:

```
> prop.table(table(tweets[,1]))

 negative   positive
0.4930362 0.5069638
> prop.table(table(tweets[indexes,1]))

 negative   positive
0.4920635 0.5079365
> prop.table(table(tweets[-indexes,1]))

 negative   positive
0.4953271 0.5046729
```

As we can see, createDataPartition has done a nice job of maintaining a similar sentiment distribution across the training and testing datasets.

Next in the line of transformations is the Document Term Matrix transformation. As we have seen in *Chapter 7, Social Media Analysis – Analyzing Twitter Data*, a document term matrix transforms a given dataset into rows representing the documents and columns of terms (words/sentences). Unlike the previous chapter, where we used the tm library's DocumentTermMatrix function for transformation and applied various transformations using tm_map, for the current use case we will use the create_matrix function from the RTextTools library. This function is an abstraction over tm's corresponding functions. We will also assign weights to each of the terms using tfidf as our feature. The create_matrix method also helps us take care of splitting sentences into words, stop words and number removal, and stemming them as well. Here's how you do it:

```
train.dtMatrix <- create_matrix(train.data[,2],
                        language="english" ,
                        removeStopwords=TRUE,
                        removeNumbers=TRUE,
                        stemWords=TRUE,
                        weighting = tm::weightTfIdf)



test.dtMatrix <- create_matrix(test.data[,2],
                        language="english" ,
                        removeStopwords=TRUE,
                        removeNumbers=TRUE,
                        stemWords=TRUE,
                        weighting = tm::weightTfIdf,
                        originalMatrix=train.dtMatrix)


test.data.size <- nrow(test.data)
```

The `create_matrix` method in RTextTools v1.4.2 has a small bug which prevents weight assignment when using `originalMatrix` option. The following small hack can be used to fix the issue till the library gets updated:

```
> trace("create_matrix",edit=T)
```

Scroll to line 42 and update Acronym to acronym.

Check the following links for more details and alternate ways of handling this issue:

`https://github.com/timjurka/RTextTools/issues/4`

`http://stackoverflow.com/questions/16630627/recreate-same-document-term-matrix-with-new-data`

Now that we have both the training and testing datasets in the `DocumentTermMatrix` format, we can proceed towards the classification algorithms and let our machines learn and build sentiment classifiers!

Support Vector Machines

Support Vector Machines, or **SVM** as they are commonly known, are one of the most versatile classes of supervised learning algorithms for classification. An SVM builds a model in such a way that the data points belonging to different classes are separated by a clear gap, which is optimized such that the distance of separation is the maximum possible. The samples on the margins are called the support vectors, which are separated by a hyperplane (see *Chapter 6, Credit Risk Detection and Prediction – Predictive Analytics* for more details).

Since our current use case for sentiment analysis is also a binary (positive and negative) classification problem, SVM helps us build a model using the training dataset, which separates tweets into positive and negative sentiment classes, respectively.

We will use `e1071` library's `svm` function to build a sentiment classifier. We start off with the default values for the SVM classifier available from the library and follow the same iterative procedure we did in *Chapter 6, Credit Risk Detection and Prediction – Predictive Analytics*, to finally arrive at the best classifier. The following snippet of code builds a sentiment classifier using the default values and then prints a confusion matrix, along with other statistics for evaluation, as shown in the following code snippet:

```
svm.model <- svm(train.dtMatrix, as.factor(train.data[,1]))

## view inital model details
```

```
summary(svm.model)


## predict and evaluate results
svm.predictions <- predict(svm.model, test.dtMatrix)


true.labels <- as.factor(test.data[,1])


confusionMatrix(data=svm.predictions, reference=true.labels,
positive="positive")
```

The confusion matrix generated as follows shows that the classifier has just *50% accuracy*, which is as bad as a coin toss, with no predictions for negative sentiments whatsoever! It seems like the classifier couldn't infer or learn much from the training dataset.

```
Confusion Matrix and Statistics

          Reference
Prediction negative positive
  negative        0        0
  positive       53       54

              Accuracy : 0.5047
                95% CI : (0.4063, 0.6028)
    No Information Rate : 0.5047
    P-Value [Acc > NIR] : 0.5386

                 Kappa : 0
 Mcnemar's Test P-Value : 9.148e-13

           Sensitivity : 1.0000
           Specificity : 0.0000
        Pos Pred Value : 0.5047
        Neg Pred Value :    NaN
            Prevalence : 0.5047
        Detection Rate : 0.5047
  Detection Prevalence : 1.0000
     Balanced Accuracy : 0.5000

       'Positive' Class : positive
```

To build a better-performing model, we will now go under the hood and tweak some parameters. The svm implementation from e1071 provides us with a wonderful utility called tune to obtain the optimized values of hyperparameters using a grid search over the given parameter ranges:

```
## hyperparameter optimizations


# run grid search
cost.weights <- c(0.1, 10, 100)
gamma.weights <- c(0.01, 0.25, 0.5, 1)
tuning.results <- tune(svm, train.dtMatrix, as.factor(train.data[,1]),
kernel="radial",
                        ranges=list(cost=cost.weights, gamma=gamma.
weights))


# view optimization results
print(tuning.results)


# plot results
plot(tuning.results, cex.main=0.6, cex.lab=0.8,xaxs="i", yaxs="i")
```

In the code snippet above, we have utilized the **radial bias kernel** (or **rbf** for short) for hyperparameter optimization. The motivation for using rbf was due to its better performance with respect to *specificity* and *sensitivity* even though the overall accuracy was comparable to *linear* kernels. We urge our readers to try out linear kernels and observe the difference in the overall results. Please note that, for text classification, linear kernels usually perform better than other kernels, not only in terms of accuracy but in performance as well

The parameter-tuning results in optimized values for hyperparameters `cost` and `gamma` as `10` and `0.01`, respectively; the following plot confirms the same (darkest region corresponds to best values).

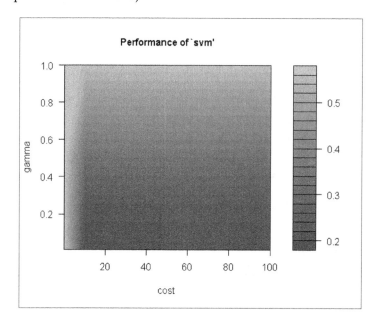

The following snippet of code uses the best model to predict and prepare a confusion matrix, as follows:

```
# get best model and evaluate predictions
svm.model.best = tuning.results$best.model

svm.predictions.best <- predict(svm.model.best, test.dtMatrix)

confusionMatrix(data=svm.predictions.best, reference=true.labels,
positive="positive")
```

The following confusion matrix shows the predictions from a much improved model. From a mere 50% accuracy to a comfortable 80% and above is a good leap. Let us check the ROC curves for this model to confirm that the accuracy is indeed good enough:

```
Confusion Matrix and Statistics

          Reference
Prediction negative positive
  negative       40        7
  positive       13       47

              Accuracy : 0.8131
                95% CI : (0.7262, 0.8819)
   No Information Rate : 0.5047
   P-Value [Acc > NIR] : 3.553e-11

                 Kappa : 0.6257
 Mcnemar's Test P-Value : 0.2636

           Sensitivity : 0.8704
           Specificity : 0.7547
        Pos Pred Value : 0.7833
        Neg Pred Value : 0.8511
            Prevalence : 0.5047
        Detection Rate : 0.4393
  Detection Prevalence : 0.5607
     Balanced Accuracy : 0.8125

      'Positive' Class : positive
```

To prepare the ROC curves, we will reuse our utility script performance_plot_
utils.R from *Chapter 6, Credit Risk Detection and Prediction – Predictive Analytics,*
and pass the predictions from the optimized model to it:

```
# plot best model evaluation metric curves
svm.predictions.best <- predict(svm.model.best, test.dtMatrix, decision.
values = T)


svm.prediction.values <- attributes(svm.predictions.best)
$decision.values


predictions <- prediction(svm.prediction.values, true.labels)


par(mfrow=c(1,2))
plot.roc.curve(predictions, title.text="SVM ROC Curve")
plot.pr.curve(predictions, title.text="SVM Precision/Recall Curve")
```

The ROC curves generated using the preceding code snippet are as follows:

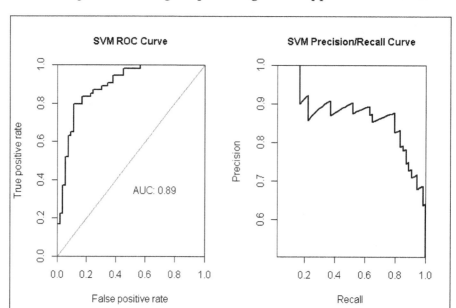

The ROC curves also confirm a well-learned model with an AUC of 0.89. We can therefore use this model to classify tweets into positive or negative classes. We encourage readers to try out ROC-based optimizations and observe if there are any further improvements in the model.

Ensemble methods

Supervised Machine Learning algorithms, in a nutshell, are about learning the underlying functions or patterns which help us predict accurately (within certain bounds) based on historic data. Over the course of this book, we have come across many such algorithms and, although R makes it easy to code and test these, it is worth mentioning that learning a highly accurate function or pattern is not an easy task. Building highly complex models leads us to issues of overfitting and underfitting, to name a few. Amidst all this confusion, it is to be noted that it is always easy to learn simple rules and functions.

For example, to classify an email as spam or not spam there are multiple rules which a machine learning algorithm would have to learn, rules such as:

- E-mails containing text such as *buy now* are spam
- E-mails containing more than five hyperlinks are spam
- E-mails from contacts in the address book are not spam

And many more such rules. Given a training dataset, say T of labeled emails, a machine learning algorithm (specifically a classification algorithm) will generate a classifier, C, which is a hypothesis of an underlying function or pattern. We then use this classifier C to predict the labels for new emails.

On the other hand, an ensemble of classifiers is defined as a set of classifiers whose outputs are combined in some way to classify new examples. The main discovery in the field of machine learning-based ensembles is that ensembles perform much better than the individual classifiers they are made of.

A necessary and sufficient condition for ensembles to be better than their constituents is that they should be *accurate* and *diverse*. A classifier is termed *accurate* if its predictions are better than random guessing (see weak learners). While two classifiers are termed as *diverse* if they make different errors on the same data points.

We can define a **weak learner** as a learner whose predictions and decisions are at least better than random guessing. Weak learners are also termed as base learners or meta learners.

The following block diagram visualizes the concept of ensemble classifiers:

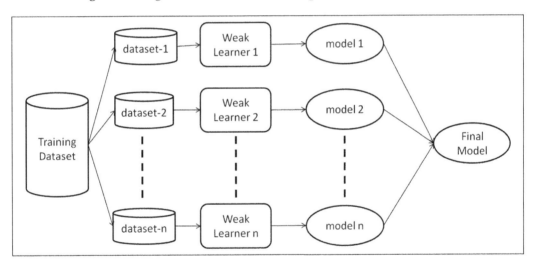

As seen in the preceding block diagram, the training dataset is split into *n* datasets (the splitting or generation of such datasets is dependent upon the ensemble-ing methodology) upon which weak learners (the same or different weak learners, again, depends upon the ensemble methodology) build models. These models are then combined based on weighted or unweighted voting to prepare a final model, which is used for classification. The mathematical proofs of why ensembles work are fairly involved and beyond the scope of this book.

Boosting

There are various ways of constructing ensemble classifiers (or regressors) and boosting is one of them. Boosting came out as an answer by Robert Schapire in his pioneering paper in 1990 entitled *The Strength of Weak Learnability*, where he elegantly describes the boosting ensemble while answering questions posed by Kearns and Valiant in their paper published in 1989, which talks about multiple weak learners that can create a single strong learner.

The Strength of Weak Learnability: http://www.cs.princeton. edu/~schapire/papers/strengthofweak.pdf.

Kearns and Valiant: Cryptographic limitations on learning Boolean Learning and finite automata: http://dl.acm.org/ citation.cfm?id=73049

The original algorithm for boosting was revised by Freund and Schapire, and termed as **AdaBoost** or **Adaptive Boosting**. This algorithm was practically implementable and empirically improves generalization performance. The algorithm can be mathematically presented as follows:

Given : $(x_1, y_1), \ldots, (x_m, y_m)$ where $x_i \in X, y_i \in Y = \{-1, +1\}$

Initialize $D_1(i) = 1/m$

For $t = 1, \ldots, T$:

- Train base learner using distribution D_t
- Get base classifier $h_t : X \to \mathbb{R}$
- Choose $\alpha_t \in \mathbb{R}$
- Update :

$$D_{t+1}(i) = \frac{D_t(i) \exp(-\alpha_t y_i h_t(x_i))}{Z_t}$$

where Z_t is a normalization factor (chosen so that D_{t+1} will be a distribution)

Output the final classifier :

$$H(x) = sign\left(\sum_{t=1}^{T} \alpha_t h_t(x)\right)$$

Source: https://www.cs.princeton.edu/picasso/mats/schapire02boosting_schapire.pdf

Here:

- **X** is the training set
- **Y** is the label set
- $D_t(i)$ is the weight distribution on training example **i** on iteration **t**
- h_t is the classifier obtained in iteration **t**
- **α** is the strength parameter or weight of h_t
- **H** is the final or combined classifier.

In simple words, boosting, in general, begins by initially assigning equal weights to all training examples. It then iterates over the hypothesis space to learn a hypothesis h_t on the weighted examples. After each such hypothesis is learned, the weights are adjusted in such a manner that the weights of the examples that are correctly classified are reduced. This update to weights helps weak learners, in coming iterations, to concentrate more on wrongly classified data points. Finally, each of the learned hypotheses is then passed through a weighted voting to come up with a final model, **H**.

Now that we have an overview of ensemble methods and boosting in general, let us use the boosting implementation available from the RTextTools library in R to classify tweets as positive or negative.

We will reuse the training-testing document term matrices train.dtMatrix and test.dtMatrix, and container objects train.container and test.container, which we created for the SVM-based classification.

For building a classifier based on a boosting ensemble, RTextTools provides an easy-to-use utility function called train_model. It uses *LogitBoosting* internally to build a classifier. We use 500 iterations for building our boosting ensemble.

```
boosting.model <- train_model(train.container, "BOOSTING"
            , maxitboost=500)
boosting.classify <- classify_model(test.container, boosting.model)
```

We then prepare a confusion matrix to see how our classifier performs on the test dataset.

```
predicted.labels <- boosting.classify[,1]
true.labels <- as.factor(test.data[,1])

confusionMatrix(data = predicted.labels,
                reference = true.labels,
                positive = "positive")
```

The following confusion matrix shows that our boosting-based classifier works with an accuracy of 78.5%, which is fairly good given the fact that we did not perform any performance tuning. Compare this to the initial iteration of SVM where we got a dismal accuracy of just over 50%.

```
Confusion Matrix and Statistics

              Reference
Prediction negative positive
   negative       40        10
   positive       13        44

                Accuracy : 0.785
                  95% CI : (0.6951, 0.8586)
     No Information Rate : 0.5047
     P-Value [Acc > NIR] : 2.128e-09

                   Kappa : 0.5698
  Mcnemar's Test P-Value : 0.6767

             Sensitivity : 0.8148
             Specificity : 0.7547
          Pos Pred Value : 0.7719
          Neg Pred Value : 0.8000
              Prevalence : 0.5047
          Detection Rate : 0.4112
    Detection Prevalence : 0.5327
       Balanced Accuracy : 0.7848

        'Positive' Class : positive
```

As mentioned earlier, ensemble methods (specifically boosting) have improved generalized performance, that is, they help achieve close to 0 training errors without overfitting on the training data. To understand and evaluate our Boosting classifier on these parameters, we will use a model-evaluation technique called **Cross-validation**.

Cross-validation

Cross-validation is a model-evaluation technique which is used to evaluate the generalization performance of a model. It is also termed **rotational estimation**. Cross-validation is a better measure to validate a model for generalization compared to residual methods because, for conventional validation techniques, the error (such as **Root Mean Square Error/RMSE**) for the training set and testing set does not properly represent the model's performance. Cross-validation can be performed using:

- **Holdout method**: The simplest cross-validation technique. Data is split into training and testing sets. The model is fitted on the training set, and then the testing set (which the model hasn't seen so far) is used to calculate the mean absolute test error. This accumulated error is used to evaluate the model. This technique suffers from high variance due to its dependency on how the training-testing division was done.

- **K-fold cross validation method**: This is an improvement over the holdout method. The dataset is divided into k subsets and then the holdout method is applied k times using 1 of the k subsets as test and the rest, $k-1$, as training sets. This method has a lower variance due to the fact that each data point gets to be in the test set once and in the training set $k-1$ times. The disadvantage is that more computation time is required due to the number of iterations. An extreme form of K-fold cross validation is the Leave-Out One cross-validation method where all data points except one are used for training. The process is repeated N (size of dataset) times.

We can easily perform K-fold cross validation on our boosting classifier using the `cross_validate` function. In general, 10-fold cross validation is used:

```
# Cross validation
N=10
set.seed(42)
cross_validate(train.container,N,"BOOSTING"
    , maxitboost=500)
```

The preceding code snippet produces the following cross validation summary:

```
Fold 1 Out of Sample Accuracy = 1
Fold 2 Out of Sample Accuracy = 0.9344262
Fold 3 Out of Sample Accuracy = 1
Fold 4 Out of Sample Accuracy = 0.9310345
Fold 5 Out of Sample Accuracy = 1
Fold 6 Out of Sample Accuracy = 0.9591837
Fold 7 Out of Sample Accuracy = 1
Fold 8 Out of Sample Accuracy = 1
Fold 9 Out of Sample Accuracy = 1
Fold 10 Out of Sample Accuracy = 0.9649123
[[1]]
 [1] 1.0000000 0.9344262 1.0000000 0.9310345 1.0000000 0.9591837 1.0000000 1.0000000 1.0000000
[10] 0.9649123

$meanAccuracy
[1] 0.9789557
```

The results show that the classifier has generalized well enough, and has an overall mean accuracy of 97.8%.

Boosting is one of the methods to construct ensemble classifiers based on weak learners. Methods such as bagging, bayes optimal classifier, bucketing, and stacking are some of the variants with their own pros and cons.

Constructing ensembles

RTextTools is a robust library which provides functions such as `train_models` and `classify_models` to prepare ensembles by combining various base learners. It also provides tools for generating analysis for evaluating the performance of such ensembles in a very detailed manner. Check out the detailed explanation at https://journal.r-project.org/archive/2013-1/collingwood-jurka-boydstun-etal.pdf.

Summary

Twitter is a goldmine for data science, with interesting patterns and insights spread all across it. Its constant flow of user-generated content, coupled with unique, interest-based relationships, present opportunities to understand human dynamics up close. Sentiments Analysis is one such field where Twitter provides the right set of ingredients to understand what and how we present and share opinions about products, brands, people, and so on.

Throughout this chapter, we have looked at the basics of Sentiment Analysis, key terms, and areas of application. We have also looked into the various challenges posed while performing sentiment analysis. We have looked at various commonly-used feature extraction methods such as tf-idf, Ngrams, POS, negation, and so on for performing sentiment analysis (or textual analysis in general). We have built on our code base from the previous chapter to streamline and structure utility functions for reuse. We have performed polarity analysis using Twitter search terms and have seen how public opinion about certain campaigns can be easily tracked and analyzed. We then moved on to supervised learning algorithms for classification, where we used SVM and Boosting to build sentiment classifiers using libraries such as `caret`, `RTextTools`, `ROCR`, `e1071` and so on. Before closing the final chapter we also briefly touched upon the highly researched and widely used field of ensemble methods, and also learned about cross-validation-based model evaluation.

There are many other algorithms and analysis techniques which can be applied to extract even more interesting insights from Twitter and other sources on the Internet. Throughout this chapter (and this book), we have merely attempted to address the tip of a huge iceberg! Data science is not just about applying algorithms to solve a problem or derive insights. It requires creative thinking and a lot of due diligence apart from domain understanding, feature engineering, and collecting data to try and solve problems which are as yet unknown.

To sum up things, ponder upon this quote by Donald Rumsfeld:

> *"There are known knowns. These are things we know that we know. There are known unknowns. That is to say, there are things that we know we don't know. But there are also unknown unknowns. There are things we don't know we don't know."*

Data science is a journey of learning the knowns and exploring the unknown unknowns, and machine learning is a powerful tool to help accomplish it. `#KeepMining`!

Index

A

active-user 132
Adaptive Boosting (AdaBoost) 306
algorithms
  family 56
  K-Nearest Neighbors (KNN) 63-65
  linear regression 58-63
  supervised learning algorithms 56, 57
analytics
  about 144
  descriptive 144
  diagnostic 144
  predictive 145
  prescriptive 145
apply function 34
Apriori algorithm 74-77
Area under curve (AUC) 196
arrays and matrices
  about 9
  creating 10, 11
Association for Computational Linguistics
    (ACL) 282
association rule mining
  about 106
  association rules, visualizing 111, 112
  dependencies and data, loading 106
  exploratory analysis 106, 107
  shopping trends, detecting 107-110
  shopping trends, predicting 107-110

B

blogs 275
boosting 306-308

C

CART 218
code flow
  controlling 29
  if 29
  if-else 29
  ifelse 29
  loops 31
  switch 30
collaborative filters
  about 116, 117
  algorithm 118
  core concepts 117, 118
  item 117
  predictions 119, 120
  rating 117
  ratings matrix 117
  recommendations 121
  similarity measure 121
  sparse matrix 117
  user 117
Comprehensive R Archive Network
    (CRAN) 95
constructs
  about 32
  apply function 34, 35
  lapply function 32, 33
  mapply function 37
  sapply function 32, 33
  tapply function 36
content-based recommender engines 115
cosine similarity measure 121

K

L

M

N

O

Open Authentication (OAuth) protocol 250
out of bag error (OOBE) 225

P

Parts of Speech (POS) 282
Pearson correlation 121
perceptron 50-55
pixel-oriented maps 248
Polarity 289-293
positive predictive value 195
precision 195
prediction operation 118
predictive analytics 145, 146, 187
predictive models
  about 188, 190
  data, features 191
  data, observations 191
  data, preparing 191
  datasets 191
  data, testing 191
  data, training 191
  data, transformation 191
  predictive models, building 192
  predictive models, evaluating 193-196
  training data 191
predictive models, building
  about 192
  cross validation 192
  hyperparameter optimization 192
  model, selecting 192
  model training 192
  predictive model 192
predictive models, evaluating
  about 193
  confusion matrix 193-196
  prediction values 193
prescriptive analytics 145
Principal Component Analysis (PCA) 139
product contingency matrix
  advanced 95-97
  data, analyzing 92-94
  data, getting 91

data, visualizing 92-94
evaluating 90, 91
global recommendations 94

R

R
  basics 2
  data structures 7
  help 38, 39
  next steps 38
  packages, handling 40
  special values 6
  using, as scientific calculator 3
  vectors, operating on 4, 5
radial basis function (RBF) 209
radial bias kernel (rbf) 301
random forests
  used, for modeling 224-229
rate of descent 125
ratings matrix 117
Read-Evaluate-Print Loop (REPL) 2
Receiver Operator Characteristic (ROC)
      curve 196
recommendation systems
  issues 115, 116
  offline-recommender engines 114
  online-recommender engines 114
  product ready 133
  types 115
recommendation systems, types
  content-based recommender engines 115
  hybrid recommender engines 115
  user-based recommender engines 115
recommender engine
  building 122
  extract, transform, and analyze 134-138
  implementing 127-131
  matrix factorization 122-126
  model evaluation 140, 141
  model, preparation and prediction 138, 139
  production ready 133, 134
  result interpretation 131, 132
recommenderlab 133
recommend operation 118

Lightning Source UK Ltd.
Milton Keynes UK
UKOW05f1458230616

276935UK00002B/48/P